成
龍

**DISCOVER WHAT MAKES JACKIE CHAN RUN—
AND JUMP, KICK, FIGHT, DIVE, AND RUMBLE!**

THE ESSENTIAL
JACKIE CHAN SOURCEBOOK

Did you know:

- JACKIE CHAN HAS ALSO BEEN BILLED AS SING LUNG, CHENG LONG, CHAN YUAN LUNG, AND . . . PAUL

- AS A CHILD, HE WAS SIGNED INTO INDENTURED SERVITUDE TO THE NOTORIOUS PEKING OPERA SCHOOL

- HE MADE HIS FILM DEBUT AT THE AGE OF EIGHT

- HE HAS INSPIRED FILMMAKERS AND ACTORS INCLUDING QUENTIN TARANTINO AND SYLVESTER STALLONE

- THE JACKIE CHAN FOUNDATION GIVES GENEROUSLY TO THE HOMELESS AND DISABLED

- HONG KONG'S FAVORITE SON WAS ONCE EXILED BY FILM INDUSTRY CRIME LORDS

- A YOUNG JACKIE CHAN WAS CAST IN ONE OF JOHN WOO'S EARLIEST FILMS

- BRUCE LEE CRACKED JACKI
  ENTER THE DRAGON?

Test your Jackie Chan IQ

D1531164

T H E _ESSENTIAL_

JACKIE

CHAN

成龍

SOURCEBOOK

JEFF ROVIN

AND

KATHY TRACY

POCKET BOOKS

New York   London   Toronto   Sydney   Tokyo   Singapore

For orders other than by individual consumers, Pocket Books grants a discount on the purchase of **10 or more** copies of single titles for special markets or premium use. For further details, please write to the Vice-President of Special Markets, Pocket Books, 1633 Broadway, New York, NY 10019-6785, 8th Floor.

For information on how individual consumers can place orders, please write to Mail Order Department, Simon & Schuster Inc., 200 Old Tappan Road, Old Tappan, NJ 07675.

An Original Publication of POCKET BOOKS

POCKET BOOKS, a division of Simon & Schuster Inc.
1230 Avenue of the Americas, New York, NY 10020

Copyright © 1997 by Jeff Rovin

ISBN: 0-671-00843-9

First Pocket Books trade paperback printing October 1997

10 9 8 7 6 5 4 3 2 1

POCKET and colophon are registered trademarks of Simon & Schuster Inc.

Cover design by Tai Lam Wong
Front cover photo credits: top, AP Photo/Butch Belair; bottom, all photos courtesy of Photofest

Printed in the U.S.A.

Text design by Stanley S. Drate/Folio Graphics Co., Inc.

All photos courtesy of Asian Film Archives except where otherwise noted

CONTENTS

INTRODUCTION

Welcome to the world of Jackie Chan.

Although Jackie's movies have enthralled a generation of fans in Asia and Europe, he was virtually unknown in America until *Rumble in the Bronx* broke down the walls. Because he seemingly appeared overnight, many people don't have a clue as to who this guy is who jumps off buildings as easily as the rest of us step off curbs.

The Essential Jackie Chan Sourcebook is here to answer questions you may have about Chan the Man, as some of his fans refer to him. The book contains a biography and a complete filmography, which can be considered his professional life story. In between, there are chapters devoted to other specific areas of Jackie's world.

Since Jackie doesn't work in a vacuum, the book spotlights the other top names in the Hong Kong action film industry and also explains the origins of kung fu and why it plays such a big part in Hong Kong movies. Directly after a glossary of martial arts terms is a quiz to test your Jackie IQ.

Now strap yourself in. It's going to be a wild and surprising ride.

THE ESSENTIAL
JACKIE CHAN SOURCEBOOK

THE
Personal

1
成
龍

JACKIE CHAN

Sometimes it seems as if Jackie has lived his entire life in the public eye. By American standards he's that rare celebrity who embraces the media and is accessible almost to a fault. Maybe it's just a function of culture. Whereas in the West we tend to tire quickly of those we see too much of in the media and often develop an overpowering urge to see the mighty fall, in the East heroes are more revered. Their continued presence is appreciated and encouraged.

People in all parts of Asia just can't get enough of Jackie Chan and follow his moves with respectful interest. Every movie release is a huge event. It has become a tradition for a new Jackie film to premiere at the time of the Chinese New Year festivities, proving his work life has become an ingrained part of people's daily life in Hong Kong and elsewhere.

Jackie's on-screen exploits are so mind blowing that they often overshadow his equally compelling real-life story—which he himself downplays. Unlike Hollywood celebrities and politicians who dwell on the miserable aspects of their private lives in interviews and on talk shows, Chan and other Asian performers tend to be much less forthcoming about personal matters. They simply were not brought up in a tell-all society where you open your soul to strangers. The intimate exposure of celebrities that Americans take for granted Asian society finds distasteful. Interesting, but distasteful.

Jackie won't tell, but we will. The following chapters will paint a picture of Chan the *Real* Man, a portrait that will help explain what makes Jackie run . . . and jump and fight and dive and tumble and continually risk his life to be one of the greatest action stars the world has ever known.

1.

成龍 THE PEKING OPERA BLUES

That Jackie has achieved and accomplished all he has is nothing short of a miracle, considering the circumstances of his birth and childhood.

Chan Kwong Sang came into the world by cesarean section on April 7, 1954, the only child of painfully poor parents, Charles and Lee-Lee Chan, who lived in a Hong Kong ghetto. They were so destitute that the Chans considered selling their son to a British doctor for the equivalent of about US$200.

Things got slightly better for the family after Charles and Lee-Lee found jobs working as domestics at Hong Kong's French embassy. Although the pay was minimal, they were able to set aside enough money to feed little Kwong Sang. But there were many other things his parents, who were in their forties, couldn't provide their son. Stability, for one thing.

Like many impoverished children, Jackie was unsupervised a lot of the time. His parents were too busy trying to keep their heads above water to be conscientious disciplinarians. He picked fights and didn't pay enough attention to his studies. Jackie roamed the streets with other young children, occasionally causing trouble but mostly just killing time and searching for companionship. Considered a chubby child, Jackie's nickname growing up was A-Puo, which means "cannonball." Actually, he had several nicknames—Big Nose was among the more painful, and it inspired more than one fight.

"When I was a child, I wanted to be a fighter, like Muhammad Ali," Chan said in an interview about his past. "He was my hero. I was training hard by eating a lot of Western food, so they called me Double Boy—everybody said I had double bone, double muscle, double everything."

Chan's father had gotten a job in the kitchen of the French embassy, so he was able to bring home thick cuts of meat to feed their daydreaming son. But life was about to change. Jackie remembers the day a family friend suggested his parents take him to the Chinese Opera Research Institute, an old-fashioned Chinese performing arts school with a curriculum that encompassed acting, singing, dance, mime, acrobatics, and martial arts. The studies would be more like torture, but Jackie didn't know that yet. All he knew was that this was a place that seemed like fun.

"In a way, the school was like the army—the children all wore uniforms of white tennis shoes and black pants," Jackie has said. "Then my father and his friend left me at the school and went to go have a drink. While I was there I picked a fight and broke some kid's glasses—I had fun."

Initially, Jackie thought he had found heaven on earth.

"They sent me there one day a week at first, early in the morning. I loved it—I was able to kick and punch and do anything I wanted. So when we went to sign me up, I was asked if I wanted to join for three, five, or ten years. At that age, I had no concept of time so I just picked ten. Besides, my mom was in Hong Kong to take care of me, right?

"Then later I was told it was good I wanted to stay because both my parents had to go to Australia to work."

After years of struggling and barely surviving, they simply couldn't turn their backs on relatively decent-paying jobs for each of them. Positions for a cook and a maid had become available at the embassy in Canberra, Australia, and Chan's parents jumped at the chance. There was one little problem, though—they couldn't take their child because the embassy didn't provide accommodations for the children of staffers. Who would take care of him? What to do?

Jackie's father had already left Hong Kong, leaving Lee-Lee behind to make arrangements for their son. Her solution was to enroll him at the Chinese Opera Research Institute, which was Hong Kong's version of the Peking Opera School, while they moved to another continent. In compensation for selling their child into indentured servitude, the school *sifu*, headmaster Yu Jim Yuen, paid the family a token amount of money. Jackie took the news like a little trouper, making the parting all the more heartbreaking.

"I told my mother it was okay and not to worry, that I'd be okay to stay there by myself."

Jackie was only six and a half years old.

It's easy from our 1990s perspective to look back with horror at the thought of leaving a small child in the hands of strangers. But life was run by a different set of rules in 1960s Hong Kong than it is today. What most people would now consider child abuse was looked upon as an opportunity for the family's future.

Despite the harshness of his upbringing at the school, Jackie never engaged in self-pity—probably because he was too busy trying to avoid beatings at the hands of his exacting teachers, which almost certainly began just days after he said good-bye to his mother.

"After my mom moved, I was crying like hell, and after about two days, the *sifu* said, 'All right—time to get started.' " What followed was a beating the likes of which the little boy had never known, kicks and punches meant to break his spirit. "All I could think about was getting away," Jackie has said to journalists. "I wanted to see my mom, I didn't want to be there anymore because everybody beat me."

Jackie tends to avoid speaking publicly about what he endured during the ten years he spent at the school, as if he doesn't want to delve too deeply into those memories. But what glimpses he does give of the brutal experience are difficult to fathom. They are as shocking and unbelievable as many of the horror kung fu films Hong Kong loves so much.

"It was tough," Chan says matter-of-factly. "It was so bad you probably won't believe it. I would get up at five in the morning and start training immediately—study voice, run, do stick fighting, knife fighting, sword fighting, work on kicks, practice jumping, hapkido, judo, karate, boxing, more singing, then dancing—just go-go-go.

"Every teacher would instruct me for two hours, and I kept running constantly from one teacher to another. I didn't have time to take my shoes off or even brush my teeth. There was no time for anything but training. This would go on until midnight. Every day."

If any of the boys had the nerve to resist the back-breaking schedule, or if they were simply exhausted, fear and pain were powerful incentives to conform, and the school's teachers doled out both liberally. Starvation was considered an acceptable punishment if a student failed to live up to expectations. And caning with bamboo sticks for a lackluster performance was practically a school tradition, as were other forms of corporal punishment.

"We had a lot of different teachers and each one would hit you everywhere—in the face, on the hands, butt, chest, feet—everywhere. You just learn to live with the pain.

"Sometimes we would have to do headstands for up to eight hours. Or we'd be required to do the horse stance (legs wide apart, feet parallel), keeping perfectly still. The teacher would place a bowl of water on your outstretched hands and head, and if any water spilled, you'd be beat.

"We learned by the stick—the stick told me when to jump, the stick told me when to kick."

Jackie says he was convinced the *sifu* had a particular dislike for him and held him up to special scrutiny . . . and torture.

"Other kids would do a trick and he would say it was okay. Then I would do the exact same thing and be told to do it again . . . and again . . . and again. Every difficult routine, I had to do first. 'Jump over that table and do two somersaults.'

"If I said I couldn't, he took out his stick and the stick would tell me I could. Again, again, again until I *could* do it."

It's easy now to see where Jackie's near-irrational sense of perfectionism comes from. It was literally beaten into him as a child.

After a while, inhumane treatment became the norm for the new students. In order to survive, the youngsters simply learned to accept their situation.

"That's the way it was, day in and day out," Jackie says with a shrug.

Ironically, Jackie's early days at the school gave no indication of what was to come in his future. While Chan was physically capable, he was not a standout student in any of the disciplines. Not even close. His greatest talent appears to have been a penchant for bad behavior and being a troublemaker. It's difficult to reconcile this image of a youthful ruffian with the gently impish Chan currently loved by billions. But it's no secret why Jackie was such a handful. Even Jackie understood why.

"I was very angry," he admits. "And bitter. Every month parents used to come out to see other students—but not mine. Every time the other parents brought food, clothes, socks—but not mine.

"I didn't hate my parents," Jackie has said in interviews, "but I was so . . . unhappy."

In between punishments and the endless training sessions, Jackie and the other students squeezed in some academic classes. Too bad they were so exhausted they could barely keep their eyes open.

"When it was time for regular school classes the next day, we all slept through them. We'd fall asleep saying the alphabet—*A, B, C, D* . . . ," Jackie has said. "So everyone *loved* school time."

Unfortunately, the Opera schoolteachers didn't seem overly concerned with the intellectual growth of the students. As long as the kids were as agile as monkeys, all was well with the world. Less than ten hours a week was spent on fundamentals. Learning to read was not nearly as important to the *sifu* as being able to do a perfect back flip. To this day, Chan laments his lack of a formal education. Because of that, he is very vocal in encouraging children to stay in school.

Back then, though, all Jackie dreamed about was finding a way out of his. Not even the nights offered any respite or comfort, except for the nearness of the other children with whom Jackie huddled. And even that became oppressive. Once their day was over, Jackie and his classmates would retire to a communal sleeping area that sounds straight out of Charles Dickens.

"Unfortunately, we all had to sleep together on this big, dirty, old rug that was so disgusting," Jackie has said. "I'm sure it had been pissed on by both people and dogs. It was really, really disgusting. And we all shared one blanket."

One blanket . . . and one dream. Among those little boys shivering next to Jackie were others who would in their own way have a major impact on the Hong Kong film industry— and thus, the world film industry—in the years to come: Sammo Hung, Yuen Biao, Yuen Kuei, Yuen Mo, and others.

(The preponderance of "Yuens" isn't a coincidence. The school had put together a performance troupe called the Seven Little Fortunes that was actually comprised of over a dozen students. Seven principals and five backups. To honor Master Yu Jim Yuen, each Fortune was required to adopt a stage name that contained the name Yuen. Jackie's was Yuen Lau—a moniker he only used while performing with the troupe. But some of the other boys, like Yuen Biao, chose to keep the names professionally even after they left the school.)

Of all his classmates, Jackie found special kinship with two very different boys—Sammo Hung and Yuen Biao. Sammo, who had come to the school in 1960 just before Jackie, was a natural leader, which earned him the nickname Big Brother. Biao, a lithe, waifish boy with spectacular acrobatic ability, came to the school shortly after Jackie and became Chan's Little Brother. Jackie still refers to them by these affectionate terms over thirty years later. And no wonder. They became

Jackie's surrogate family, with all the pluses and minuses that come with that kind of forced intimacy.

"My relationship with Jackie is hard to define," Sammo admits. "Through all those years of sleeping together, eating together, fighting together, we became closer than family. Even though we still argue at times, I think we've remained connected."

Although he didn't know it at the time, Jackie's future literally came knocking on the school door one day in 1962 when a local director showed up in search of a new young face to use in his movies.

"I was very lucky—I was the child they picked, so I became an actor," Jackie says. "I didn't know what to expect, but it was so easy—it didn't require any additional training on my part. I could do whatever they needed. At the school we had learned both the southern style, which emphasizes hands, and the northern style, which uses feet more. *My* style now has a lot of jumping and footwork, but back then I used both when working."

This is exactly what the school had been preparing him for: a life of performing. Initially, Jackie liked working in films simply because it meant he could sleep a little later on the days he had to report to work.

"At that time I didn't know what I was doing, I didn't know about films. To me, it was just a way to make a living. You give me a part and I'll do it. I was very young, so I just followed direction. Whatever he tells me to do—cry, walk—I did. But it was very good training."

But slowly, the process of making movies itself began to steal his heart.

"After five or ten years I began to love movies. They'd tell me it was okay, that I could go home, but I'd say no, I wanted to stay. I enjoyed going to the studios and watching and learning. I assumed I could grow up to be a stuntman, no problem. Since I didn't really need any additional training for that, I literally fell into the movie business. I loved all those early films and I think they were all good."

Jackie eventually appeared in well over twenty films during his tenure at the school. To his chagrin, Jackie admits he can't remember the titles, and he assumes most of the films don't even exist anymore.

"I wish I did know," Jackie has said. "But at that time in Hong Kong, it took only seven days to make one movie. *Seven days*. They'd never even move the camera—it was very much like the Opera. They'd just set up two cameras and the actors would act. Then it was finished.

"If I could only find them, I'd love to find copies of all those movies and put them in my collection so I can say that's Jackie Chan back when. But I cannot find them, not even my first childhood film. I think they've disappeared. I'd be happy with just a poster, but so far, nothing."

Naturally, his teachers encouraged his career. Not only was Jackie a physical showcase for the school, he was also a cash cow.

"By the time I was a teenager, I had become a stuntman and was working regularly. Some director would say, 'Okay, Jackie—you die here, you die there.' I'd do it and get paid seventy-five dollars for the day. But I was still a student at the school, so I'd have to give my earnings to my *sifu*, and he'd let me keep maybe a dollar. But to me, that was a lot of money, considering that before I didn't have any money at all."

Between working in films, performing, and the school's rigorous training schedule and his earlier appearances as a Little Fortune, Jackie's formal education dwindled from next to nothing to nothing. He's lucky he was able to read and write, and any higher learning was a luxury he would never experience. It's a void he's still acutely aware of today.

"In China education and knowledge are very important—there is nothing more important than education, even in the martial arts," Jackie has explained to reporters. "But there is obsession with being number one. Everybody says they're number one—nobody says they're number two. So I always say I'm number three. Why? Because it doesn't matter, as long as you keep learning.

"The Chinese have a saying, 'Clever men move mountains, stupid men must move.' I believe that."

Then one day, Jackie's hard youth was over. The time had come for Jackie and his brothers to graduate from the school. Regardless of the hellhole it may have been, for ten years it had also been home. For the second time in his young life, Jackie was cut loose and left to fend for himself. Only this time, he wasn't even given a filthy rug to sleep on. As fate would have it, just as Jackie left the confines of the school, the Opera had gone out of favor as a performance art. The action, color, and scenery of the movies had effectively killed the stage-bound opera and its glory days. So a life in the Opera was suddenly not a viable option. And since these young men had not received a well-rounded education, they could not easily find employment in another field. All they knew how to do was fight and perform. That left them just one choice: to go into the movie business. With a mix of hope and dread, Jackie joined the multitude of young men jockeying for movie stunt work.

Jackie had grown enthralled with the movies and set his sights on being a stuntman and fight choreographer. He also secretly dreamed of being a star, a goal that would have seemed highly unlikely. He was skinny, had crooked teeth and very small eyes, and lacked any immediately apparent charisma. Details.

However, he also had a fire-hot desire to succeed plus a willingness to do absolutely anything necessary to achieve his dreams. Those qualities would ultimately make all the difference.

Ironically, shortly after Jackie graduated from the school, his father returned to Hong Kong to present his son with a house. The younger Chan was speechless.

"For ten years, my parents suffered and saved to buy me a house. This is why I know my mother and father did everything for me."

When asked if there's any way a system like the Opera School—which Jackie himself has said is accurately depicted as nothing short of a torture chamber in the 1993 film *Farewell, My Concubine*—could ever be made suitable for children by today's standards, Jackie doesn't hesitate.

"No way," Jackie has said in interviews. "It's too tough. If you are older, say thirteen to sixteen, you're at an age where you're considered too old to be taught; but if you're a young child, it is far too tough to go through. When I was seven, I had no energy, but my training still lasted the whole day, almost twenty-four hours.

"We don't have schools like this now. You hit a kid like that now, you sue, right? Instead, I would teach children how to exercise and martial arts techniques—but I wouldn't teach them how to kill or hurt people.

"Before 1972, a lot of young people wanted to learn martial arts, but they just wanted to fight—that's no good. Too many young people today can't understand that the techniques aren't to be used aggressively, that you should only use the force necessary to get out of a situation.

"Martial arts are a great thing to know—but only if you also learn that they're not just for fighting. It's a different age now, and martial arts are for health and for fun—not hurting people. You might study for forty years and never once use them in a fight but you will still have used them because they improve your mind and help you to learn other things more quickly.

"If you master martial arts, then you can go on to master almost anything."

But Chan admits not everyone was able to overcome the lack of a formal education the way he was.

"It's true—me, I'm happy. But I look at some of my other classmates and they're not doing so well. They have no education—they don't know English, and even their Chinese isn't very good. That's because we spent all that time studying other things."

Never one to dwell publicly on the negative, Chan is quick to point out that his years at the school taught him almost everything he knows about martial arts and the other skills he needed to become the superstar he is today.

"My *sifu* was a very good teacher and he taught me a lot. He trained my mind as well as my body, and when I would see him he was still my teacher—I am still scared.

"But," Jackie has said, "I have paid back what I owe to him. All my creativity for choreographing fights comes from those years of training, it's true. All the things I use in my movies I learned from the school. But I would *never* put my kids, or any kids, through it nor would I tell anyone else to go through what I did.

"It's just too much."

2.

成
龍

A STAR IS BORN

The Hong Kong film industry up to the 1970s was not highly competitive, at least in terms of the number of big studios. There was only one major studio: Run Run Shaw's Shaw Brothers. The lack of competition was not necessarily the best thing for the studio. Without any competition, it was easy to fall into a creative rut, which is exactly what happened to the house that Run Run built. By the time they noticed that the audience was hungry for something fresh, a new kid had taken over the block.

Raymond Chow was hardly an unknown commodity. He had been a Shaw Brothers executive for years until he struck out on his own and created Golden Harvest. It was a production entity that he envisioned would take films in a new direction rather than continue mass producing what were becoming tired retreads.

Almost immediately, the studio hit pay dirt after somebody—Chow now says it was *him*, though others beg to differ—saw Bruce Lee doing a martial arts exhibition on television. Chow claims to have assigned the job of tracking down Bruce to actress Liu Liang Hua, who just happened to be married to up-and-coming director Lo Wei (who also laid claim to Lee's discovery). Liu found Lee in Los Angeles, signed him to a Golden Harvest contract, and in the process changed the course of Hong Kong cinema forever. (See 3. Gangster's Paradise, page 23, for more about Bruce Lee.)

Jackie was right when he assumed he would have no problem finding stunt work once he had fulfilled his contract with the school. He worked on dozens of movies, eagerly jumping at any chance to do any small acting roles tossed his way. For the most part, Chan was considered either too young or too short for the parts available, so he became a "dead body" specialist because he could lie perfectly still.

There didn't seem to be a lot of career advancement playing corpses, so Jackie concentrated on getting stunt work. He hoped to work his way up to action director, a very important position on kung fu films.

"In those days, the pay was sixty dollars for each stunt, but the action director would ask for twenty dollars back to pick you. Even the directors sometimes asked for kickbacks," Jackie has recalled.

"When we were on the set, I was always beside the action director. If he wanted to wash his car I would help him, if I wasn't doing a stunt. I did lots of stunts, all kinds of stunts— jumping off buildings, bouncing on trampolines, anything. I would do stunts for several characters in the movie—I'd just change clothes."

Thanks to his training at the Opera School, Jackie was able to learn stunts quickly and rapidly rose through the ranks. In 1971, a seventeen-year-old Jackie was hired to play the lead in a picture called *Little Tiger from Canton*. Little is known about why he was chosen or what happened to the film's producer, Li Long Koon. It was reportedly an amateurish film that did absolutely nothing for Chan's career or reputation. It would be years before he'd get another chance to star in a movie. Until then, it was back to bit parts and action directing gigs on a string of similarly forgettable films.

Although movies provided a steady income, the young Chan was antsy. His ambitions had grown since leaving school . . . and since getting a taste of being the "star" of a film, even a small, unnoticed movie like *Little Tiger*.

"I'd see the way people were making films and see how directors were directing and I'd say to myself, 'This is not good—they're doing it the wrong way.' Then I would tell myself that if I ever got the chance, I would do it differently. I would do it *my* way. But I was just one of hundreds of stuntmen—when would it be my turn?"

Exactly. Who in their right mind was going to give a no-name stuntman a chance to set the industry on its ear? Especially an industry that in 1973 was reeling from the shocking death of its greatest star. Bruce Lee's body was barely cold before the search for his replacement was under way. And none was looking harder than Lo Wei, the director who took credit for discovering Bruce. Finding the next Bruce Lee would vindicate Lo and boost his production company's profile.

Jackie had crossed paths with Bruce in *Fist of Fury* and *Enter the Dragon*, nearly getting his neck broken by Lee in the latter. He used the opportunities to study Bruce closely, to see what made him so magical on screen. He realized that Lee stayed completely true to himself on screen as well as off. In person, Bruce was not exactly a laugh-a-minute guy. He was a serious person and had developed a fighting style that fit his personality perfectly. The movies he starred in perfectly complemented his on- and off-screen personas. Plus he had undeniable charisma and was handsome to boot. No wonder he become famous the world over.

With Lee's sudden death, there was now a huge hole in the heart of the Hong Kong action film industry.

"The films that followed Bruce Lee's death were known as Bruce Lee–style films—but Bruce wasn't in them and nobody went to see them," Jackie explains. "So action films went out of favor and love stories became popular instead."

As far as the American market was concerned, the Bruce Lee imitators further sullied the perception of "chopsocky" films as cheap and tacky entertainment. For all intents and purposes these even cheaper productions drove them out of mainstream theaters. For a while, it seemed as if the Hong Kong action film genre might never recover from Bruce's untimely demise.

Maybe that explains why Jackie agreed to go way out of character and do the non–martial arts film *All in the Family*. The script required Jackie to do sex scenes in the buff.

A better experience came that same year in *Hand of Death*, directed by a then-unheralded John Woo. Besides giving Jackie some meaningful screen time, the film also gave him a chance to work with two of his Opera School brothers—Sammo Hung and Yuen Biao, both of whom were also forging careers in film.

It's ironic to note that at this point it was Sammo who looked to be the sure bet as a star of the future. He was already making a name for himself as an actor and even more so as a fight choreographer in films like *Hapkido* and *When Tae Kwondo Strikes*. If he had one major obstacle it was his unconventional looks. Beefy and cherubic, he was definitely not leading man handsome. But in action films, that's not necessarily a requisite. You have to be able to jump, kick, punch, juggle, and fall. So it was quite conceivable that Sammo would be the Next Big Thing.

Hand of Death gave Jackie an opportunity to tackle a major acting role, as it were. The actual star of the film was Dorian Tan, who had a short and undistinguished career. On *Hand of Death*, Chan took a wicked kick and suffered a nasty bout of internal bleeding. Being young and ambitious, he shook it off and went back to work. Toughness as well as skill was another legacy of the Peking Opera School. Besides, working with Sammo and Yuen was something he wanted to savor.

Unfortunately, the fun of working with his good friends notwithstanding, *Hand of Death* was yet another box office failure. The film itself was not that bad, but because so many chopsocky films were bad, audiences simply stopped going to them. Jackie began to feel as if everything he touched went bust. His pride and ego were taking a beating—along with his hoped-for marketability. He *knew* he had the right stuff, and it was frustrating to be lumped in with every other struggling action director/stuntman/would-be filmmaker.

"None of the films I was in was successful, so I began to consider giving up and moving to Australia to join my parents. Also, action movies were going downhill, and there was no more work."

Chan in fact did leave Hong Kong and join his parents Down Under, believing his future would be spent working as a cook. But fate had other ideas.

First of all, Jackie found Canberra, Australia, stifling and dull.

"After five in the afternoon you could go to sleep in the middle of the street and not worry about getting run over."

Chan decided to go back home and take his chances one more time with Hong Kong's stagnant film industry. Besides, he was suffering a kind of physical withdrawal being away from it.

"Once you make movies, once it gets inside your skin, it is like a drug," he has said. "You can't *not* do it."

Not that Jackie was going back empty-handed. Hong Kong executive Willie Chan had been in contact with Jackie about appearing in a movie his company was producing. The company belonged to a director named Lo Wei. (Years later, Willie Chan would become Jackie's manager.)

The story about how Lo claims he "discovered" Jackie is vintage Lo: pure hyperbole. The director claims he had been fretting about who he should cast in his pet project, a sequel to *Fist of Fury* creatively titled *New Fist of Fury*. Lo was skulking around various Hong Kong sets like an Asian Fagin looking for someone, anyone, to pick up where Bruce had left off.

One day after Jackie had returned from Australia, Lo happened to be visiting a set where Jackie was showing another actor how to do a death scene. Lo says he was hit by a thunderbolt of precognition. He yelled, "Sign that boy up!" and announced he had found the man to fill Bruce's *Fist* shoes.

Of course, Willie Chan, Jackie's manager of twenty years, tells a slightly different story about how *he* was the one who thought Jackie had potential. In 1976, Willie had just joined Lo Wei's company as an executive and was working on the *Fist of Fury* sequel.

"We were looking for a new star and I thought of him," Willie has said in interviews. "But he was in Australia so I had to convince him to come back. We've been together ever since."

New Fist of Fury was made quickly and without much care. Lo didn't give his "discovery" a chance to strut his stuff. As a result it hit the ground with a resounding thud. So much for Lo's big plans. But at least Lo had a new property to promote. From Bruce Lee–style films like *New Fist of Fury* and *Dragon Fist* to poor imitations of the period kung fu flicks being made by the Shaw Brothers, Lo Wei couldn't get a handle on how to best use his protege's unique skills and bubbly personality.

Not that Jackie didn't give the director not-so-subtle hints. In fact, after the failure of their first collaboration, they argued over it. To Jackie, it was so clear he wanted to scream. But no matter how loudly he spoke, his ideas fell on deaf ears.

"One day, when we were talking about a script, we tried to think of ways to change all the Bruce Lee–style films that were ruining the movies. My idea was to add kung fu and comedy, too. Lo Wei wouldn't hear of it.

"This is why I wanted to direct myself. Lo Wei wanted me playing the part of a hero, so he put me in older roles. Terrible stories, terrible casting—I'm only twenty-one and he wants me to play a forty-year-old.

"He also wanted me to do Bruce's kick, Bruce's punch, Bruce's yell, be serious like Bruce—but I knew it was wrong. I'm just not this kind of person.

"Nobody can imitate Bruce Lee. Even now. Bruce is still considered the king of kung fu films and back then more so. I tried to tell Lo Wei that we should change, but he wouldn't listen. He insisted on doing it *his* way."

Lo Wei finally got tired of listening. To teach Jackie a lesson, he teamed him with a young director he also had under contract, Chan Chi-hwa.

"He was a young guy who didn't know anything about kung fu and just listened to me. But Lo Wei always wanted to change me into something else. I had a lot of ideas, but he always told me I didn't know anything. I began wondering why I was still making movies with him, but I had to for then. But I knew one day *I* would direct and then I'd do things my way. So from that point on, I kept all my ideas to myself. And Lo Wei did it his way.

"Of course it was totally wrong—and none of the movies was a success."

The one time Lo capitulated and allowed Jackie to do a film his way, the old-school director was horrified at the results. After viewing *Half a Loaf of Kung Fu*—a spoof on the kinds of movies Chan had been making the previous few years—he pronounced it unreleasable and shelved it. Now Jackie knew for certain that Lo Wei would never allow him to put his full vision on film. He was serving time in creative prison and Lo Wei had no intention of relinquishing the key.

But working with Lo did have its advantages. First of all, he encouraged Jackie to "cinematize" his appearance by having dental work done to straighten his teeth and cosmetic surgery to make his eyes look more open—less Asian, if you will.

Second, because the director had never been a martial artist, the busier he became the more he deferred in that area to Jackie, who worked hard at coming up with creative and innovative bits wherever he could sneak them in past Lo Wei.

"I directed the action and fight scenes, which really helped me. And when I was doing that, Lo Wei was usually asleep or somewhere listening to the radio, so I sometimes directed other parts of the film, too.''

Jackie has said repeatedly that the secret to his success was his calculated decision to be diametrically opposed to Bruce, in both fighting style and screen persona. Instead of being an intense, nearly invincible hero, Jackie assumed and developed the underdog position, the guy who feels pain, gets confused, and isn't always sure about the outcome. And, most significantly, he was a guy who has a sense of humor.

Jackie's viability as a film star was running out at the box office. He bombed with films like *Shaolin Wooden Men*, *Snake and Crane Arts of Shaolin*, *To Kill with Intrigue*, and *Killer Meteors* (a/k/a *Meteor*), in which Jackie actually played the evil bad guy.

When he least expected it, Chan got the break he'd been working so hard to get. Not surprisingly the film was *not* directed by Lo Wei.

When director Yuen Woo-ping and producer Ng See Yuen approached Lo and told him they wanted Jackie to play the lead in their next film, he was more than happy to oblige. Lo Wei had just about run out of ideas of what to do with Jackie and had little hope that he would become a Bruce Lee–size film star.

Chan couldn't believe his luck. *Snake in the Eagle's Shadow* was intended to be a comedy, and he would finally get a chance to make an audience feel good. However, even after Lo agreed to let him go, Jackie almost didn't get a chance to.

''The distributors begged me not to hire Jackie,'' producer Ng recalls. ''They were very concerned because he'd never been in a hit film. They wanted me to use anybody but him.''

Ng stuck to his instincts. He was familiar with Jackie's work and felt Chan's problem was that he'd never been given the proper vehicle to showcase his talents. He believed that Jackie was one of the new generation poised to take the reins and save the sagging genre.

Under the careful direction of Yuen and with Jackie's enthusiastic performance, *Snake in the Eagle's Shadow* was an immediate hit. Suddenly, after almost twenty years in show business, Chan was an overnight sensation. He had no doubts why.

"Nobody could beat Bruce Lee—but everybody can beat me. Bruce never smiled—I smile all the time. That's me. I'm always smiling. I like comedy. The action I do is real action a human being can do.

"I finally got to do all these things in *Snake in the Eagle's Shadow*, and it totally changed action films," said Jackie, if he does say so himself.

"People were really surprised after the film came out. All of a sudden, they wanted to know who I was. It gave me the confidence I needed to keep doing it my way. Before nobody would listen to me, I had to listen to everyone else. But after I finally had a successful film, then everybody started listening to me."

Which in time would prove both a blessing and a curse. But initially, it allowed Jackie the freedom to spread his wings and nurture his emerging film character. And make no mistake: Any time Jackie stars in a Jackie Chan film, he's essentially playing the same character. John Wayne did the same thing and became a screen icon and an American hero in the process, a fact that was not lost on Chan.

Jackie's success thrilled Lo Wei, who suddenly saw Chan as being a new cash cow. Now that kung fu films had been given a fresh, comedic, decidedly non–Bruce Lee spin, the action film community enjoyed a renaissance of excitement. *Snake in the Eagle's Shadow* clones were produced by the dozens as moviemakers scrambled to get their feet into the new wave.

But Ng and Woo-ping were already working on their next idea, which would be based on Wong Fei-hung, a revered Chinese historical figure known for his martial arts skills and his social activism. Wong had been the subject of over a hundred films, so coming up with a fresh take on him required some creativity. What Ng had in mind was to do a film about Wong in his younger days, before he was a legend.

The result, *Drunken Master*, was a turning point in martial arts film history and in Jackie's life. The movie catapulted Chan to the top, turning him from a sensation to a full-fledged star. However, he was still bound contractually to Lo Wei. So *Drunken Master* ended his collaborations with Ng and Yuen.

That was okay with Jackie. Thrilled to be the focus of so much positive attention, Chan went right back to work. *Fearless Hyena*, which was produced by Lo Wei, marked Jackie's directorial debut and further established comedy kung fu as the way to go in the post–Bruce world.

"I want to make people happy," Jackie says. "But I don't want my films to just be comedies, so there must be at least one serious fight to let the audience know I am more than just funny. The fight comes either in the middle or toward the end, but the very end must have comedy so the audience leaves happy.

"The way I look at it, if you come out laughing, you have something to talk about."

Jackie and Lo also had things to talk about. Chan's multi-picture deal with Lo Wei was just about up. After some arm twisting, and against all common sense, Jackie agreed to sign a new deal with Lo, who in turn agreed to loan out Chan so he could work on outside films. Jackie's manager, Willie Chan, couldn't believe what Jackie had agreed to. What the *hell* was he thinking?

It's difficult for anyone to understand what made Jackie do something so obviously detrimental to him professionally. Lo had proven totally inept at handling Jackie's career. Yet here he was turning his future over to him again. The deal struck, Jackie started work on the sequel to *Fearless Hyena*. He didn't get very far.

Whether he came to his own senses or was convinced by Willie Chan that staying with Lo was not in his best interests, Jackie abruptly bolted from *Fearless Hyena II* shortly after filming began. He signed a deal with Raymond Chow's Golden Harvest and immediately went to work on setting up shop, the world suddenly his movie oyster.

Jackie's first project for Golden Harvest was *Young Master*, which is a continuation of the theme of Wong Fei-hung as a youth started in *Drunken Master*. This movie further enhanced Jackie's rising star. He was now without question Hong Kong's biggest kung fu star. However, Jackie was about to learn a lesson. His sophomore effort for Raymond Chow and Golden Harvest was *Dragon Lord*, which was shot on location in Taiwan and Korea. Displaying a proclivity for expensive production indulgence that would dog him throughout his career, Jackie spent a lot of money on *Dragon Lord*, which then fared poorly at the Hong Kong box office. It wasn't that the film wasn't up to snuff. Rather, because of Jackie's success there was a sudden surge in similar films. It taught Jackie that to stay on top one must always top oneself. Each subsequent movie must have some new, fresh element the one previous didn't. Then the audience wouldn't know what to expect. That was the way to keep 'em coming back.

It was a creed Jackie would make the cornerstone of his career.

While Jackie was moving forward, not everyone was cheering the new hero. His decision to jump ship had left Lo Wei in the lurch and furious. The first thing he did to get back at Jackie was to make money off of him whenever possible in whatever way possible. In the coming years, Lo would patch together several compilation films, utilizing footage from old Jackie films. This is how he completed *Fearless Hyena II*. This sad excuse for a sequel didn't exactly heat up the box office but it did warm the embittered cockles of Lo Wei's heart.

Unfortunately, financial gain wasn't recompense enough for Lo Wei, who was a lot more enraged than Jackie thought he would be over the loss of both revenue and face that Chan's rejection caused. He wanted his former star to pay dearly for his breached promise. It's been said that Lo Wei was out for blood. Literally.

Jackie was about to be introduced to the dark underbelly of the Hong Kong film industry.

3.

成
龍

GANGSTER'S PARADISE

Just as Jackie was achieving everything he had dreamed of, he abruptly left Hong Kong. The official reason that's been given for years is that he wanted to set sail for America and conquer her shores. This was partially true. In the back of his brain, Jackie knew that capturing the hearts of U.S. moviegoers would be one way to effectively dispel the posthumous shadow he believed Bruce Lee still cast.

But there was another, more basic incentive to take the next train out of town: survival. Lo Wei had carried his grudge to lethal levels and had put the word out that Jackie's life was worthless. If any of Lo's cohorts caught him making movies in Hong Kong, he'd be following Bruce Lee's career path to early retirement *exactly*.

Lo's fury wasn't solely based on loss of professional face. To Lo, Jackie's defection to Raymond Chow and Golden Harvest was a huge betrayal. Lo felt he had plucked Jackie from the gutter and had salvaged a career that was headed nowhere. Lo made him a leading man when nobody else would give him a chance. Chan was an ingrate who needed to be taught a lesson.

There were also the financial rewards that Lo had seen slip through his fingers along with his biggest star. Never the sharpest businessman, Lo was near bankruptcy at the time Jackie left him high and dry.

The director had planned to cash in on Jackie's sudden fame and popularity by flooding the market with B movies—a Lo Wei specialty. He really couldn't care less what that plan would do to Chan's long-term career, he wanted a big payoff immediately.

Not surprisingly, Jackie didn't want to see all his hard

work wasted by Lo. So he took his manager's advice and made a break for it and steeled himself for the consequences, which were certain to come. One doesn't anger a Triad boss and get away clean.

The Triads are the organized crime mobs of Hong Kong. Also called the Chinese Mafia, the Triads were founded in the seventeenth century by a monk of the Shaolin monastery in order to rid China of her barbarian conquerors, the Manchus. In the beginning, they were actually viewed as patriots. But as the decades and centuries went by, the Triads were less concerned with nationalism than with bettering the Triads. Since they started out as subversives, the leap to criminal activity was a small one. Eventually they infiltrated any area where money could be made.

Like the American Mafia, the Triads of today see themselves as businessmen—businessmen who negotiate with knives and guns instead of attorneys. And in modern times, nowhere have they made their presence more publicly known than in Hong Kong's film industry. Shaw Brothers' tight-fisted economics forced many of the actors and crew members in the film business to moonlight for the Triads. Because of that, the Triads gained a prominent foothold in Hong Kong's film industry.

"Entertainment is big business and wherever there's lots of money to be made, you're going to find organized crime," says one industry source. "Plus, there are other advantages. For one thing, making movies is a perfect way to launder large sums of drug money. A 'production company' can always claim they made or lost however much money they need to balance the books. And as long as the actors cooperate, there's virtually no way for the government to keep track of what's truly being spent where.

"In addition to that, Hong Kong drug dealers often use entertainers as carriers, since they travel frequently and are usually accorded special treatment by foreign customs officials. The Canadian government in particular has started taking a much closer look at entertainers who fly in regularly from Hong Kong precisely for that reason.''

Although all of this is common knowledge and/or lore to anyone working in the Hong Kong film industry, the actors themselves tend to be rendered mute whenever the topic of the Triads comes up. Spilling their guts might lead to just that.

Lo Wei himself was believed by most to be a high-ranking member of the Sun Yi On Triad, which according to authorities has forty-five thousand members. And Lo intended to get even with Jackie the old-fashioned way. He contracted out for it.

The fallout wasn't immediate, but it came quickly enough. Chan was able to finish *Young Master* without incident, but by the time he was ready to start production on his next film, things had started to heat up. Lo Wei had put the word out to his associates that Jackie was a marked man.

Jackie took the threat seriously enough that he went on location to film *Dragon Lord*. He had little choice. Like the Mafia, the island's organized crime lords were not people to take lightly. They were brutal and remorseless and everywhere.

Stories have long circulated that Bruce Lee's death wasn't merely a tragic accident, and in each version the Triads play a prominent role. One of the more sinister theories is that Lee was murdered after he made it clear he wanted to make a break from Golden Harvest and work autonomously. Somebody along the financial food chain took umbrage at that notion and made sure that Bruce didn't go anywhere.

The picture painted of the top brass in the Hong Kong movie business makes even the more notorious American studio executives look like petty schoolboys. The stories of Triad intimidation and control can be found everywhere. There's hardly a big-name Hong Kong actor who hasn't eventually had to deal with organized crime at some point in his or her career. For example, martial arts star Jet Li is no stranger to Triad violence. His manager, Jim Choi, was murdered in his office building by two men dressed as security guards. There are differing stories as to why. The first is that Choi had argued with a Triad boss who wanted Jet for a movie. The other is that a former manager, upset at being dumped in favor of Choi, demanded the man's life as payment for the slight. After Choi's death, Li turned to members of Sun Yi On, who became Li's new representatives. They stepped in and settled the dispute with the first manager, who was now threatening a lawsuit, by buying him out.

Gordon Chan, who directed Jackie's recent *Thunderbolt*, says he used to try and hide in order to avoid being "offered" a chance to make a Triad-backed film.

"I'd even disguise my voice when I answered the phone," he has admitted. "But finally, one day they put a gun on the table and told me they wanted to make a film with me."

Film producer Choi Chin Ming was also the victim of a 1993 contract murder. Director Wong Jing, who made the critically acclaimed *Return of God of Gamblers*, had his teeth literally bashed in as punishment for talking too much about certain gangsters.

But perhaps the most notorious Triad case involved the murder of mobster-turned-movie producer Wong Long Wai. The Wong case reverberated throughout the industry because one of the players was among Hong Kong's best known performers, Anita Mui. A poor-girl-made-good as both singer and actress, Anita Mui is often called the Madonna of Hong Kong because of her sultry concert performances. She has been linked with many men, including a long relationship with Jackie Chan. The story of how she became entangled in a Triad murder case illustrates the vulnerability of Hong Kong actors who live in a mob-ruled society.

As reported by Fredric Dannen in *The New Yorker* magazine in an article about the Hong Kong film industry, in the early morning hours of May 4, 1992, Anita Mui and some friends were hosting a birthday party for Mui's assistant in a private room at Take One, a karaoke club in Kowloon, an area of Hong Kong where many in the film industry rent offices. As it happens, karaoke bars are a favorite hangout for Triad gangsters. Anyway, Wong Long Wai was also at the club, accompanied by his wife and another man. Wong belonged to the 14K Triad, a powerful gang known for their predilection toward especially brutal violence.

When Wong heard that Anita Mui was also at the club, he invited her to join him for a drink and asked if she would sing for him. She declined. And not politely. According to witnesses, she addressed Wong in English. When he told her he couldn't understand English, she reportedly shrugged and said, "So what?"

Wong then slapped her across the mouth.

Word of the incident was everywhere by morning, and people could smell trouble coming. Intriguingly, it was other Triad members who were most upset over Wong's actions. They all have a heavy financial interest in the movies, and assaulting a big-time actress in public is simply bad business.

The next evening, Wong was leaving a restaurant when three men approached him, including one who introduced himself as Andy Chan, better known as the Tiger of Wan Chai. He was a former race car driver who was considered one of Mui's closest friends. Like every other halfway powerful male in Hong Kong, he was also Triad. The encounter ended with one of Chan's cohorts slashing Wong's arm with a knife and the Tiger punching Wong in the face.

Two nights later, Wong was shot in the head as he lay sleeping in his hospital bed. Anita Mui got on the first plane out of town, with little more than the clothes on her back. Although nobody had any proof that she had asked for Wong to be killed, there was bound to be speculation. A woman suddenly without a country, she wandered aimlessly through America, Europe, and parts of Asia.

Proof or not, the 14K Triad allegedly had a contract out for her. They were not calling for death. Rather they simply wanted to maim her by cutting off a leg. Authorities initially arrested the Tiger for the murder but had to drop the charge for lack of evidence. However, they wanted to put him on trial for the initial knife attack.

It never happened. On November 20, 1993, Andy Chan was shot dead outside a hotel in Macao. Nobody has ever been charged in either the Wong or the Chan murder. Anita Mui eventually returned to Hong Kong and to this day refuses to discuss what happened.

With the Triads known to have no qualms about wielding their knives, the mere threat of violence is now enough to keep most actors and filmmakers in line. Chow Yun-fat, "the Cary Grant of Hong Kong," happily made movies for Huang Wah Sing, a well-known gangster-turned-producer.

"Of course Huang used force to get actors to work for him—otherwise they wouldn't have anything to do with him," one Hong Kong film critic has said. "But these days, Wah Sing and his brother Wah Keung act like real businessmen."

Huang is actually considered a "good Triad" because of his apparent reasonableness. He has won the loyalty of many in the business by coming to their aid against "bad Triads," those who will slash first and talk later.

"He makes twelve movies a year and they're always successful," the critic continued. "He's proven his credentials and realized that you get better work from your actors if you don't use violence and agree to pay people properly."

Chow Yun-fat had his own brand of trouble with mobsters a while back, when he was allegedly threatened with serious, potentially career-ending injuries if he didn't stop associating with some of the crime bosses' women. Another time, according to Dannen's New Yorker piece, Yun-fat received a script from a particularly notorious Triad producer named Chan Chi-ming. When Yun-fat failed to respond, someone threw a newly severed cat's head into the actor's yard.

It has also been reported that Yun-fat was once forced to sign an exclusive three-year contract with one Triad boss, who then let him languish without work for the duration of the contract. Yun-fat, who is married with three children, apparently thinks this is no way to live. He recently chose to start over in Hollywood rather than stay in Hong Kong, where he's a big star. The price of fame is just too high.

Another tale of Triad control involves the so-called Kings of Concerts, a reference to Hong Kong's top pop singers, which include Andy Lau (who has also made a name for himself in films) and Aaron Kwok. Kwok is a rising star who has recently been named as Golden Harvest's choice to be the "next" Jackie Chan when the day comes that Jackie's worn-out body forces him to quit his high-risk action movies, or he decides to move to America full-time.

According to one Hong Kong insider, "A lot of times the Kings have to make movies for the Triads, sometimes for free. The situation with actresses, though, is much worse. Many of them are under Triad control, especially if they are not from a wealthy family or already have a strong background. They are also forced to sleep with the bosses in exchange for not having their careers ruined. Or worse. Many have reported being raped if they refuse to appear in a film.

"It's a rough, rough business."

One actress told her story to the South China *Morning Post*. After refusing to star in what she thought was a silly, ridiculous movie offered to her by Triad producers, she was attacked on the set of a movie. In full view of the cast and crew, five men pounced on her.

"They came over and without saying a word, they began punching and kicking me. I was screaming and crying with pain but the people who saw it didn't dare give me a hand until after the men left."

She ended up doing the silly, ridiculous movie.

Pushing the Triads out of the movie business has proven next to impossible over the years, in part because the crime syndicates appear to have very close ties with the mainland Chinese government. In fact, Tao Si Qu, the Chinese minister of public security, called the Triads "patriots" in a recent documentary about Asian organized crime. Crime can be responsible for a lot of economic growth both personal and national.

But an event in 1992, reported in Dannen's *New Yorker* article, was so outrageous that it broke the silence in the film community. Chan Chi-ming, the man who cuts the heads off of cats, had his black little heart set on having Leslie Cheung star in his next movie. But Cheung was busy working on a film, *All's Well, Ends Well*, scheduled to be released for the Chinese New Year, which would be equivalent to America's busy Christmas movie season added to the summer season. In other words, a lot of money is at stake with New Year's film releases.

Chan, of course, is not a man who likes being told no. It is believed that to get back at Cheung's movie company, Mandarin Films, for refusing to yank Cheung off of *All's Well, Ends Well*, he sent armed men to Mandarin's film laboratory to steal the negatives of Cheung's film. For once, one of the thieves was later caught and in his confession—later retracted—he named Chan as his boss.

Chan was never arrested or charged, and *All's Well, Ends Well* premiered without a hitch. The hapless thieves had stolen the wrong negatives. But the incident was too outrageous to be ignored. Triads who supported the likes of the extreme Chan had to be stopped.

A large group of actors and filmmakers organized a march, demanding the police do something about the worst of the Triads terrorizing the industry. Some believe that the united show of force has made a slight difference.

''It made an impact and forced the police to treat our complaints seriously,'' says actor Tsui Kam-kong. ''A new department called the O Shop—Organized Crime and Triad Bureau—was formed and it has forced the mob to be much more restrained.'' (It also served as the basis for a gritty, very popular 1993 film called *Organized Crime and Triad Bureau*.)

More to the point, it forced the bad Triads to cool their heels. But the police cannot take full credit—the good Triads also realized the situation was getting out of control. Many believe Chan Chi-ming's jail sentence for having sex with a minor was orchestrated by the Heung brothers in order to teach Chan a lesson.

Even so, some filmmakers still prefer the *See No Evil* attitude. John Woo, who has made a career out of movies dealing with, and often glorifying, the underworld, says for the record, ''I myself have never known of any underworld involvement in the movie industry.''

However, after a long career and close collaboration with

Chow Yun-fat, Woo came to Hollywood in 1993 to make *Hard Target* with Jean-Claude Van Damme and *Broken Arrow* (1996) and *Face/Off* (1997), both with John Travolta. He has no plans to return to Hong Kong anytime soon.

Interestingly, in the latter stages of his career, Jackie Chan has been curiously Triad-proof. Part of it is because he's represented by a large, stable company in Golden Harvest. The other has to do with the type of movies he makes. Since most bad Triads are only concerned with a quick buck, Jackie's films are a bad investment. They take a long time to make, cost a lot of money, and as such take years to recoup expenses and become profitable.

But that's now. In 1980, Jackie was still a relatively small fish and fair game for an angry Triad boss. For Chan at that time, the possibility of violence was very real and impossible to ignore.

Having a price on his head made coming to America suddenly a very appealing, no-time-like-the-present, great idea to Chan. Temporarily relocating in Hollywood would serve the dual purpose of letting Jackie test the American waters and give his friends and business associates back home some time to try and defuse the potentially deadly feud with Lo Wei.

So just as his stardom was peaking in Hong Kong, Jackie Chan was a young man headed east. In a hurry.

4.

成龍 HOME ON THE RANGE

Even if a sore-losing producer-gangster-director hadn't forced the issue, Raymond Chow would still have financed a Chan assault on the American market, though probably not as early as 1980. Chow was the man who had successfully marketed Bruce Lee's films a few years earlier, and he was eager to get back into the lucrative North American market.

For Jackie's U.S. debut, Chow reassembled the same production team that had worked on *Enter the Dragon*, including Fred Weintraub as producer and Robert Clouse to direct. The vehicle was *The Big Brawl*, also called *Battle Creek Brawl* in some areas. (If there's a Hong Kong production company involved, there are bound to be multiple titles. Part of this is due to vagaries of translation. Part is also due to the challenge of finding the most commercial title for each country.)

Jackie arrived in America full of hope about the future and relief at having left his troubles behind him. Confident that this was the beginning of a beautiful friendship with the American public, Chan bought a house and prepared for a long, possibly permanent stay. He really believed this was to be the next great phase of his career—Jackie Chan, American Movie Star. He was getting paid like one. A $1 million payday in 1980 was substantial cash.

But from the beginning, things weren't quite what Jackie expected. To begin with, he wasn't prepared for the way a Hollywood studio film was made.

The upside to the U.S. system is that movie sets are much better organized, with every crew person possessing a high level of professionalism and technical know-how. America then and now leads the world in production values. It also leads the world in action movie budgets. And the best part, for Jackie at least, was that there were no knife-wielding gangsters lurking outside waiting to turn him into shredded cabbage.

The downside of working in America was the tight scheduling. Jackie was accustomed to the free-wheeling Hong Kong style where timetables were ignored. But American film crews were under tremendous pressure to finish on time. For Jackie, that meant he could no longer take a few extra days to work out a complicated fight sequence that was needed to spice up a scene. Time was money, and the studios held the purse strings. This clearly hampered his creativity, and Jackie is a man who hates to feel rushed.

Then there was the matter of the stuntmen. In Hong Kong,

movie stuntmen are martial artists who have grown up fighting. To them, taking a punch is part of life. In America, stuntmen had perfected fake hits to avoid contact, and possible injury, at all costs.

"They come from a different school of stunts than I do," Jackie said to reporters in an interview given during the filming of *The Big Brawl*. "In Hong Kong I can hit one of my stuntmen and he's able to block every punch. But American stuntmen are so slow—they are able to only block every third punch." (Of course, most American stuntmen can ride and fall off a horse better than anyone. It depends on how they've been trained.)

Chan also expressed his fascination with how much job security American stuntmen received from their unions.

"When I was starting out, stuntmen were always getting hurt, but you couldn't admit it. When the action director asked if you were okay, you'd say sure. Because if you said you were hurt, they'd fire you.

"In Hong Kong, human life is so cheap."

Communication may have also hindered Jackie. Even though he had learned enough English—he had worked around the clock with three tutors to learn English—having to deliver convincing English dialogue over the course of a working day took up precious time and energy.

"My acting was not good," Jackie has said without hesitation. "In fact, it was pretty bad. In my native language, Cantonese, all my acting can come out. But I had to speak English, so my acting suffered."

But he tried, determined to do the best job he could.

And he was surrounded by people who genuinely wanted him to succeed, a fact Jackie recognized.

"In Hong Kong, I felt I knew everything. I could pick up a white tablecloth and say black and everyone would say, 'Yes, black.' But here, nobody knows who I am, still people helped me when I went on the set. They made me feel like I was home."

Which is just what Chan needed because personally as well as professionally, Jackie was a bit overwhelmed by his new

surroundings. *The Big Brawl* was filmed on location in San An-
tonio, Texas. Chan was awed by the vastness of the Lone Star
State.

"Texas is like a country, and yet it is only one state. When
you've lived in Hong Kong and then come here, it's impossible
to comprehend the size of America. Also, it's not crowded here
and there seems to be less tension than what I see in Hong
Kong.

"There the individual is very crowded—but very lonely at
the same time. There is a strong feeling of alienation. Here,
people seem to care much more about each other."

Feeling awed and also a little displaced made Jackie contemplate his future beyond the movies—an indication of the
unease he felt being far from home and facing a very uncertain reception from the U.S. film market.

"I will go back to school," Jackie announced shortly after
finishing *The Big Brawl*. "I must learn more about acting. I
will get a British teacher, I will learn to ride a horse and how
to fence."

But even Jackie realized that these were still action-ori-
ented goals.

"I'm young now, but what about when I'm old? I must
learn to read, to talk, to write. I must learn something because
martial arts is of no use [when you are older] . . .

"My father says, 'The clever man moves his mouth, the
stupid man fights.' When young people write to me and tell
me they want to be like me, I tell them to stay in school."

In his heart, even as shooting progressed, Jackie sensed
that *The Big Brawl* had missed the mark because he knew he
hadn't been able to be himself—in one area especially. It had
to gall Chan that he was not allowed autonomy to direct the
fight scenes on his own—the studio hired an American, Pat
Johnson, to "supervise" Jackie. The result was predictable.

"Pat Johnson would tell me what American audiences will
believe and what they won't believe," Jackie explained in an
interview soon after the film was completed. "He said Americans want to see power, they wouldn't believe that a real kung

fu punch, that has little movement, would really be powerful. So instead I had to use a roundhouse punch, even though real martial artists would never do it this way. But he said that's how the audience likes it.''

Touring the country while promoting the film introduced Jackie to the more aggressive nature of some Americans. Jackie has told in interviews how, on three separate occasions, he was confronted by guys challenging him to a fight.

''The first troublemaker was at the City Center in Detroit. When I walked in the first thing I saw was a banner that said 'Jackie Chan—Master of Kung Fu.' I sensed an unpleasant atmosphere, I sensed some people were offended by the words on the banner.

''As my interview was coming to an end, I was asked to perform a few kung fu techniques. Right then a guy jumps onto the stage and shouts, 'Jackie Chan, what would you do if someone attacked you?'

''The guy wasn't tall, but he did have a sturdy build. I figured he was trying to make a name for himself by striking me. I looked over to see what the staff was doing—nothing. They wanted to see the duel. I had no choice but to keep calm and ready myself. I decided to go for his legs.

''He made the first move, swinging his fists, like a feint move. Anyhow, before he finished I had already struck his legs. He hit the stage with a loud 'bang!' That's when the staff finally came and got the guy.''

Jackie's response was a smart, classic martial arts reaction. Hold the enemy's eyes with your own, don't let him see which part of you is moving, then drop him with a low kick.

The next incident occurred in Cincinnati, Ohio, on a local television show. Chan was giving a demonstration on how to free yourself from being strangled from behind.

''My performing partner was this man who was about six feet tall. During the rehearsal, everything was fine. But when we did it on camera, he squeezed my neck as tight as he could, and I was really almost suffocated. So I put an elbow in his ribs to loosen his grip, then I twisted my body, and with my hands over his back I pulled and rolled his body in a complete circle, heels over head. It was a terrific move. That two-hundred-pound man landed right in front of me, knocked unconscious for a moment. But he was all right."

The last confrontation took place at a party in Jackie's honor held in Portland, Oregon.

"Right at the party a guy asked for a duel, and of course I refused. I thought he was going to shake my hand good-bye, but he was being cunning—once he had my hand, he held on as tight as he could. I immediately moved my hand into a defensive position. He was actually strong, so I gripped his veins to lower his blood circulation, and gradually his grip loosened.

"Just as I was about to free my palm, I saw him raise his left fist, so I grabbed his thumb and commanded his wrist. At that point he couldn't move."

The action between Jackie and his three would-be challengers sounds a lot more fascinating than the fight choreography staged by Pat Johnson for *The Big Brawl*. Unfortunately, it was Jackie's face on the movie poster and Jackie with the reputation as a great action star. So it was Jackie who took the critical heat for Johnson's misguided decisions. Here's one L.A. reviewer's impression of *The Big Brawl*:

> Like Lee, Chan choreographs his own fight scenes but unlike Lee he is not a true super-master of the martial arts. . . . He is not nearly as interesting as Lee was on screen. He does not project the power as a fighter that could create a cult following and he has not achieved the humor in his second language that could give him a following as an action comedy star.

Although it wasn't a bomb, *The Big Brawl* didn't make the hoped-for splash. As a result, it was an obvious disappointment to all concerned.

Of course, the last thing Jackie wanted was to be like Bruce, but it was a hook critics could hang their headlines on.

And people taking a look at Chan hoping to see "the next Bruce Lee" were sure to be disappointed.

After *The Big Brawl*, Jackie was signed to do a cameo in *Cannonball Run*, a Burt Reynolds vehicle that was billed as a wacky road comedy. In it, Chan played a Japanese car driver who participates in a brawl with bikers.

"I thought if I did something special, people in America will remember me. If the movie works, then I will get a chance to do another leading role."

Even though the slam-bang film was inexplicably popular, it presented Chan as little more than a curiosity. This was not the showcase material Jackie needed.

A film analyst opined:

> Jackie Chan's appeal is limited to the Asian circuit. He is very Hong Kong oriented, whereas Bruce Lee, who had spent many, many years as an actor in America, possessed an instinctive feel for the American audience. Bruce Lee had an emotional impact on the audience, while Jackie Chan could merely dazzle them with stunts for the duration of the movie.

Bruce Lee was simply too fresh in people's minds, and Jackie wasn't given the right projects to establish his own identity in America's film-going psyche—yet. This opinion was echoed by Rigo Jesu, who distributes Western films in Hong Kong:

> Chan is very refreshing, a combination of innocence, power and technique. However, all of his previous efforts in the international market have been B-Grade movies with bad scripts. He needs a unique role that will make him stand out.

The grand experiment had failed through mishandling, a lack of vision, and bad timing. Plans to make *Why Me?* with Robert Clouse were scrapped as the Golden Harvest brain trust pulled the plug.

Returning to Hong Kong presented an obvious problem for Jackie—he was still a marked man. But he didn't have a lot of options, so there was really only one thing to do—figure out a way to make peace with Lo Wei.

Back in Hong Kong, attempts were under way to try and resolve Jackie's Triad troubles. For reasons not completely clear, actor Jimmy Wang Yu, who had worked with Jackie and Lo on *Killer Meteors*, intervened. Wang Yu had his own movie ties to a Triad in Taiwan, where he lived. Jimmy arranged to meet with Lo Wei in Hong Kong to discuss the matter and see if they could come to a resolution. But once he arrived, Wang Yu found himself in his own pickle, confronted by a dozen or so Sun Yi On hit men brandishing nasty-looking "watermelon knives."

Jimmy was in trouble, but he turned out to be the luckiest man in Asia that day when an English police sergeant on patrol happened by and saw the impending attack. He arrested the lot of them and ran everyone into the station to find out what the heck was going on.

The next day, a Hong Kong newspaper carried a short news item about the bust, along with this tidbit:

> The director Lo Wei and actor Wang Yu have been summoned to the police station for questioning.

It was obvious that the Jackie Chan/Lo Wei situation had gotten way out of hand, and it was time to settle the matter in whatever way necessary. Raymond Chow finally offered to ante up enough cash to satisfy Lo Wei's ego and pocketbook. The final settlement was said to be HK$13 million. In addition, Chow secured the rights to some—but not all—of Jackie's early movies.

Chow effectively "bought up" the hit and in so doing bought up Jackie as well. Chan would have to spend the rest of his life indebted to Chow and, to a lesser extent, Wang Yu, who had literally put his life on the line to help Jackie.

This is one reason Jackie continues to work under the Golden Harvest umbrella. There are also those who believe that Raymond Chow's hold over Jackie is why Chan keeps putting off retirement. As long as Golden Harvest believes him to be a viable product, he's obliged to keep working—no matter how battered and bruised his brand of moviemaking makes him.

It gives new meaning to the old Hollywood term *contract player.*

5.

龍 LET THE ACTION BEGIN

Before Jackie resumed his movie life in Hong Kong, he showed his gratitude to Jimmy Wang Yu by appearing in *Fantasy Mission Force*, a soldier-of-fortune war flick. Jackie's presence gave this rather ordinary film more pizzazz than it would have had. That done, he went to work on *Dragon Lord*, a film that once again featured his Dragon character, the lazy boy who'd rather play hooky than learn to fight.

The film was in the *Drunken Master* vein, a kung fu period piece jazzed up with clever fights and some more modern-looking action sequences. Jackie's stuntmen were the first to notice his new intensity. He pushed his men to the limit, unconcerned with the body count. While shooting a sequence showing a martial arts tournament, almost a hundred stuntmen were injured. It would be one of the last costume kung fu films Jackie would do because he had decided it was time to move in a new direction, time to set the industry on its ear again.

Dragon Lord exorcised some demons for Jackie. First of all, it gave him back the face he felt had been lost by his failure to conquer America. More than that, it freed him of the anxiety that he had lost all his fans during his absence. He hadn't. If anything, their hearts had grown fonder. There was a lot of anticipation to see what Jackie would come up with next.

Chan already knew what it was. It was an idea that had begun to take shape while he was in the United States.

"To pass the time there, I watched a lot of old Hollywood silent movies," Chan has said. "Buster Keaton, Harold Lloyd. And what they did was amazing. Buster Keaton gave me a lot of ideas, new things I could do that were physical and funny—but weren't fighting. Some of the things I saw or thought of I wrote down and saved—sometimes for years. Sometimes it's just a bit of an idea, and I'll work on it for years until I come up with the best way to use it.

"It made me think it would be good to use physical stunts in my movies—to combine action with comedy, the way I had combined kung fu and comedy. I knew I had to be different, I knew I would have to keep thinking to stay ahead. I always wanted to do something nobody else can do. With special effects, anybody can be Superman—but without them, nobody can be me."

Released in 1983, *Project A* was the result of Jackie's vision and is still considered by many to be his best film ever. For this grand experiment, Jackie turned to the tried-and-true for assistance—his Opera School brothers Sammo Hung and Yuen Biao. In the film, set at the turn of the century, the three friends play soldiers and sailors who end up fighting a band of pirates. The story line is secondary to the amazing action and stunt sequences in the film, including Jackie's now-infamous fall from a clock tower, which nearly broke his neck.

And just to make sure there was no doubt about who was doing his stunts, ever since *Project A*, Jackie had begun showing outtakes of missed stunt attempts under the closing credits and always made sure his face was visible on the stunts themselves.

Beyond helping to conceive and direct the stunts, Sammo's presence on the set guaranteed some excellent screen fights as well. For many, it was a near-perfect film experience. And on a larger scale, it brought kung fu movies into modern times.

Time magazine's film critic, Richard Corliss, has commented on Chan's silent-era pedigree:

> Chan's study of the silent masters taught him the universal language of film: action and passion, humor and heart.

His movies are so simple, so fluid, so exuberant that they are easily understood by people who don't speak Cantonese.

If anyone had thought Jackie was a one-note wonder, *Project A* proved he was one of the film world's most creative and influential forces. The next few years were a whirl of activity, with Jackie often working on two projects at once, in roles large and small.

Two of his more popular films during this period, *Wheels on Meals* and *Winners and Sinners*, were directed by Sammo, who had become a highly respected filmmaker in his own right with films like *Enter the Fat Dragon*. However, he was better known for his fight choreography as opposed to directing and starring in stunt and action work. Jackie had cornered the market on *that*.

If there is one recurring complaint American Chan fans have about Jackie's early movies it is the lack of a cohesive plot. This was often a result of Jackie coming up with a new scene well into the shoot—scenes that had to be shoehorned in whether they made sense or not. But Jackie had been aiming for the heart of his Asian audience. For them, Jackie's charm and stunts were enough.

"People like Jackie because his films are pure action and adventure—he's like a local Steven Spielberg," explained George Chang, who was the head of the communications department at Hong Kong Baptiste College in 1987 when he gave an interview.

If that's what they wanted, that's what Jackie would give them. And he seemed to have the Midas touch when it came to pleasing his audience. By the mid-1980s he had become without question the most popular actor not only in Hong Kong, but in the world—with the annoying exception of America.

For a variety of reasons, Asian films were hitting a glass wall in the United States, making access incredibly difficult. Fans either had to travel to the local Chinatown to see his films or rent badly produced videos, *if* they were even available.

His earlier failure in America still stung Jackie, which is the only plausible reason he agreed to do *The Protector*, a cop drama to be directed by a man who was hardly well versed in martial arts, James Glickenhaus. Jackie was the one who initiated the collaboration. After seeing Glickenhaus's *The Exterminator* and *Code Name: The Soldier*, Chan thought this might be the right director to work with.

He wasn't.

This time, the situation was reversed. The movie was predominantly shot in Hong Kong, and it was Glickenhaus who was reeling from culture shock.

"Working that way was incredibly hard. We shot the exteriors in New York, then two months later filmed interiors, which made matching it up hard to do.

"Right from the beginning I told Jackie that this was *my* film and *I* was going to direct the martial arts sequences and we were going to do them *completely* differently than he did.

"They never shoot masters, they shoot very short sections and they do a lot of under-cranking to speed up the movement on screen, which I refuse to do. I told him I wanted to shoot the fights in masters and then, if they didn't work, go back and cover them."

Jackie didn't get mad—he simply began planning the ways he'd reshoot the film once Glickenhaus was out of the way. Which is exactly what he did. Chan hired the film's "villain," Bill Wallace, to hang around and shoot extra footage, which was then edited into Chan's edited version, which was released in Asia.

Glickenhaus wasn't amused.

"Technically, I had the right of final cut on the picture—they didn't have the right to add footage and change what was there.

"I've seen a lot of Hong Kong cinema and I think it's very interesting, terrific stuff—but it doesn't have a chance in America."

Well, neither did *The Protector*. Although it turned out to be Jackie's most successful international release to date, it was still a disappointment. More than anything, it was a frustrating experience for Chan. Because of his still-shaky English, a dialogue coach was brought in to help Jackie with his dialogue and reaction shots.

"The coach is down here, kneeling down next to me so he can touch my leg here when I should be smiling, then touch me there when the script says I should be angry. Then there was a signal for when I was supposed to walk away.

"How could I possibly be any good like this?"

But there was one positive outcome—Jackie's thoughts on how the movie *should* be made planted an idea that blossomed into what would be the most notable film series in his career.

Police Story was Jackie's answer to *The Protector*. Considered by most followers of the genre as a modern-day classic, *Police Story* stars Chan as a Hong Kong cop who takes down a drug-running crime lord. It includes some of the most spectacular stunts and action sequences ever filmed, including Jackie's death-defying slide down a pole decorated with very juiced-up electric lights.

"First I did comedy and everybody starts doing comedy," Jackie has said to reporters. "Then I do action and everybody does action. So then I start doing dangerous stunts—and nobody follows me. It's mine alone."

Amen to that—although others weren't above "borrowing" some of Jackie's stunt and action ideas. One of the most obvious appropriations is in Sylvester Stallone's *Tango & Cash* (1989), which re-created a *Police Story* sequence where Jackie single-handedly stops a bus full of bad guys. It only proved that while the general American population might not know about Jackie Chan, those in the business of making action films watched his every move. (Years later, Yuen Biao's martial arts laundry scene from the classic *Dreadnaught* [1988] was "borrowed" for *Batman Forever*. And as has been reported in the mainstream press, Quentin Tarantino also "borrowed" plot, character, and structure for *Reservoir Dogs* from director Ringo Lam's classic *City on Fire* [1987].)

"*Police Story* is my favorite film as a finished product,"

Chan says. "It's got the best director, best martial arts director, best choreography. A lot of work went into this film, I
spent a lot of time thinking through the script and working
on the editing.

"It's also the first action/dangerous stunt movie. In Asia,
everybody was very shocked. The first time it was showing in
the theater, it was a midnight show, and nobody was talking,
they were just staring at the screen in awe. Then when it was
over, they went wild."

Police Story is not only Chan's personal favorite, it was also
a *huge* international hit that cemented his hold on the title of
Most Popular Actor in the World. Of course with such monu-
mental success comes the drawback of having nowhere to go
but down. The real trick now for Jackie was to find ways to
top himself from movie to movie—a daunting project even for
someone as gifted as he.

Jackie surprised a few people by next starring in a drama,
First Mission, directed by Sammo. The movie contains little
fighting or action but for once gave Jackie the chance to show
he really could act if need be. It's just that his thespian skills
were not why Chan fans paid money to see his movies. They
came to see their real-life superman do the seemingly impossible. And Jackie was determined to give them what they
wanted—even if it killed him. Which, in fact, it almost did.

Armor of God was Jackie's version of Steven Spielberg's Indiana Jones character—an adventurer who must confront
dangerous and occasionally mystical obstacles in his quests. It
was a big-budget monster of a shoot being filmed on location
to improve the production values.

Jackie arrived in what was then Yugoslavia and headed directly for the set to prepare for that day's scene. It was a relatively routine stunt that called for him to jump from a wall to
a tree branch, then jump down to the ground. Later, Jackie
admitted that he was probably a bit fatigued and jet-lagged
from the long trip and that he had also drunk some beer on
the plane. But he insists he was not impaired.

Whatever the cause, on an extra take Jackie insisted on, he

missed the branch and crashed headfirst into the rocky ground below. If you look at the outtakes at the end of the film it is obvious that Chan was gravely injured. Unlike a lot of people who suffer head trauma, Jackie vividly remembers the accident and its aftermath.

"I had already done the stunt several times but I wanted to do it again so I could land in a certain way. But I didn't grab the tree limb tightly enough and I fell. There was blood coming from my ear and I knew I was badly hurt."

Frantic crew members called an ambulance and tried to stem the blood flow.

"They rushed me to the hospital, then later transferred me to another one. Fortunately, the best brain surgeon in Europe was in Yugoslavia, and he rushed to the hospital to operate on me.

"I woke up in the middle of the night, around two-thirty, and I was so happy to see the face of a nurse rushing into my room because then I knew I had survived. I wasn't in heaven or hell."

Jackie's father flew in to keep vigil over his son, along with the ever-present Willie Chan. Once he was stable enough to travel, Chan was flown to France for extensive tests. The tests took eleven days, and the prognosis looked good. Other than some hearing loss in one ear, Jackie would recover.

The news was so optimistic that Jackie started making plans to return to work, completely ignoring the doctors' warnings not to do any more stunts until his wounds were healed. His father put his foot down and absolutely forbade it—Jackie was taking two months off whether he liked it or not. He didn't like it. But for once, he had no choice.

He passed the time by editing the footage already shot and working on stunts for when he returned to work in January of 1986. Chan also formalized the completion of his own production company, Golden Way, which would operate under the Golden Harvest umbrella.

Jackie also took the time to reassure his fans and the film

community in general that they had not seen the last of Jackie Chan, Action Daredevil:

> The show will go on and I will continue appearing in dangerous stunt sequences in my movies in the future. I consider it a new challenge whenever I appear in any action or stunt sequence. I want to show my best to the world and I'm not giving up because of one accident.
>
> I started doing dangerous stunts when I was 17 and a movie stand-in. I'm an experienced and professional stuntman and I want to show my audiences the most challenging and most exciting shots in all my movies.
>
> Unless I call it a day in my acting career, I will not hesitate to try more stunt shots. I want to thank all my fans in different parts of the world for their concern and support. I am so glad to be back home.

Even though the press release was authored by a public relations writer, the sentiments behind it were pure Jackie. Movies had become his passion in life, and nothing short of death would keep him from returning to work.

Incidentally, while having such a brush with mortality makes many people suddenly religious, at least temporarily, Chan says he doesn't subscribe to any religion. Nor does he have faith that there is a Supreme Being looking out for his welfare.

"No, I don't believe in God," Jackie has said. "When I was young I was religious—everybody had religion. But I only liked going to church because they handed out milk and food. Then later, in school, we learned about Buddha.

"But as an adult, I don't believe in anything. I see so many wars—Iran, Iraq, Yugoslavia—people fighting and killing *because of* religion. That's why I don't embrace any religion. I just believe in myself.

"I work hard and I help people. If I do that, then every Buddha, every god will smile on me. I don't have to go to a judge—I believe in myself."

The instant he got the green light to return to work, Chan was back on the set. He fired the original director and took over the reins himself—not out of vindictiveness, but from the need to channel all his energies into the project. If anyone thought the accident would temper Chan's on-screen daring, they were in for a shock. If anything, it seems to have spurred Jackie on, as if he felt the need to prove just how unafraid he was. As a result, *Armor of God* features vintage Chan stunts, including one where he free-falls from a mountain onto a hot air balloon, grabs the rigging, then climbs into the gondola. It showed the world Jackie was back and intended to stay.

Jackie regularly tries out variations on his screen persona to see which ones will be best received by his fans. In *Dragons Forever*, he plays a borderline shyster lawyer who starts out defending an unscrupulous company run by gangsters but ends up on the side of righteousness. One of the highlights of the movie is a fight between Chan and American kickboxing champ Benny ''The Jet'' Urquidez, with whom Jackie had filmed a memorable fight in *Wheels on Meals.*

But the negatives outweighed the positives on *Dragons Forever.* Because of the tradition of releasing a new Chan film on Chinese New Year, Sammo and Jackie were under tremendous pressure to deliver the movie on time. Although they were longtime collaborators, they had distinctly different styles—Jackie is an impulsive stunt performer who believes in winging it; Sammo is a meticulous director with a savvy sense of fight choreography and film structure. It's no secret why Jackie tends to come across better when someone who really knows him, like Sammo, directs him. And despite his success, Jackie tended to turn to Sammo in times of uncertainty.

''Even now,'' Sammo has said, ''if Jackie has a difficult stunt to do, he sometimes calls me to come on the set. He'll say, 'Big Brother, come and give me strength.' I go and encourage him and tell him he can do it.''

But as with most siblings, complicated and occasionally conflicting emotions run deep. Despite having worked together for so many years, this time out their differences became a wedge. Jackie and Sammo had a bitter falling out, and the movie ended with a black cloud hanging over it. Yuen

Biao, for one, thinks it was an accumulation of feelings that had gathered over the years before finally exploding.

"Sammo has always been the Big Brother," Yuen explains carefully. "He was the first one of us to be very successful as an actor and a director. Then all of a sudden, Jackie became a huge star internationally, so of course Sammo is going to ask why Jackie and not him. That caused friction, especially on *Dragons Forever*."

Sammo's question was valid. There were others who *were* better actors, better directors, better fighters, and better choreographers than Jackie. Yuen Biao is arguably the best acrobat of the three. Yet Jackie's ability to synthesize various cinematic elements into new forms had made him the surprise cream of the crop.

Few would argue with the idea that Sammo was a superior mainstream film director who himself was considered a comic innovator. But stardom is a quality that's impossible to quantify. For whatever reason, Hung didn't capture the audience's imagination the way Jackie did, and therein lay the difference.

The fallout between the brothers became common knowledge in Hong Kong—not a good omen. Fan reaction cemented the perception that it was an ill-fated production—although it did decent business in Hong Kong, *Dragons Forever* bombed throughout the rest of Asia. Stunts couldn't erase the specter of Jackie in a suit and tie playing a lawyer.

The box office drubbing he took with *Dragons Forever* sent Jackie scurrying back to the tried and true, in this case sequels to *Police Story* and *Project A*. *Police Story II* was a fine film on its own merit but paled for many when compared to the stunning original.

Although *Project A, Part II* was successful, Sammo's and Yuen's absences were noticeable, and the movie suffered for it.

It's interesting that Chan chose to direct the corny, mushy *Miracles* after his breach with his older brother. It's as if he felt compelled to show off *his* directing muscle as a counterpoint to Sammo's strength. And indeed, although the movie's story meandered at times, many critics praised Jackie's direction of this musical retelling of *Pocketful of Miracles*.

American musicals have long been a passion for Chan. *Miracles* was a chance to live out a special fantasy.

"The first movie I ever saw as a child was a musical—*The Sound of Music*. 'Doe a deer, a female deer,' " Chan has said. "I saw it seven times. I didn't understand any English but I loved it anyway."

One could well imagine Jackie feeling a oneness with the apple-cheeked Von Trapps and doting Maria. So it's no surprise that Chan says as far as directing goes, *Miracles* is his favorite film. Unfortunately for Jackie (though fortunately for us!) the film was a bust.

Jackie was learning a sad truth that many an American actor already knew. Action film fans won't be supportive of action film stars who go off and dabble in self-indulgent projects. They want you to go home with the date that brought you to the dance, so to speak.

Jackie got the message.

6.

UNDER PRESSURE

Before he could start work on his next project, he had an obligation to fulfill—an appearance in Jimmy Wang Yu's big screen comeback. *Island of Fire* co-starred a slew of big Hong Kong names, including Sammo Hung and Andy Lau, who were there after being informed it could be unhealthy to do otherwise. Although his name figures prominently in the credits, Jackie has only about ten minutes of screen time. Which was about nine too many for his taste.

"That film was rubbish," Chan has said flat out. "Jimmy says he needs my help and I agreed to do it because he is a friend who helped me a great deal when I had problems with the Chinese Mafia years before.

"To be in the movie would help sell it to a lot of countries, so I said fine. I really wanted to do something good for him. But when I got to the set, all his friends, the director, everyone is just fooling around. I can't make a good movie by myself."

Jackie ended up buying the Hong Kong rights to the movie, then shelved it. He believes the lax attitude displayed on the *Island of Fire* set is an insidious virus slowly destroying the Hong Kong film industry.

"If all I was interested in was money, I could put out ten movies a year. But I'm not. Instead, I concentrate on one film every year. And in that one film, I oversee everything—music, directing, locations, art design. I make sure that at least *I'm* happy with it.

"But too many movies are being made that satisfy *nobody*. They are just made to make whatever money they can. And they die. The film industry is dying because of it. One thing— you can count on a Jackie Chan film to do good box office business. The audience knows what they will be getting. It's important they can count on that."

Hoping to appease the restless natives and give them what they wanted, Chan began work on a big budget *Armour of God* sequel called *Operation Condor*. In it, Jackie made a conscious effort to minimize fighting elements and maximize action instead.

"Kung fu belongs in the past," he said in a 1991 interview. "In Hong Kong, films are getting faster and we don't care about fighting as much anymore. I think the change is good because it makes the films more modern. What people want are stunts.

"I'm always trying to come up with funny, interesting stunts—and I want them to be as dangerous as possible. While working on a project I always work on the stunts first and figure out how many I'll be able to put in the film. I describe the scenes I want in the movie to my writer, then they start working on the story."

No wonder the plot always seems like an afterthought in Chan films. It is.

Even on paper, *Operation Condor* was an ambitious undertaking, with locations literally spanning the globe. But Jackie felt he had to compete with the mega-budgeted American films Steven Spielberg, Sylvester Stallone, and Arnold Schwarzenegger were putting out. Seeing dollar signs, Golden Harvest gave the project a green light.

As mentioned previously, Jackie is not burdened with an acute sense of promptness nor is he driven by financial efficiency. It took over eight months to make *Operation Condor*, and the film had a final price tag in excess of HK$80 million. The stress of trying to control such a behemoth took a tremendous toll on everyone involved. Directors came and went, and Chan was buffeted by the sheer logistics.

The size of the project spread Jackie way too thin and caused countless delays.

"We had two units working—but there's only one Jackie Chan," he said in an interview. "Everyone wanted to get direct orders from me, and that was a problem. It took too long and the delays cost a lot of money. There was also a lot of rivalries among the stuntmen, and I was obliged to fire some of them so I could finish shooting the movie in peace."

If people weren't wearing out his patience, then the elements were beating him down.

"The Sahara is a wonderful location, but it is so hot! During preproduction, we had gone there and it was beautiful— but it was winter. We came back to work during the summer and the heat was just terrible."

The fact that nobody considered that the desert might be a tad warmer during the summer just proves how badly organized the preproduction was on this film.

"We didn't have enough water for the crew and actors, either," Jackie admits. "Then when the sandstorms came, it was impossible to work. The camel didn't want to obey, and the scorpions . . . they came out every night. One of our crew was bitten by one but he was saved because we had a doctor with us.

"If you like action, try the Sahara."

Instead of being in the desert for one month as scheduled, it took three months to wrap shooting at that location. The heat was so brutal, they had to stop filming at noon. Then fifty-eight crew members fell ill after contracting a mystery ailment. At the end of the three months, Chan shipped ten tons of Sahara sand back to Hong Kong so he could simulate the location.

All in all, Jackie spent three times the original budget—not that he didn't receive some spectacular results. *Operation Condor* includes a fight finale that takes place in a wind tunnel. But the cost was staggering by any nation's standards. For Hong Kong, it was nearly insurmountable. Luckily for Chan and Golden Harvest, *Operation Condor* was an international hit. The all-important Japanese market devoured it. Even so, the sky-high price tag meant that despite being one of the most popular films in memory, it turned a relatively low profit.

Studios the world over have one thing in common. They exist to make money. Although Jackie had made his studio extraordinary sums, all that mattered was the most recent profit statement. And as far as Golden Harvest was concerned, his profitability was down.

Jackie had been in the business long enough to know that he was walking a thin line, so he promised to be a better boy and not spend cash like so much Monopoly money anymore. To that end, Jackie realized he had to turn over control behind the camera to others. Even though actually doing it would prove to be a constant struggle for the control-oriented actor, he knew it was necessary to at least make the attempt.

"I spent too much time location hunting, casting, and doing meetings," Jackie admits. "I would have to listen to everything big and small—this actress wants this, this location won't work for that. It's not like being an American director—an Asian director has to know everything.

"Now I hire different directors to do different things, then they keep me informed. If I don't like something, I tell them to change it. But when we're on the set, I don't have to listen to all the questions. I say, 'Go ask the director.' ''

What Chan really means is he turns over control until he disagrees with something, then he pulls rank. Surprisingly, this has worked more often than not but it has also resulted in more than one director being out-and-out fired mid-film when they dared to try and hold their ground against Jackie's wishes.

With the start of a new decade, Jackie knew it was time to regroup. Although his films still routinely outperformed American action films abroad and he was still the number one box draw worldwide, he also knew that you don't stay on top by playing it safe.

Whatever direction Jackie chose to take, he knew his fans would be there waiting with open minds and wallets. The one constant in Chan's career has been the unconditional loyalty of his followers, who span continents and cultures. To some he is a kind of god, insofar as they find inspiration from his exploits on films, while for others he's a hero they can live vicariously through. Jackie hopes his fans know how much their devotion means to him.

"When someone knows me I am so *happy*," he has said. "I've been recognized in Moscow airport by Red Army soldiers, and once when I was in Morocco for *Operation Condor*, there was a riot in the market—and I was so *happy!*

"Whenever I get hurt or when it's my birthday and my office fills up with flowers and chocolates and gifts—it's wonderful! Everybody in Asia really adores me—they call me Sunkist Orange and other pet names."

Chan fans wait anxiously for every new movie release and immerse themselves in Jackie lore and minutiae. The Internet is filled with homepages dedicated to Jackie, intricately designed by devoted fans. His international fan club is more organized than most small businesses and at its height had over ten thousand members—mostly girls. His followers will spend $169 for the latest laser disc version of one of his films even if there's no subtitling and they don't understand Cantonese.

To be fair, most Chan fans are otherwise rational, stable people who simply find Jackie's movies to be a wonderful escape and fantasy. Here is a regular guy doing incredible things, *really* doing it, without benefit of blue screens or computers. And to show his fans how much he appreciates their overwhelming support, twice a year Jackie hosts a party for the Jackie Chan International Fan Club, with a majority of the members being young Japanese women.

But Jackie's fans span the range and include people of both genders from all walks of life. Director Quentin Tarantino positively gushed when presenting Jackie with MTV's Lifetime Achievement Award:

> When you watch a Jackie Chan movie, you want to be Jackie Chan. You want to run through glass as only he can. You want to fight twenty-five guys, lose up until the last moment and then take them all on, as only he can. To jump through glass, to jump off buildings, to be drug behind buses and handle it all—he's one of the best filmmakers that the world has ever known. He's one of the greatest physical comedians since sound came into films.
>
> If I could be any actor, I would have the life Jackie Chan has!

Barbara Scharres is a Chan fan who bared her soul in an essay that appeared in a national trade paper:

> Like the audiences with whom I've watched Hong Kong movies, I'm getting carried away without a pang of regret or a thought of restraint. For one thing, I can hardly remember when watching movies was quite this thrilling. It's a magic that catches me by surprise every time.
>
> When I'm watching Jackie Chan's *Project A* or *Police Story*, I don't have to care or analyze whether these films were made for art, money, or ego gratification. They unstintingly deliver the goods in terms they establish.
>
> By the time the credits roll, I feel grateful for the rare and pure excitement of going crazy with delight in unison with several hundred other people.

Art in any form has always been capable of eliciting a certain type of single-minded passion. People have been known
to steal or kill in a quest to possess a great work of art; lovers
of Renaissance art will travel to foreign countries just to visit
museums while others will spend ghastly sums of money to
own a drawing, painting, or sculpture created by an admired
artist.

Obviously, though, there is a difference between passion
and obsession. Admirers of great art focus on the created object itself whereas obsessed fans tend to focus on the person
who is creating the art. Besides, Michelangelo admirers don't
have the option of stalking him.

"Right now, I belong to the people," Chan said in a 1987
interview. "I won't even contemplate any serious romantic
commitment because there is no guarantee what my fans
would do."

For the individual fan who is a step or two past stability to
begin with, fixation on a celebrity can grow into delusion,
where the line between reality and fantasy breaks down completely. No star in the world is safe from fans who have created a fictional relationship with them that is as real to the
obsessed fan as the morning sun.

"Jackie Chan is the best, I love to watch his wonderful
stunts," says one fan. So far, so good. But then you find out
this Japanese college graduate has given up her life in Tokyo
and moved to Hong Kong for the sole purpose of being closer
to Jackie.

"I am learning Cantonese so I can talk with him in his own
language," the young girl adds.

Technology has made it easier to think we "know" a celebrity. Our ability to process information grows ever more efficient and with it the ability to keep track of a celebrity's daily
movements. Television is filled with entertainment news
shows that tell us everything we wanted to know and more
about actors. Via the Internet, we can read translations of the
Hong Kong newspapers and find out up-to-the-moment dish
about Jackie or any other Asian film star. Privacy is a thing of

the past for any person wishing to pursue a public profession, whether it be acting, sports, or politics.

Unlike American actors, who grab the money and perks accorded them by their celebrity status with one hand while pushing away the fans who are responsible for it with the other, Jackie has always been accessible—another reason fans begin to feel as if they have a personal relationship with him. He has freely and routinely talked about everything from his impoverished childhood to his film failures to intimate matters of his health. Nothing seems off limits—except his love life, which has usually been kept in shadows.

He gives conflicting reasons for the secrecy. Sometimes Chan says his movies are so important that his personal relationships are secondary. But other times he admits it's simply too dangerous to be open about whom he may or may not be dating, may or may not be married to, may or may not lust after, because it might cause problems. He worries about inflicting unintentional pain on his female fans who then might be driven to hurt themselves. And he's serious.

He claims that concern over fan reaction is also a reason why none of his film characters ever gets involved in a serious romance. Even in *Police Story*, the relationship between Chan and his on-screen girlfriend, played by Maggie Cheung, has absolutely no fire. To the contrary. She's always getting slugged, dropped, or kidnapped, and Jackie merely rescues her. There's no hint of intimacy between the two—and apparently that's just how Jackie's most ardent female fans like it.

Culturally speaking, it's a bit of a relief to discover that deranged fans in serious need of a life are not just an American phenomenon. But there is one important cultural difference between obsessed film fans in Hong Kong and those in the United States. In America, demented fans kill the stars. In Asia, demented fans kill themselves.

"I always would say to journalists, please no personal questions," Jackie said in one interview. "But they would, so I lied:

"Do you have a girlfriend?"
"No!"
"Do you have a wife?"
"No!"

"That's because the first time I talked about having a girl-friend in an interview, one of my fans committed suicide. She jumped beneath a subway train because she read I was seeing someone. Then it happened again! Another girl came to my office, stood in front, and drank poison.

"I was very scared because I have a responsibility with all my fans. I cannot say I have a girlfriend or am getting married or I have a son—how many people would die? So all these years I was very quiet about my private life. It was a secret, which was very hard on me but it seemed better to hurt the person I was seeing instead of many, many fans."

Whether it was the fact that he was getting older and de-veloping a life-is-too-short attitude, whether Chan is simply worn out from all the intrigue, or whether he's taking a cue from Americans who routinely bare their soul, he's lately adopted a new, open policy.

"Now, I do answer," Jackie says. "You cannot keep lying about your life. And I believe all my fans are growing up and having families of their own. So now I do tell the truth—I have a girlfriend—and a wife. And I have a twelve-year-old son."

His wife is Lin Fung-chiao, a Taiwanese actress. Despite his newfound honesty, Chan is vague when it comes to details on how they met. However, they were married in 1981, which was during the time Chan was exiled from Hong Kong because of his problems with Lo Wei but was able to work in Taiwan, where he was protected by his friend Jimmy Wang Yu.

Together they have a teenage son named J.C. Although Jackie is secretive about where his family lives, some associ-ates say Chan has relocated them to America, in part because he wants his son educated here.

By American standards, Chan has an unconventional fam-ily life. Although he and his wife continue to be legally married, they live separate lives, and it's no secret that Jackie dates other women—he says so himself. Nor does he go out of his way to spend time with his son, whom he admittedly sees infrequently, only three or four times a year. While that *is* more than his own father saw Jackie, the circumstances are different. Still, Jackie says he's simply too busy working, usually on location in some part of the world. Even when he's in Hong Kong, he often sleeps at Golden Harvest, using his office as a small apartment, instead of going home to his penthouse condo in Hong Kong's exclusive Repulse Bay area.

Jackie offers something of an explanation for the estrangement from J.C.

"I work all the time because . . . I don't like not working. Every movie I treat like my son. It's *more* important than my real son," Jackie was quoted in one interview.

When asked why he doesn't have his family join him on location, Chan loses some of his ever-present jocularity.

"I don't like my family around when I work. It bothers me," he says, possibly referring to the experience of letting his wife and son visit the *First Strike* set while on location in Australia. The press dogged them, invading Jackie's privacy and breaking his concentration.

It's not that he wants to be alone when he works. Quite the contrary. The bigger the entourage the better. Just as long as they're not relatives.

"I like having people beside me, behind me, and around me. I don't like staying at five-star hotels—I'd rather stay at an apartment with my screenwriters and stunt guys and bodyguard and everyone. I like to open the door and see everyone there.

"Young guys come to me to learn. They are with me for a long time as my driver or my secretary and all the years they're with me they're learning to become stuntmen. When I am editing I tell them to come sit with me. Forget sleep. When they know everything then they can sleep. I train them. They become martial arts directors."

Jackie certainly practices what he preaches. He's usually

the first to arrive and the last to leave. His work consumes every waking moment.

"Sometimes, when everyone else is asleep, my mind is still working. If we're in Hong Kong, I'll come downstairs in the middle of the night and edit. Sometimes I shoot all night, drive to the day location, park my car, sleep, then wake up and start filming."

Not that he's driving around by himself. Chan has at least one full-time bodyguard, Kenneth Low—the anglicized name of Lan Hui Kuwong—who also appears in Chan's films, most notably *Drunken Master II*, in which he's Chan opponent for the spectacular fight finale. Because he's so easily recognizable and because of the fervor of his Asian fans in particular, Jackie doesn't venture out alone very much. But beyond that, it seems obvious he prefers to hang out full-time with his stunt-men and bodyguards.

Which doesn't leave a lot of time for romance, even if he were so inclined. But there have been a couple of notable women Jackie has been linked to romantically—Maggie Cheung and Anita Mui, both costars. The relationship with Maggie has only been talked about by others—neither Chan nor Cheung has publicly confirmed it.

However, his romance with Anita Mui has been more public, with the two actually going out together and showing up hand in hand at functions. Jackie was one of the people most critical of Anita when she got into that scrape with the Triad leader. But as far as any entanglement that's going to sweep Jackie off his feet, don't count on it. Chan's life, his fuel, his reason to get up in the morning, his very existence, is making movies. Without that, he would be lost. It is more important than friends, lovers, or even children.

"Maybe my philosophy is different than some other people but today, for me, work is the most important thing. My most important relationships are with my staff because they help me in my work. A wife, son, girlfriend, doesn't help me. I do everything for my public, then I think about family.

"You think I'm happy always running around?" Chan said

to one reporter after revealing he had spent only two weeks in Hong Kong in 1996 and five days with his family. "I wish I could be more like Tom Cruise, just sitting around not worrying about my life, but I'm too busy working. You can't have the best of both, so one is sacrificed.

"Perhaps my wife is unlucky having me as her man—although I *will* make her happy when the time comes for me to slow down. That's why she is still here."

Some might argue that Jackie's priorities are skewed or that he's using movies to avoid the adult responsibilities and relationships the rest of us have to deal with daily. Maybe so, but he's also turned this single-mindedness into his own personal art form, which no amount of criticism can undermine.

7.

成
龍

RESURRECTION

By 1992, Jackie decided the time had come to give special effects a closer look. Not that he intended to make a sudden conversion, but he was hoping to learn about the techniques being used by some of Hong Kong's New Wave directors, Tsui Hark in particular. In movies like *A Chinese Ghost Story*, Hark had popularized the "flying" martial artists film genre, in which the period heroes and villains soared through the air like Peter Pan. The breathless albeit improbable action in most of these films left audiences craving more and more elaborate special effects.

As it happened, Jackie, Tsui, and nearly every other Hong Kong director you could think of had been recruited to make a film to raise funds for the Directors Guild. The film was *Twin Dragons*, in which Jackie played identical siblings separated at birth. From his perspective, the shoot was a disaster. Tsui Hark and Ringo Lam shared directing chores while Chan handled the stunt and action end. Anyone who has seen how differently these men approach filmmaking would know there was bound to be conflict. Despite the behind-the-scenes tensions, the film itself was a big hit, but it did nothing to whet Jackie's appetite for newfangled film techniques.

"In Hollywood, they still have sixty-year-old action stars, but I'll probably have to retire in a few years. So when people like Spielberg and George Lucas say they want to make movies with me using special effects, I don't know what they're talking about. I don't know how to do it. That's why I do *Twin Dragons*, to learn. Too bad.

"I was totally disappointed about the whole Hong Kong special effects ability. From now on, I'll learn from people in Hollywood."

Disappointed by the gimmicky nature of special effects films, Jackie became a man possessed. He kicked his film production into high gear. He was determined to kick butt without tricks. It was a rerun of the time when he was trying to escape Bruce Lee's legacy: Do what the other guy *wasn't* doing. If they were using special effects, he'd use no special effects. He'd use nothing but guts. It may also have been that Chan felt hot breath on his neck—his status as top dog was being threatened by the likes of Stephen Chow, Andy Lau, and, mostly, Chow Yun-fat. Chan was still the stunt king, but he wanted to be the most popular actor, period. Like a cornered animal, he lashed out—creatively.

First up was *Supercop*, the third *Police Story* installment. Jackie turned the reins over to director Stanley Tong who, like Chan, started out as a stuntman. He went on to stunt double for Leslie Cheung and Chow Yun-fat. It was the first time in years that Jackie wasn't going to direct and stunt coordinate himself. But he had too much on his plate to devote that much attention to *Supercop*. Tong was thrilled.

"I was his fan since I was a kid," Stanley Tong said in one interview with reporters. "But I had never had a chance to work with him in the film business because he always worked with the same group of people. But then Jackie's producer at

Golden Harvest, Leonard Ho, thought my style was similar to Jackie's so he arranged a meeting.

"Now, I feel like we're brothers."

Supercop is an amusement park ride of nonstop action that adds a new twist for a Chan film—a female equal to Jackie. Michelle Yeoh (renamed Khan for the U.S. market) matches Jackie's every kick, punch, and stunt. In fact, Yeoh was so good that from all appearances Jackie actually felt competitive enough with her that he tried to talk her out of doing a stunt. But she insisted, and one of the more memorable scenes is of Michelle jumping a motorcycle onto the top of a moving train. The bruising spills she took filming the scene are presented under the film's closing credits.

After bringing a Japanese "anime" cartoon to life in the silly *City Hunter*, Jackie indulged his own creative needs and did a bleak cop drama called *Crime Story*, which was based on an actual Hong Kong crime. It was a jarring turnabout for Chan, who has to carry the film with his acting instead of just action. Jackie surprised a lot of people when he was able to pull it off so well that he won the Hong Kong Film Award for Best Actor.

Finally, Jackie needed a break from playing cops. In fact, he needed a break from modern life. The time had come for a trip down memory lane. *Drunken Master II* was an event before it even started filming. Jackie had recruited the venerable Liu Chia-liang, one of Hong Kong's greatest filmmakers and one whose work is largely unknown in the West.

Unfortunately, Chan and Liu were not a compatible mix. Although Chia-liang is responsible for some of the film's more amazing fight sequences, his resistance to Jackie's vision led to his departure from the movie midway through filming.

"Liu decided I shouldn't drink in the film," Jackie said in an interview given after the film was completed. "So I asked some people if they thought the character should drink in the film. They look at me like I'm crazy—it's *Drunken Master*. The last scene is impossible without it."

Interestingly, though, Jackie himself was concerned with

the film's central theme: The more staggering drunk the character is, the better he fights.

"Now I have to have more education for the children—don't fight and don't drink. It's wrong. But it's a comedy and I have to drink but mostly just at the end."

The finale Jackie's referring to is a grueling fourteen-minute confrontation between Jackie and the villain's lead henchman, who was supposed to be played by Ho Sung-park until the fighter failed to pass Jackie's personal litmus test.

"He had no rhythm, none," says Chan, who has often compared staging a fight to dance choreography. "After a few shots, he wants to take a break because his leg hurts. Then, he wants to take a couple of days off because he twists his leg. He tried but he wasn't able to finish the movie, so I fired him. He was very surprised."

Jackie didn't have to look far for a replacement—he simply summoned his bodyguard, Kenneth Low. It was a brilliant choice.

"We had fireworks!"

Literally. In a scene that took four months to film, Jackie and Kenneth staged a battle of the titans. Hot pokers, furniture, crates, and bodies fly. Among the sequences is one where Chan falls on a pit of burning coals and another where he actually consumes industrial alcohol to get drunk.

Drunken Master II is considered Chan's best film and was a welcome return to where his career began. But Jackie didn't dwell on the plaudits for his kung fu gem. He was already thinking about his next projects. And there was something else on his mind.

Slowly, Jackie Chan had been infiltrating the American film consciousness. Not that he was even remotely a known commodity to the average moviegoer, but his work *was* well known within the film community. So much so that several filmmakers had been "borrowing" his stunt and action sequences for several years. Sylvester Stallone paid overdue tribute to Chan in his 1993 film *Demolition Man*. In it, Stallone wrote a line of dialogue for costar Sandra Bullock where she explains how she learned some kung fu moves.

"I love Jackie Chan movies."

Film retrospectives of his career had been organized in various cities, most notably New York, Chicago, and Dallas. His videos were becoming slightly easier to find, and articles about his vast contribution to the genre appeared in not-so-fringe publications like New York's *Village Voice* and the *L.A. Weekly*. An eponymous Nintendo game, big in Japan, was released in the United States.

In other words, Jackie had become a cult figure. It was now hip to be a Jackie Chan fan. The change had happened so gradually that it sneaked up on people, Jackie included. Chan was understandably hesitant about what it all meant. He happily gave interviews and appeared at the film festivals and retrospectives, but he refused to get his hopes up that this fringe movement would blossom into something more grand. At least, that was the face he put on in public.

A seminal moment for Chan happened in 1995. Quentin Tarantino, who just a few years earlier had been working in a video store, was basking in the warmth of being Hollywood's hippest new director when MTV asked him to participate in its annual offbeat Movie Awards. He agreed only on the condition that Jackie receive MTV's Lifetime Achievement Award and that he be allowed to present it to him.

The *Pulp Fiction* director was a longtime film fanatic and had discovered Chan's movies while working at the video store. He made no attempt to hide his childlike idolization of Jackie, and it was this heartfelt tribute that America heard the night of the awards ceremony.

"Thank you for the speech. Actually, I'm not that good," he told the audience as he accepted the award from Tarantino. "When I first heard I was getting the Lifetime Achievement Award, I was surprised because I am very young. I have a long way to go.

"Because of this, I will do more kicking and more punching, more dangerous, crazy stunts and continue to make movies the rest of my life. I believe that many people don't know me, but it doesn't matter. Go see *Rumble in the Bronx* and you will know me better."

Backstage, Chan appeared happy but nervous facing the curious American press corps, many of whom had no clue who he was. But enough did, and Jackie couldn't stop smiling as he answered questions about when he was going to market his films for wide release in the States. At the time, Jackie had no answer because he had no idea. But the fact that people had cared enough to ask made his heart soar.

"I want people in America to see my movies. I want an audience here. I need an audience here. When I walk the streets here and someone recognizes me and tells me I'm the greatest, it makes me so happy!"

If that's true he must have been ecstatic for most of 1996. Although many in this country still don't know his place in film history, Jackie Chan has become a mainstream personality in America, and his movies are finally getting a general release. This is thanks to two distributors who believe the time is finally right for Hong Kong films to find a place with a wider audience.

New Line Cinema opened the gates by picking up the rights to *Rumble in the Bronx*, which opened in the U.S. February 1996 and earned a dazzling $10 million in the first weekend. Miramax tossed their hat in the ring and released *Supercop* in July, which also did respectably at the box office. It should be noted that *Rumble in the Bronx* was made with a hoped-for U.S. release in mind, witness the U.S. setting (though it was shot in Vancouver) and the fact that the bad guys spoke English (which was dubbed for overseas release). That film lent itself to "Americanization" more readily than *Supercop*, which was Hollywood big but still very Asian in its sensibilities and, of course, its setting.

Suddenly, Jackie was a happening thing, and he rode the wave of publicity like a champion surfer, appearing in nearly every national entertainment magazine. He made the rounds of talk shows, showing up on both Letterman and Leno. Quite a difference from when he was trying to promote *The Big Brawl* and a national morning news program interview was canceled when the producer decided Jackie's English wasn't good enough. Instead, they suggested he just show a few of his moves. Silently. Now that same program was competing with the others to get Chan back, and like the good sport he is, he went because he was too happy to carry a grudge. Not when years of frustration were about to be erased.

Now that Jackie has established enough of a mainstream fan base in America to guarantee more of his movies being given a general release, a bigger question looms. What does Jackie see in his future? The death-defying stunts that made him famous have taken a tremendous physical toll. Even though he's supremely fit, he's also in his forties and knows he has to once again make a shift in his career.

American fans may be more amenable to a shift than his Asian followers because they're not as tied to his high-risk style. Chan fans, however, are already mourning what they fear will be the demise of Chan films as they know them. They worry that mainstream commercial success will be the ruin of what made Jackie great. They're possessive of Jackie and don't want newcomers to claim his artistic soul.

What they have to keep in mind is that the inevitable is approaching. Jackie needs to plan for his movie life when the risk of jumping off tall buildings becomes too great. One solution may be to protect himself better, and that doesn't have to mean the end of Jackie Chan as we know him.

Dar Robinson is considered by many in Hollywood to have been one of our greatest stuntmen. He was a free-fall specialist who was adamant that stunts be made as safe as possible and found a way to do it without diminishing their excitement quotient. Among his more famous stunts was free-falling from one airplane onto another, meticulously planned via painstaking mathematical calculations and test run-throughs.

While the use of wires is anathema to many Hong Kong

film fans, when used properly and creatively they can actually help create spectacular stunts that are no less dangerous.

In the film *Stick*, Dar was working as both stuntman and actor for director and star Burt Reynolds. The climactic confrontation between Burt and bad-guy Dar at the end of the movie contains a stunt where Dar is seen falling backward off a hotel ledge 150 feet high.

The camera's point of view is looking down from the ledge, and as he falls, Robinson's villain futilely empties his gun as he plummets toward certain death. Below you see people running for cover. It is one shot with no cuts until the split-second when Robinson would be hitting the ground.

What prevented a disastrous crash landing was a small wire, one-eighth of an inch in diameter, attached to his ankle that was controlled by a hydraulic pulley Dar himself spent months creating. The use of a wire allowed Robinson to perform this otherwise impossible stunt. Not even Jackie could fall off a 150-foot building and survive with no net below. Yes, it's not the same as Jackie jumping off a mountain onto a hot air balloon—though he *was* wearing a parachute just in case. But in Jackie's hands, a contraption like that could work wonders. Mixing American technical know-how with Jackie's physical skills and inventiveness could be the dawning of a new film age.

Jackie and his fans alike will eventually have to decide if a New Age Jackie is something they can both live with—either that, or he keeps on until he suffers a career-ending injury. For those who love his creativity and cleverness, the answer seems obvious.

The idea of spending more pre- and post-production time in America also has an appeal for Jackie beyond finally realizing his dream of being accepted. Although there are plenty of would-be deranged fans in this country, it is unlikely his popularity here will ever approach the dimensions it has in Asia, where, as earlier noted, it has reached uncomfortable levels.

Jackie talks about a woman who stalked him for three years, showing up at parties he was attending—in different countries, no less. In each case she walked up to Chan, slapped him across the face, and then walked away with a satisfied smile.

"One time, a fan comes to see me and tells me he had come from Germany and that he wants to work with me as a stunt-man. He says this over and over, so I tell him if he's serious, he can come to the set and watch.

"But when he talked, his eyes were always shaking. He stayed for three days, then leaves. I was relieved that he was gone but in two days, he comes back."

Irritated, Jackie asked the young man why he'd come back.

"He said none of his friends had believed I had been so nice to him so he had to come back to take a picture with me. Crazy, huh? This is why I don't go out much anymore, and when I do, I don't stay in one place. When people pass by, they're not sure it's really me, and by the time they realize it is me, I've already run away."

Because Chan's movies are now primarily shot on location, Jackie spends less and less time in Hong Kong, making it hard for any potential stalkers to catch up to him. He checks into hotels under an assumed name (even in the United States), and his movie sets are secured by his own staff of protectors.

Whatever his new ties to America may be, Chan has said repeatedly that he has no intention of abandoning Hong Kong, as so many others in the film industry have done due to concern over its political future under Chinese rule. But his reasons are practical, not political.

"If my country is no good, I should stay and help it, not leave. People watch what I do there, so if I leave, it would be scary for many people. A lot of people moved to L.A.—then moved to Quebec after they feel the earthquakes. For me, it's different.

"My movies are not political, so they are accepted by China. My movies are good for children—I always consider the children when I make a movie. That's why I don't make love in my films. Yes, there's violence, but I show children that fighting *hurts* and my characters fight only because they have to.

"When people come out of my movies, nobody wants to

fight, they want to laugh. I don't want children to watch me and then go home and fight. I like to entertain. I don't even want somebody to die in my movies, and I only like a little blood.

"In Asia my films are special because for all these years, parents were able to bring their children. They knew what a Jackie Chan film was going to be. I never speak dirty, there is no sex—so all these people grew up knowing me. So now when my movies come out everybody sees it—and now they're bringing *their* children.

"And yet in America, they give *Rumble in the Bronx* an R rating so the children *cannot* see. I don't understand this."

The bottom line is, Jackie wants it both ways. He wants to capture the hearts of Americans without having to give up the adulation he has in Asia and the creative autonomy he has in Hong Kong—a perk and power base he simply would be loath to relinquish.

"In Hong Kong, it's *my* movie so nobody tells me I can't do something. Every action scene usually takes between two and three months to film, and they will never do this in America. To make *my* films I need to be able to do everything, anything—even risk my life if I want. In Hong Kong I can die for my movie."

Not that he intends to. One of his greatest concerns is how to balance the physical need to take better care of his body with the expectations of his ever-loyal fans. Jackie admits he's already started being more careful than he was early in his career out of sheer physical necessity. For example, he will have members of his stunt team do practice runs on stunts while the kinks are being worked out, then Jackie will step in for the money shots.

"Of course I'm scared. After a while, I began to ask myself, why am I doing these crazy things? I had to develop more technique and learn to plan my stunts better," Jackie has said in an interview with the press. "I will continue to make action films for as long as I can, and I will keep surprising people even if I make changes in how I do them."

While his days of falling off a clock tower may be over, this should not be interpreted as an announcement that he plans to start using special effects or stunt doubles like his American counterparts.

"I would lose face if I used a stunt double," Chan has said. "Now I can show my movies to my children and grandchildren and say, 'That's your grandfather doing that.'

"And I don't know anything about computers, I don't know how to use one. Today I am special because you know it's really me doing it. I'm special in Asia because I'm different. You can't find what I do in any American movies because they're done with computers, not people, so I will keep my current standard—with a change here or there.

"But I don't want the audience coming *just* to see Jackie doing dangerous stunts. Before, yes. But not now. Now I'm more clever. I know other people who can fight better than me, but they cannot do these other things. That's my value.

"And that's why I'm changing my style so I can do things besides dangerous stunts. Now I'm more clever than crazy."

For now, Jackie is taking the future slowly, maybe because for the first time in many years he feels uncertain about where his career is going. He fantasizes about being summoned by his personal idol. "If George Lucas calls and says he wants me for *Star Wars IV*, I would say yes. I think Lucas and Spielberg are geniuses."

However, that kind of team-up seems unlikely. Jackie is way too independent. Indeed, a story that has been picking up steam tells of a developing rift between Chan and Raymond Chow. Hong Kong newspapers have reported that Jackie wants to be paid US$8 million, a salary more in keeping with his value to Golden Harvest.

"I feel I'm worth $22 million," Jackie is quoted as saying. "But the actual amount is hard to nail down. Many years ago people wanted to give me a blank check to leave Golden Harvest—but I didn't."

Other reports have surfaced indicating that Chan is insulted that Chow has decided to groom Jackie's "heir apparent," a young actor/pop star named Aaron Kwok. Chan has developed a certain philosophical attitude toward the vagaries of the movie business.

"The new Jackie? In this world, nobody can replace Jackie—just like nobody could replace Bruce. Or Aaron Kwok. Every person is unique.

"Before, I really wanted to be an American star, and I was totally lost when it didn't happen. But now I believe I'm successful enough that people respect me. This time, I'm very comfortable to try the American market. And if I don't make it, I can go back to Asia. Or maybe if after five years I can't do it, I'll find a new talent and teach him how to do it. I'll be the director, and I'll just put my dream into somebody else and take him to big success.

"If I do make it, I'll still go back to Asia. But maybe then I'll have more money to make bigger-budgeted films, then I can hire more professional people to help me."

Jackie's immediate plans are to get his next film, *A Nice Guy*, ready for release and to travel the world promoting it. It was directed by Sammo Hung, with whom he has done some long-overdue fence mending. Jackie also wants to work with Yuen Biao again. He told the magazine *Hong Kong Film Connection*, "Yuen was a success but when he left Golden Harvest, he followed the wrong road. Brothers have success in Golden Harvest. When they had success in Asia, all the production buyers came out. Give them a blank check. They think they are a success. . . .

"Then Sammo and Yuen Biao go out and make their own company. The buyer doesn't have to put up with the problem. Golden Harvest would say, 'You want to buy Jackie Chan movie, then you have to buy ten rubbish movies. So now they just buy one Yuen Biao movie and they don't promote it. That's when Yuen Biao went down . . . they say, 'Ah, he's finished.'

"So as soon as they are down, Golden Harvest would not let me make a movie with Yuen Biao anymore. . . . But I've brought Sammo back and later I'll bring Yuen Biao back. Then all three brothers will be back together again."

As for specific future projects, Chan recorded the theme song for a new Hong Kong TV series *Interpol 1997 (Kwok Ja Ying Gaing)*. Then he went back to feature-film work, starring in and directing *Who Am I?* (originally known as *Safari*). Shot in South Africa and the Netherlands, it's the story of a man who wakes up in the jungle with no idea who he is or how he got there. He also has written a script about firemen and has met with some of the experts who helped create *Backdraft*, with the idea of possibly enlisting their aid. He is also developing a western that he has had in mind for over a decade, and scores of actors have contacted him about possible collaborations. Jackie would also like to work with Jet Li. "The film with Jet Li and Sammo Hung is at best an idea in Jackie's head," says Willie Chan. "As you probably know, the movie market in Hong Kong and Southeast Asia has been a downward trend—with the exception of Jackie's films. Jackie feels that if he can work together with other stars like Jet Li, Stephen Chow, or Chow Yun-fat, it may create new chemistry and thus help boost sales for the entire industry."

He refuses, though, to feel any pressure to make up his mind. "You see, I'm a happy-go-lucky type of guy. Since my accident on *Armour of God*, I've decided to live one day at a time without worrying about tomorrow. I only make plans one year ahead. Who can say how things will turn out—I might die later today. But I don't worry about it.

"I've always been lucky and I trust my lucky star."

His most compelling problem is working out what he calls the "dilemma" of keeping true to his way of making movies while making them spectacular enough to keep roping in the American audience. *A Nice Guy*, which was shot in Australia, is filmed in English, a first for Jackie. Then he'll dub it for Asian release, something he usually does anyway.

The question is not whether Jackie will physically work within the borders of America. It seems unlikely he could ever adapt his style to conform to the myriad of regulations governing filmmaking here. Indeed, after at first agreeing to make *Beverly Hills Ninja* with Chris Farley, Jackie withdrew. He was replaced by *Mortal Kombat* star Robin Shou. Now he's considering making *The Bee*, written by John Hughes *(Home Alone)*. It's like a *Popeye* cartoon come to life, the misadventures of an architect who is trying to develop some land and is harassed by a bee. The question is, can he make films geared toward the U.S. market that will also do well in Asia?

"The thing about my movies is you don't have to understand the dialogue to understand it. That's why people from all over Asia go see them. In my philosophy, the more people who see a movie, the more successful that movie is. That's why I would say *Schindler's List* is not a 'good' movie but *Jurassic Park* is.

"It's very difficult to get an Oscar, right? But when you can make one movie that everyone around the world wants to see, that's even more difficult."

It seems like a fragile juggling act, but Jackie has proven many times before that he's agile enough to pull it off. The problem of trying to balance all these elements gives Jackie a new mountain to climb, and he seems energized at the prospect. What else is there for the man who literally has everything he could materially want, including a fleet of over twenty cars—pared down from sixty—and a thousand pairs of shoes, his fashion passion?

"Before, when I made a film, it was for money," Jackie has said. "But now when I make a film it is my hobby, the thing I love. Money is secondary. I have enough money. So I don't think about that anymore. Instead I make sure that I leave something for the film industry, for myself and my family.

"I hope one day to be remembered like James Dean is. If in the film books you see the names Charlie Chaplin, Steven Spielberg, and just a small note with the name Jackie Chan, then I'll be so *happy*.

"I want people to remember me like I remember Buster Keaton. When they talk about him or a Gene Kelly, people say, 'Yes, he was *good*.' If they remember Jackie Chan that way, it will be enough."

THE
Professional

2

JACKIE CHAN

成
龍

*C*han's devotion to films and filmmaking doesn't end when the cameras stop rolling. For over ten years, Jackie's been as active in the business aspect of the Hong Kong film industry as he has been in making movies.

Below is a list of the positions Chan has held or continues to hold in various professional organizations.

Jackie Chan Charitable Foundation, Hong Kong
1987—founder

Jackie Chan Charitable Foundation, Japan
1988—founder

Hong Kong Directors Guild
1989–1991   executive committee member
1991–1993   vice president
1993–present   president

Hong Kong Stuntmen Association
1992–present   executive committee member

Hong Kong Society of Cinematographers
1993–present   honorary president

Hong Kong Performance Artist Guild
   1993–present   vice president

Motion Picture Association, Hong Kong
   1994–present   president

THE 3 Entrepreneurial

成
龍

JACKIE CHAN

*T*he Hong Kong entertainment community calls Jackie "Dai Goh," Cantonese for Big Brother, because of the success he continues to bring to the Hong Kong film industry and the number of jobs he provides. But his economic influence reaches beyond moviemaking.

Today Jackie Chan is not just a world-famous actor, he's also a cottage industry. Using his massive popularity as a springboard, Chan has spawned numerous businesses that span the consumer horizon.

RETAILER

Taking a page out of Disney's marketing department, Chan has opened a Jackie Chan Shop, where he cashes in on a devout legion of fans hoping to own a little piece of their idol.

The Hong Kong boutique is brimming with Jackie paraphernalia. If you want a Jackie baseball cap or Jackie T-shirt or Jackie coffee mug or Jackie wristwatch or Jackie key chain or Jackie photograph or Jackie . . . you've come to the right place.

Interestingly, one of the more popular items is a Jackie Chan ruler made from unused film from one of Jackie's movies. For US$12, you too can own a laminated strip of 35mm movie film made from movie outtakes, each little frame bearing the likeness of Jackie.

JACKIE'S ANGELS

No, this is not a group of Good Samaritans or latter-day Mother Teresas. Think more along the lines of *Charlie's Angels*. Jackie's Angels is the name of Chan's Hong Kong–based modeling agency. Beautiful young girls from Hong Kong and beyond clamor to be signed by Jackie's Angels, many hoping that Jackie will cast them in his next picture and make them the next overnight sensation.

Chan does actually hire girls from his agency, but usually to work as extras or bit players in his TV commercials.

PLANET HOLLYWOOD INVESTOR

Considering Jackie's appreciation of American movies, at least the ones made before the advent of sound, and his fondness for Sylvester Stallone, it's not surprising that Chan is one of the major investors in Hong Kong's local Planet Hollywood.

Besides the money, being in the Planet Hollywood family gives Jackie an added perk. Planet Hollywoods everywhere are ready to lend a hand should Jackie need a venue for a premiere party or publicity event. Hence, when Jackie was in New York to promote the opening of *Rumble in the Bronx*, the festivities were held at the Manhattan Planet Hollywood, with many of its other illustrious investors present, including the Sly one.

Entertainment synergy at its most obvious.

FILM PRODUCER

In conjunction with Golden Harvest, Jackie's Golden Way Production Company is more than just a vanity label. Golden Way produces not only Chan's films but also a number of other filmmakers, both well known and up-and-coming.

One of Golden Way's proudest moments was the company's production of the critically acclaimed 1987 film *Rouge*, for which Chan's longtime friend and coworker Anita Mui was honored with a Hong Kong Film Award for Best Actress.

POP STAR

Of all Jackie's many hats, this is the one that bemuses people the most. On the one hand, Jackie's records and CDs have sold well enough—in fact, he's had a few bona fide hits. And in Cantonese versions of his films, you can often hear him crooning over the end credits.

Still, not everyone is taken with his musical abilities. Here's how one reporter put it:

> Judging by Jackie's impromptu rendition of Willie Nelson's "You Were Always on My Mind," he shouldn't clear a spot on the shelf for a Grammy.
> Then he begins singing Richard Marx's "Right Here Waiting."
> "Oceans apart, day after day . . ."
> This time it's not Chan looking for a building to jump off.

Before Chan fans rise up in indignant protest, even Jackie's manager, Willie Chan, acknowledges his client's strengths lie elsewhere.

"He's not a very good singer," Willie has bluntly said.

But that hasn't stopped him from being a pop star.

BEVERAGE MARKETER

Jackie and Chua Lam, who coproduced *Armour of God*, are partners in the Bo Bo Tea company, which markets a line of teas and snacks. In an attempt to tap into Jackie's broad international appeal and to reach the thousands of on-line Chan fans, Bo Bo teas are sold via the Internet (http://www.bobotea.com.hk) as well as in a Hong Kong specialty store nearest you.

According to the company's ad copy, "Bo Bo Tea (International) Limited aims at reintroducing the lost treasures of Chinese heritage into modern life. Highly concerned with consumers' health, natural ingredients are what we insist on. Through the wide variety of products that we provide, you can once again explore the forgotten treasures of Chinese heritage."

Not only does Jackie sell everyday Pu-erh and Oolong tea, he sells sugar-free canned tea, Bo Bo crackers, Bo Bo Camellia cooking oil, and even the Zen Tea Series—*for vegetarians.*

Huh?

There's one last product Bo Bo Tea Limited sells that we do understand—even though Jackie's image is that of teetotaler supreme, his company markets Lipo's Hangover Terminator, a Chinese herbal hangover cure.

So far, Bo Bo Tea Limited is grossing over US$250,000 a year.

AUTO PITCHMAN

Having one of the most recognizable faces in Asia, Jackie is constantly being sought out by companies wanting him to pitch their wares. But since he spends so much of his time abroad filming and stumping for his movies and is concerned about the image he projects, Chan is selective about what products he lends his name to. Don't hold your breath waiting to see Chan hawk cigarettes or the latest alcoholic beverage. That would be too un-Jackie, regardless of whether or not he indulges in those types of products himself.

But cars—that's a different story. Chan has been a spokesman for Mitsubishi for years, and the arrangement has worked out handsomely for both sides. The car manufacturer gets to use Jackie's good name and have his likeness associated with its cars all over China and the rest of Asia. In return, Jackie gets a king's ransom *and* has gotten to film in Mitsubishi car manufacturing plants on a couple of different occasions. Which, knowing Jackie, is actually the best part.

Naturally, when Jackie needed to spend over US$2 million on autos to demolish in *Thunderbolt*, Mitsubishi happily provided the cars.

That's how smart business is supposed to work.

THE
Notable

JACKIE CHAN

4

成
龍

Over the course of his career, Jackie has been bestowed with a roomful of awards, citations, medals, trophies, and prizes from an assortment of groups the world over. Below is a list of Chan's professional achievements.

RoadShow Magazine (Japan)

1983   Best Actor, Foreign

1984   Best Actor, Foreign

1985   Best Actor, Foreign
              Best Director, Foreign

1986   Best Actor, Foreign

1987   Best Actor, Foreign

1988   Best Actor, Foreign
              Best Director, Foreign

1989   Best Actor, Foreign

Hong Kong Artists Guild

1989   Best Actor

Cine-Asia

1994   Best Actor of the Year

Hong Kong Radio & Television
    1990   Ten Most Popular Performers of the 1980s

    1992   Ten Most Healthy Personalities of Hong Kong

Hong Kong Junior Chamber of Commerce
    1986   Ten Outstanding Persons of Hong Kong

City of San Francisco
    1986   Jackie Chan Day, September 6

Jaycees International (Japan)
    1988   The Outstanding Young Persons of the World

British Government
    1989   Member of the Most Excellent Order of the British Empire

Le Cinémathèque Française (France)
    1990   Insignes de Chevalier des Arts et des Lettres

Taiwan Government
    1992   Five Most Outstanding Young Chinese of the World

Asia Pacific Film Festival
    1993   Outstanding Contribution to Movies Award

MTV
    1995   Lifetime Achievement Award

Postage Stamp
    1996   The Gambia

THE *Mythical*

5

成龍

JACKIE CHAN

*I*t happens with nearly any larger-than-life personality who spends too much time in the public eye: They develop an image that may or may not have any basis in reality. Entertainers like to call it a mystique; the less charitable might prefer the word *fiction* to describe some aspects of the celebrity persona.

Take insult-*meister* Don Rickles. In his case, he has cultivated the persona of an equal opportunity king of insults. By all accounts, the "real" Don Rickles will give you the shirt off his back and never has a harsh word to say about or to anyone. What we see when he's in public is his shtick. Marilyn Monroe was supposed to be some ditzy blonde, but history has shown her to be far more calculating, and tragic, than anyone could have guessed. Things are not always as they seem.

Whatever one chooses to call it, the phenomenon is usually a result of two synergistic forces: public expectations based on the actor's film or television character, and the celebrity's carefully orchestrated publicity effort.

Maybe more than most, what you see with Jackie *is* a fairly close representation of the real man. However he, too, has some great myths that swirl around him. In Chan's case most of the fictions are professional rather than personal, but a myth is a myth is a myth. Below are Jackie's.

MYTH 1

Jackie Doesn't Drink or Smoke

Nobody's caught Chan guzzling vodka on a street corner, but there's celluloid proof that he's no stranger to nicotine. Check out the bizarre film *36 Crazy Fist*, which uses behind-the-scenes footage of Jackie working as a fight choreographer.

Not realizing the footage would be released to the public, Chan didn't bother to hide the ever-present cigarette dangling from his lips.

Chan has said he doesn't drink or smoke (he forgot to add "in public") because he doesn't want to be a bad role model for children. And that is to his credit. On the other hand, it's also good for children to learn not to lie for the sake of convenience.

MYTH 2

Jackie Never Does Love Scenes

What he really means is he won't do love scenes *anymore*. One of the odder movies in Jackie's long career is *All in the Family*, a softcore film about relatives waiting for their rich grandfather to die so they can battle each other over the inheritance. In it, Jackie has a nude sex romp with a mother-and-daughter team.

Granted, in 1975 Jackie would have probably done just about anything to get a job, but what's funky about this is that he tries to hide the fact that he *ever* accepted this kind of role. Many Chan fans would think somebody's slipped you too much ginseng if you told them Jackie had ever stripped naked to star in a sex romp.

MYTH 3

Jackie Invented "Comedy Kung Fu"

Although it might not seem like it at times, kung fu films have been parodied or contained humor long before Jackie came on the scene. Comedy in kung fu films can be seen as far back as the Wong Fei Hung series, in which the Ah So character was there for little more than comic relief. Years before Jackie would become the Clown Prince of Hong Kong Action Films, a man named Sam Hui was making 'em laugh in otherwise "straight" kung fu flicks. And in 1978, Liu Chia-liang directed and starred in the amusing *Shaolin Challenges Ninja*. It's not a comedy per se, but it certainly has comedic elements. It's interesting to note that in the film, which predates *Drunken Master* by a year, Lui plays a drunken master.

However, Jackie certainly made the genre his own and influenced a generation of filmmakers that have followed. Jackie's greater contribution is his modernization of the kung fu genre and his incorporation of nonfaked stunts within the context of humor.

MYTH 4

Jackie Has Never Used Wires or Stunt Doubles or Cinematic Tricks.

Not so, by a long shot. Not only did Jackie use wires on occasion early in his career when he had no control over the situation, *Hand of Death* being an example, but he has resorted to trickery on occasion after he had all the control in the world. A case in point: the scene in *Project A* where Jackie is trying to run up a hill that is almost vertical to the ground.

In the outtakes, you see him try and fail several times before finally succeeding. But if you look at his shirt, it's easy to see where the attached wire is pulling him chest first up the hill. In fact, his body kind of rolls back in response to the wire being pulled.

Wire work was also employed in *Drunken Master II*.

And as far as stunt doubles go, it's not as uncommon as Chan fans might want to believe. His most frequently used double is a man named Chan Chuen. Obviously, on the "money stunts," that is Jackie hanging on for dear life at the end of a helicopter's hanging ladder. But in *City Hunter*, to offer one example, he used a stunt double for a fight sequence because he had previously injured his foot and was unable to do what the scene called for. In *Armour of God II*, it isn't Jackie doing all those motorcycle stunts. In long shots on *Thunderbolt*, Jackie doubles were used in nondangerous scenes so that the star could film other scenes simultaneously, thus saving a little time.

Chan has also resorted to "cinematic tricks" like quick editing or undercranking (to slow the film and thus speed up the action) every now and then. Again in *City Hunter*, a skateboard stunt that has Jackie leap up and over a car speeding at him, then land perfectly back on the skateboard, is obviously accomplished through editing. Most likely because they didn't want Jackie killing himself, which is a perfectly fine reason.

Undercranking seems to be a constant hot topic of debate when discussing kung fu scenes. Can they really move that fast or is it mechanically enhanced? Did they "speed up" the fight scene under the train in *Drunken Master II*? On and on. But it appears fairly obvious parts of *Project A, Part II* are speeded up, and there's one instance in *Supercop*, at least, where there's no denying undercranking was used, mainly because director Stanley Tong—not Jackie—has admitted it in interviews.

The technique was implemented during the scene where Jackie and a cohort are descending a mountain via a cable. Tong says it was for safety considerations—he worried that the cable would snap and his actors would plummet to injury or death.

The point of this is not to say, *Told you so.* The only quibble is against the fallacy that Jackie never, ever, *ever* uses tricks and that he *always* does all his own stunts without any outside help. Nobody is denying he's the greatest action actor alive. That's a given. The use of occasional movie tricks in no way diminishes his status. All it proves is that Chan is human and not Superman. And isn't that one of the reasons why Jackie fans love him in the first place?

THE
6 *Charitable*

成
龍

JACKIE CHAN

For someone in Chan's position it would be unseemly not to donate some of his time and money to a charitable cause or two. But in Jackie's case, his generosity is heartfelt and not driven by a desire for photo opportunities.

Not surprisingly, the organizations Jackie has aligned himself with are geared to help those most in need such as the homeless and children. Below is a brief outline of Chan's pet passions.

THE H.O.M.E. PROJECT

This group is devoted to assisting the disabled of Hong Kong. Like any densely populated urban area in the world, Hong Kong has more than its share of social ills, and helping those unable to help themselves is important to Jackie. Considering his brushes with debilitating injury, it's easy to see what attracted Chan to this particular charity.

At the on-line "ribbon cutting" ceremony, Chan sent out this message to explain the goals of H.O.M.E.:

> This project will provide hardware, software, communications technology, training, and employment for the disabled of Hong Kong. It consists of a central bulletin board service in Hong Kong, with a disabled system operator and links to the world through AT&T Easylink. It also involves

87

the business community as well as the education and social welfare departments.

We see it as a way for the disabled to socialize, learn, and work, without ever leaving home, except through the marvels of technology. There are disabled here with me today who have already derived some benefits from the project and the early work of the Hong Kong Users Group for the Disabled (HcUG).

Thank you at AT&T for making it possible and here's a big 'HcUG' for all of you.

Jackie Chan

Hoping to get others involved, Chan has been set up with an E-mail address for H.O.M.E-related communications: jackiechan@attmail.com.

THE JACKIE CHAN CHARITABLE FOUNDATION

Provides scholarships to young people for the expressed purpose of education and training in the arts as well as funding for a wide range of projects including hospitals.

THE ANNUAL JACKIE CHAN BENEFIT

A car race extravaganza that raises money for various Hong Kong charities.

THE
Uninsurable

7

成龍

JACKIE CHAN

*C*han's litany of serious injuries and occasional brushes with death is the stuff of legend and has in no small way contributed to his popularity. Despite Jackie's breezy, it's-all-in-a-day's-work attitude toward continually putting himself in harm's way, nearly twenty years of mishaps have taken their physical toll.

"It's okay—if I don't have to go to the hospital, it's a piece of cake. But I hate it when I have to go to the hospital."

He's been in the hospital more than some doctors. Like professional football players who don't suffer the full effect of their brutal sport until they suddenly can't get out of bed a few years after retiring, it's inevitable Chan will ultimately pay a heavy price for his on-screen exploits. As it is, Chan admits his body is already in constant pain—and he's only forty-three. His back is so troublesome he sleeps on the floor, even in five-star hotels. And when he wakes up in the morning, he has to hang by his fingertips from the bedroom door to work out the stiffness.

Jackie's not the only one who carries battle scars. Many members of his stuntmen team have been injured, some seriously. Although Chan won't confirm it, stories have appeared in Hong Kong claiming that at least one of his men was permanently paralyzed in a stunt gone wrong and still requires full-time hospital care. Chan has told reporters that he takes care of any medical bills of seriously injured stuntmen.

"We are like a family and I am like the father and take care of all the stunt guys. I have a responsibility to do that because we can't get insurance because I'm blacklisted and so is my team. They will do everything for me, so if they get hurt on *my* films I take care of them for as many years as necessary."

Jackie has given interviews about his attempts to improve the lot of Hong Kong stuntmen.

"Back when I first started as a stuntman in Hong Kong films, there was no safety in our stunts. We'd crash to the floor, maybe with a T-shirt on our arm or back to protect us. We got hurt a lot. But when I first came to America, I learned that you can use a shoulder pad or an elbow pad and I brought them back to Hong Kong.

"American stuntmen are smart, they think about safety. When they do a jump in a car, they calculate everything—the speed, the distance. It's very good. But in Hong Kong . . . there is no math, everything we do is a guess. If you've got the guts, you do it. If you don't have the guts, you don't. I'm the leader and must show them what I can do.

"It's true all of my stuntmen have gotten hurt. I say, 'Rolling camera, action, jump! Boom! Ambulance! Hospital! Next stuntman!' "

On a more serious note, Chan has admitted, "Sure I get hurt a lot but I also get a lot of respect. Yes, I'm playing with my life to do these stunts. But it's all worthwhile. One take and I never have to do it again. I break my ankle? Good. I'll be recovered in three months. And that movie will survive for hundreds of years. Your children may see me doing a stunt and maybe they'll say there was never a better action star than Jackie Chan.

"I live for pain. Even when I was young I loved pain. And if I get hurt, I have to keep going because even though I'm a star and could take a break to recover, the whole production would shut down and I just can't have that happen. The producers would lose money, and of course the crew is counting on me to get paid."

The most obvious result of his King of the Stunt Hill status is that no insurance company in the world will touch Chan, at least while he's doing high-degree-of-difficulty stunts. Which means that if he sustains a career-ending injury in the middle of a $20 million film, it's bye-bye to the production company's money if they can't somehow finish the film.

That's not as big a risk as it may seem to a company like Golden Harvest, which has made zillions off of Jackie. However, it *would* be a big deal to an American studio. The odds are, if Jackie ever does hook up with an American studio or production company, he would either have to appreciably tone down his let's-see-just-how-dangerous-I-can-make-this-stunt bravado, or he'd have to guarantee financing somehow.

Ironically, although Hollywood today is known for its super-duper special effects and blue screen techniques, Chan is really a throwback to the "real" Hollywood.

For example, that was no stunt double half freezing to death on an ice floe in *Broken Blossoms*. Nor was Lillian Gish simply "acting" frightened as her chunk of ice floated slowly toward a waterfall—she was probably terrified. One never knew just what D.W. Griffith might think would be a swell shot. Jackie is much more the standard-bearer for Hollywood's golden age than Tinseltown's current crop of action heroes.

But for how much longer? Even Jackie realizes the day is fast approaching when he will perform his last outrageous stunt and hang up his book of over-the-top stunt tricks and concentrate on something less dangerous. Hopefully, when that happens it will be because his body is simply worn out or he decides the risks finally outweigh the benefits—rather than it being forced on him because of a stunt gone terribly wrong resulting in cataclysmic injury.

Until that time comes, though, Jackie continues to rack up injuries by the emergency roomful. Below is an accounting of the major injuries he's received during his career. The key word here is *major*. On the Jackie scale of physical damages, things like sprains and minor cuts hardly register. The most amazing thing about the catalog of pain listed below is that Chan is able to move at all anymore, much less regularly push his body to the limit—and beyond.

CONCUSSION—*Hand of Death* (1975)

Even before he became well known, Chan had earned a reputation for doing overly dangerous stunts. In this case, not even the help of wires prevented injury while costarring in this John Woo film.

In the stunt, Jackie jumped off a truck onto a trampoline, and a wire was supposed to pull him back. But Chan lost his balance during the jump. When the wire yanked Jackie back, he hit his head and had no idea where he was.

Chan admits it hurt so badly he cried. But instead of taking a break, he went back and did a second take immediately—and promptly passed out when it was over. It took over a half hour for Jackie to regain consciousness, during which the then-new director Woo was convinced Jackie was critically injured and going to die.

Instead, Chan woke up, and when it was discovered he was passing blood, Woo insisted he receive immediate medical attention. All things considered, it's kind of ironic that Woo would be so upset at the sight of a little blood, isn't it?

FRONT TOOTH—*Snake in the Eagle's Shadow* (1977)

When this film was made, Huang Cheng-li was famous far and wide for his lightning kicks—a fact Chan discovered firsthand. During one of the fight sequences, Huang kicked Jackie in the face, knocking out a tooth—actually a cap—and injuring Chan's ego. Jackie claimed Huang disfigured him on purpose and actually demanded the kick-*meister* be fired.

Not surprisingly, Chan's overreaction was ignored and the filming went on.

BROKEN HIP—*Magnificent Bodyguard* (1978)

Another clue that life on the silver screen wasn't going to be a walk in the park happened when Jackie broke his hip performing a stunt while making this film. On the upside, being a very fit twenty-four-year-old, Chan healed quickly. And having learned mind over matter techniques at the Opera School meant Jackie would simply work in spite of the pain.

BROKEN NOSE—*Dragon Fist* (1978)

As if it wasn't bad enough that during a fight scene using weapons Chan got womped on his face so hard his nose broke, to be injured in a turkey like this added to Jackie's already considerable pain.

CONCUSSION; CUT EYE—*Drunken Master* (1979)

Unable or unwilling to control those happy feet, Huang Cheng-li whacked Chan in the head so hard Jackie ended up hospitalized. Again, this was too much realism even for Chan. While he was furious with Yuen Woo-ping for refusing to fire Huang, that anger pales when compared to the antipathy he felt for Huang himself.

On top of that, Jackie also managed to severely cut his eye in another scene, leaving a scar that's still visible today.

Coincidentally or not, after Jackie established himself as *the* man in Hong Kong action cinema, Huang Cheng-li's career evaporated like a drop of water on a hot wok. Last time anyone checked, Huang was said to be working at a golf tee manufacturing plant in his native Korea. He also put out a series of instructional tapes called the "Art of High Impact Kicking"—or how to detonate a career in one easy kick.

BROKEN FINGER—*Project A* (1983)

It's ironic that Jackie walked away stunned but unscathed from the stunt where he free-falls off the clock tower, but he managed to break his finger during a standard fight scene.

IMPACTED BACK; BURNS—*Police Story* (1985)

This unusual back injury occurred when Jackie jumped through a plate of glass to land two stories below. Chan said later that the problem started when he momentarily "thought about" the jump in the moments before he did it. That nano-second of hesitation threw all his timing off and he landed flat on his back.

Jackie has said to reporters that this was the only time he really thought he wasn't going to survive—this from the man who has a hole in his head the size of a marble, incurred during the filming of *Armour of God*.

For some reason, nobody seemed to notice the distress Jackie was in. In fact, the crew kept yelling at Chan to get up because the cameras were still rolling. Well, he did—only to have blood suddenly gush from his mouth. His crew realized maybe it was time to turn the cameras off and get Jackie some help, so he was rushed to the hospital.

Doctors diagnosed an impacted back, gave Chan some fluids, and within a couple of hours he was back working on the set.

Ditto for the little mishap that occurred during the scene where Chan slides down a pole strung with Christmas lights. Instead of powering the lights with a low-voltage car battery as planned, the knuckle-headed electrical crew plugged them into a wall outlet. The juiced lights exploded with vigor, generating a searing heat. Not only did Jackie have to pull out tiny glass fragments from his hands, he also had to be treated for second-degree burns.

SKULL FRACTURE—*Armour of God* (1986)

Jackie had just arrived on the set, coming directly from a flight from Japan. Chan was confident enough in his abilities to shrug off the jet lag and fatigue he felt from his journey and immediately set out to film a stunt that seemed simple enough. And Jackie indeed did the stunt several times with no problem—jumping from a ledge to a tree branch, then swinging down to the ground.

Ever the perfectionist, Chan wanted to try one more time so he could add a little monkeylike twist as he landed. It was one time too many. He slipped off the branch and headfirst hit the ground below, smashing into at least two rocks, blood pouring from his ear.

In addition to a fractured skull, Chan broke his nose, shattered his jaw, lost several teeth, and had a bone chip lodge dangerously close to his brain. It's not an understatement to say doctors weren't sure he'd ever fully recover, much less return to stunt work.

The aftereffects of this injury are a virtually nonfunctioning right ear and a hole in his head.

IMPACTED ANKLE—*Dragons Forever* (1987)

This film featured a rematch between Chan and Benny "The Jet" Urquidez, a grudge match that left both fighters battered, although Jackie came away the worse for wear, having jammed his ankle so badly he couldn't flex it without excruciating pain. But, as usual, he was able to function despite the pain.

LACERATIONS—*Police Story II* (1988)

As if his head hadn't gone through enough already, it was the recipient of more damage during the filming of the first *Police Story* sequel. The stunt begins with Chan crossing the street by jumping on top of vehicles cruising back and forth on a busy street. The stunt ends with him diving through a plate glass window. And was the window made of safe spun glass? Of course not.

The impact shattered the glass pane, and despite his trying

to protect his head, Chan's scalp was sliced and diced by the flying shards.

PUNCTURE WOUND—*Armour of God II: Operation Condor* (1991)

Chan had a deep hole punched into his leg by a wire rigging during a stunt. (Kind of makes it difficult to deny Chan ever uses wires during his stunts.)

CUTS—*Twin Dragons* (1992)

There are injuries—like having a nose or finger broken during a spirited fight, or cracking an ankle giving an opponent a too-mighty kick—that evoke a kind of macho image. Then there are injuries like the one Jackie suffered here, which simply evoke chuckles—glass shards in the butt.

Granted, having pieces of knife-sharp glass piercing skin anywhere on your body is painful and necessitates medical attention. But it's not particularly ego boosting to need somebody to pluck glass out of your butt.

DEEP BRUISING; BROKEN SHOULDER—*Supercop* (1992)

By the time this film ended, Chan was battered and bruised. In the outtakes at the end of the movie, there's footage of Chan being clipped by a helicopter as he is hanging off a train. The accident occurred because the wire that was supposed to pull Jackie to safety got tangled.

However, despite being smashed into by a helicopter, nothing broke—although Chan had a deep bruise that turned most of his back a rich shade of purple. Bruises like this can lead to a host of potential health problems, including arthritis and, rarely, irregular cell growth (i.e., cancer).

Jackie wasn't so lucky when he was dangling from the rope ladder of the helicopter in another scene. His shoulder was broken when Chan was sent crashing through an assortment of billboards while flying through the skies over Kuala Lumpur.

BROKEN INSTEP—*City Hunter* (1992)

There's been a lot of disheartening discussion among Chan fans regarding the very obvious use of a stunt double by Chan in this film, during a fight in the cruise ship's dining room. But even though Chan is a stunt phenomenon, he's not Superman.

As mentioned above, Chan's body had just been pummeled during the *Supercop* shoot, then, making matters worse, he broke the top of his foot relatively early on in the shoot. This would explain why he had little choice but to use a double for a skateboarding scene, as well as for a fight scene that required a fair amount of up and down movement—the kind that a cracked instep would make difficult, if not impossible.

BURNS—*Drunken Master II* (1994)

The most serious injuries Jackie sustained in this film occurred while shooting the marathon fight scene at the movie's end when, among other things, he was thrown on a bed of hot coals. Twice.

The sequence called for Chan to fall backward onto a pile of burning coals, then scoot across the embers to get away from his opponent. After the first take, Jackie decided he didn't think his reaction to feeling his skin burn had been "right," so he insisted on doing it again. Not surprisingly, he suffered serious burns on his lower back and butt.

Of less obvious consequence was his insistence on actually drinking industrial alcohol in the scene, rather than a less harmful substitute. There does come a point where method crosses the line into madness.

ANKLE—*Rumble in the Bronx* (1995)

Jackie brings new meaning to the expression "walking off the pain." While filming in Vancouver, Chan designed a stunt where he would jump off a bridge and onto a hovercraft roaring by. Unfortunately, he landed wrong and broke his ankle. The injury was obviously serious, as Jackie appeared at the Vancouver Film Festival in a wheelchair.

Even so, it didn't stop Chan from working, employing a specially designed cast, which he later donated to Planet Hollywood for its collection of celebrity memorabilia.

CONCUSSION; NOSE INJURY—*First Strike* (1996)

This film was another stunt spectacular, so all things considered, Chan came away relatively unscathed. And again, it's curious that Jackie can jump off a mountain onto a helicopter with no mishap, then get knocked unconscious while working with a ladder. The outtakes show Jackie having to be peeled out of the ladder after he gets entangled and crunched.

It's a medical fact that repeated concussions can lead to permanent brain damage, resulting in a condition that makes the person appear to have wet brain (damage due to severe alcoholism). Football players most commonly suffer from this ailment, and in fact, Dallas Cowboy quarterback Troy Aikman has been advised he might have to retire if he suffers another concussion on the field.

What on earth does American football have to do with Jackie Chan? Just this: Injuries have a cumulative effect, especially head injuries of all kinds. How many more concussions can Chan endure before he turns into Lenny from *Of Mice and Men?* And how many more times can he break his nose until he either can't breathe or it slides at will around on his face? As it is, his nose has been so battered it would need reconstructive cosmetic surgery to resemble the schnoz he had when he began his career.

Ultimately, the biggest factor in all this will be time. Now in his forties, Jackie has already discovered how much longer it takes his body to heal now, as compared to twenty years ago. So expect to see him relying more and more on stunt doubles—except for the spectacular money shots.

NECK—*A Nice Guy* (1996)

What started out as a relatively routine stunt ended up deadly serious. Chan was lucky to walk away from this one—literally.

The stunt took place on an upper floor of a construction site. It called for Jackie to be pushed backward into a wheelbarrow and then for him to fall out of the wheelbarrow and down to the ground. The stunt crew put mats down that were supposed to break Chan's fall, but the mats were not positioned correctly, and when he hit the mats, he rolled off and smacked into the ground.

Wanting to show everyone he was fine, Jackie jumped up—and promptly passed out. Crew members called an ambulance, and Chan was rushed to a local hospital where X rays revealed torn neck ligaments and several dislocated vertebrae. He came uncomfortably close to a career-ending injury.

Even so, Chan only missed a couple of days' work and was able to finish the film with no additional problems.

THE
Fit

JACKIE CHAN

8

成龍

So, you say you want to start jumping over cars or free-fall off your roof and want to know how to get in shape for being the neighborhood daredevil? Well, if you're Jackie Chan, you devote at least three hours a day to working out. And you thought it was easy being a super stuntman.

"It takes a lot of work to stay in shape," Jackie has said in interviews. "I must keep my body very flexible. I lift weights for my chest, shoulders, and arms about one and a half hours but I have to be careful—if I get too big then I won't be able to move fast.

"Then I work on my punching and kicking, working out watching myself in the mirror. I kick for forty-five minutes—which is very difficult. After that I spar with my trainer. There's contact, but we don't hurt each other."

Everything is relative, we're sure.

"I also love to jog, but not up and down hills, just level, like a park. I usually run about three and a half miles. And when I run I wear three layers of clothes to make sure I work up a sweat. Working up a sweat is very important because when you sweat you burn fat and it keeps you thin.

"So does drinking lots of water. That is also very important."

Kind of makes you tired just reading about it, doesn't it?

But there's one obvious advantage to this daily torture regime—you get to eat anything you want.

"Oh, yeah—I eat everything," Jackie has said. "Meat, vegetables, chocolate, pizza, ice cream—sometimes five full meals a day. Of course, some days I eat no meals. I'm not really careful about my diet. . . . But I don't worry about weight—the workout takes care of that."

THE
Transliterate

9 成龍 JACKIE CHAN

*D*espite being recognized the world over as one of history's most unique filmmakers, the irony is that for years Jackie Chan and his films were virtually shut out of the movie-crazy American market. Before *Rumble in the Bronx* broke the logjam, to see Jackie's films you either had to travel to Chinatown movie houses—which, if you didn't understand Cantonese or Mandarin, could present a problem—or ferret out video copies, which opened a new Pandora's box of troubles.

Videos of Hong Kong films often have subtitles that are nonsensical translations, or even if you can actually make sense of the sentences, the subtitles are often frequently impossible to read—they are either cut off at the bottom of the screen or the white lettering is projected against a white background an amazingly high percentage of time. In recent years, laser discs have been an alternative, although not everybody has the equipment or can afford the steep disc prices.

Thanks to the growing numbers of Hong Kong fans, some of them well known and vocal, like Hong Kong film fanatic Quentin Tarantino, the situation is finally changing. More video stores are stocking better-produced copies of Asian action films, and more Hong Kong films are finding their way to mainstream theaters, where they're shown with halfway decent subtitles. But even with these welcome improvements language will continue to be a problem, bedeviling the efforts of those who want to introduce Asian films to mainstream American audiences.

It could be argued that it was the Chinese language that gave kung fu movies a less than stellar reputation to begin with. It's not just the terrible dubbing and the cheap production quality of many Asian films that have kept people from shelling out good money to see them.

Language is indeed the root of much Asian film difficulty. Or rather, the lack of a uniform spoken language dialect. And by this I don't mean dialect like we have in America. Although there are some snooty northerners who swear folks in Alabama are speaking a different language, we all speak the same language and use the same words, even if the pronunciation of certain vowels is different.

Not so in China. China is comprised of several ethnic groups such as the Tibetans, Turks, Russians, Mongols, Thai, Koreans, and a bunch of others, but the Hans make up 90 percent of the population. And in fact what most Westerners consider "Chinese" culture is actually Han culture, which also dominates Hong Kong, Taiwan, and the overseas Chinese communities in Europe and America.

While the Han Chinese share the same culture—meaning the same general values, religion, and, most importantly, a shared written language—what they don't share is a common spoken language.

The written Chinese symbols that we're all familiar with are called Hanzi, and they have the same meanings for all Chinese. You could give a diverse group of Chinese a newspaper or a book or have them watch movie subtitles written in Hanzi and they'd all be able to read them. However, they wouldn't be able to talk about it to each other afterward because over thousands of years each group has developed different sounds for the written characters.

Imagine if America were a thousand years old and the residents on the east and west coasts of the country rarely interacted—the way it was in China because of the country's vast size. Over the course of that time the regional dialects of the east and west American coasts would have changed, since language is a continually evolving form of communication. So now Californians pronounced the letter *D* as "duh"—no wisecracks—while New Yorkers pronounced *D* as "goh." Well now, that would cause a bit of a problem talking to each other, wouldn't it? In simplistic terms, that's what has happened in China.

This is why there is so much confusion when it comes to translating Asian movies—not to mention actors' names—into English. Translating is done by applying our alphabet sounds to the "spoken interpretation" of the Hanzi symbols. So the translated version changes depending upon whether the translator is speaking Mandarin Chinese or Cantonese or some other lesser dialect. Hence, Jackie Chan's name in Mandarin is Cheng Long, while in Cantonese it's Sing Lung.

At least 70 percent of the Han population speaks Mandarin as their first language. The entire coast north of Shanghai falls within Mandarin domain. The rest of the Han Chinese who reside on the southeastern coast speak ten mutually unintelligible languages. All in all, there are seven major Chinese dialects. Since the 1920s, an attempt has been made to unify the spoken language with campaigns waged to promote Mandarin, which is the official language of mass media and education. A modified version of Beijing Mandarin has been declared the standard for the nation—mainland China and Taiwan as well as the Chinese communities of Malaysia, Singapore, and Vietnam.

From the early days of the Chinese film industry, which was in Shanghai in the 1930s, all major film production was done only in Mandarin. And the dialogue had to be spoken in *perfectly* accented Mandarin—although media was given more leeway. And up until the 1970s schoolchildren were forced to speak only Mandarin—or face severe punishment.

However, in Hong Kong, films were also made in Cantonese. But these efforts were generally looked down upon by the cultural elite. Even those who spoke Cantonese avoided those films and went to see only Mandarin or American films. American films were held in disregard, so one can imagine that Hong Kong cinema was considered by many to be a rung above porno. Or perhaps below. This cultural blacklisting led to the demise of Cantonese cinema in the early 1960s.

But with the rise of communism, the Mandarin movie industry relocated to Hong Kong, where it continued producing films in Mandarin—despite Cantonese being the island's language. As a result, actors were required to speak perfect Mandarin, forcing them to undergo crash courses in Mandarin.

But as the older generation of Mandarin-speaking Hong Kong actors began to retire or die off, the new generation coming up presented a problem—having grown up in less stringent political times, most did not speak Mandarin. Nor did they particularly want to. Technology offered a solution.

Instead of recording the dialogue at the same time they shot the film—which is called shooting with synch-sound—they dubbed in the dialogue later. Usually badly. An actor would move his mouth, but the words wouldn't be heard until many seconds later. Or the words would start when the person first began talking, but then would continue long after his lips stopped moving.

This creates a cheesy production value, which affects the perception of the film's quality, especially to film-savvy Americans. This poor quality was the result of Hong Kong filmmakers having to work for years with relative shoestring budgets. The result was that Asian films became the butt of jokes.

Fortunately, Cantonese cinema made a triumphant comeback in the 1970s, giving the genre a popularity it had never before enjoyed. Many Mandarin-speaking stars from China and Taiwan swarmed to Hong Kong trying to get work in its rejuvenated film industry—making reverse dubbing necessary. So from the 1980s to the present there have usually been two versions produced of each film: Cantonese for Hong Kong, Japan, and the United States, and Mandarin for Korea, Taiwan, Singapore, Malaysia, and other parts of Southeast Asia.

Whether the Mainland's takeover of Hong Kong will change this current arrangement is a question nobody can answer. The overall view of many of the artists involved is that the language of a film should be an artistic choice, not the result of a decree by the government. But they obviously won't have the final say on the matter, and many filmmakers are already beginning to shoot their movies in the Mandarin dialect so it at least *feels* like it was their choice.

In the meantime, life goes on and movies keep getting made. Over the past few years more and more Hong Kong filmmakers have gone back to making films in synch-sound, in part because of the increased ability of Mandarin-speaking actors to handle the Cantonese dialogue themselves. Although synch-sound dramatically improves the production value appearance of a film, it means that even Asian viewers elsewhere in the world have to deal with subtitles. But most filmmakers consider subtitles the lesser of two evils.

Interestingly, one of the last holdouts against filming in synch-sound was none other than Jackie Chan. His attitude was, in a nutshell, why bother? Since he still dubbed the movies for Mandarin release anyway, why not dub the Cantonese version at the same time? Again, remember that Jackie's main concern was creating the most spectacular stunts and action film possible—his movies are about doing, not talking.

But even he has now seen the synchronized light—and it is shining on the American movie market. And Jackie's most recent movies are being shot in English, which completely eliminates the dubbing and subtitle problem for American audiences.

10

Cinematic

JACKIE CHAN

成
龍

*I*f nothing else, Chan has to be one of the more prolific filmmakers of our time, as his extensive filmography bears out. His movies are presented chronologically, as best as could be determined from the information available.

The format of each listing: First comes the title that the movie is best known by in this country plus the year the movie was released locally in Hong Kong—which is not necessarily the same year it was released anywhere else in the world. When possible the Cantonese name of the film is also given under the English title, since that is the most common language of Chan videotapes available in this country.

After the plot summary is a section of anecdotal and/or production information about the film and, if warranted, commentary on its place in both film and Jackie Chan history.

The third section includes tidbits, including production credits, any awards the film may have won, U.S. release dates, and a Mandarin translation when possible.

The data on some of the older, more obscure films is admittedly sketchy with many informational elements missing. But since this *is* the complete Jackie Chan filmography, a little information is better than none.

Truth is, not even Jackie himself can tell you the names of every film he has been involved with over the course of his career. Chan has said he believes the total number is somewhere around a hundred and assumes many of his early films have probably disappeared forever or languish forgotten in some Hong Kong warehouse. And as far as the chronology of films he made as a child and teenager—forget it. Even he can't provide an accurate listing.

One of the biggest obstacles to overcome when tracking down some of Jackie's films is the multiple titles an individual film often has. For example, even the American-made *The Big Brawl* is known some places as *Battle Creek Brawl*. The result is that many titles listed on various filmographies are simply additional titles for the same films.

Thus the difficulty in creating a complete and precise filmography. Still, this is as complete and accurate a list as is currently possible. In some cases, the film's title was the only piece of information available at this time.

成龍 FILMS 成龍

BIG AND LITTLE WONG TIN BAR (1962)
"Huang Tian Ba"

Here's where it all began. When he was just eight years old, Jackie made his screen debut in this Cantonese melodrama. It is unknown whether any print still exists. His Little Fortunes brother Sammo Hung was also featured in the film.

CAST: Jackie Chan, Sammo Hung

LOVE ETERNE (1963)
CAST: Jackie Chan

STORY OF QIU XIANG LIN (1964)
CAST: Jackie Chan

MASTER WITH CRACKED FINGERS (1971)

PLOT: Chan plays a young waiter who battles local punks after he befriends a young girl. Making matters worse by refusing to pay them, he incurs the wrath of a Chinese extortion ring that controls the docks where he works. After he learns these are the same goons who burned his house to the ground—with his adopted father still in it—Chan vows revenge and trains under an eccentric Master. After learning to fight with fists that strike with the deadly speed of a coiled snake, he goes after the bad guys with a bloody vengeance.

It is difficult to pin down an accurate date for this movie. As often happens when dealing with films from Asia, release dates vary from one account to another, and in this case, there's even inconsistency about the director's credit. One reference book lists the director as a Wei Hui Feng; others state that Chin Hsin directed the film. Chin also happened to write the screenplay for *Shaolin Wooden Men*, one of Jackie's other early efforts, and is most likely the director of this film.

The reason for the confusion probably stems from the Frankenstein-like rebirth this film went through several years after it was originally made. Accurate documentation took second place behind the rush to make money off Chan's name. And the original film was such a disaster, those associated with it probably wanted it to disappear without a trace.

In what is considered his first starring role, Chan (listed in the credits then as Chan Yuan Lung) was only a teenager when he made this low-budget, low-quality kung fu picture that was released for a nanosecond in 1971, then again in 1973. No doubt Jackie hoped it would help establish him as an up-and-coming kung fu movie star. But the finished product was so subpar and unimpressive that it languished unreleased for a couple of years.

Fast forward a few years. *Drunken Master*, released in 1978, is a major hit, and Chan is now super-hot. A Chinese distributor with questionable artistic ethics acquired the film footage and set about to renovate his purchase. Additional footage was shot using a Chan lookalike and Simon Yuen, who had appeared in the original film. Among the added scenes are one of the stand-in doing kung fu in a dimly lit shack and a final, climactic fight where the pseudo–Jackie and the bad guy cleverly use blindfolds to cover their faces.

The new creation was released again in Hong Kong and for the first time in the United States under the title *Snake Fist Fighter*.

None of it helped—the film in either incarnation was terrible. In addition to being ho-hum, the gussied-up version was insulting because of the attempted sleight of hand concerning Jackie. All of this intrigue may explain why there's no mention of this movie on Chan's *official* filmography.

CAST: Jackie Chan, Tien Feng, Hon Kwok Choi
DIRECTOR: Chin Hsin
PRODUCER: Li Long Koon
FIGHT/ACTION DIRECTORS: Jackie Chan, Se Fu Tsai
PRODUCTION COMPANY: Solar Films
DISTRIBUTOR: 21st Century
U.S. RELEASE: 1981 (video—"reconstructed" version)
A/K/A:

- *Little Tiger from Canton* (original title)
- *Snake Fist Fighter* (U.S. release title)
- *Cub Tiger from Kwang Tung*
- *Stranger in Hong Kong*
- *Marvelous Fists*
- *Ten Fingers of Death*

FIST OF FURY (1972)
"Jing Mo Moon"

PLOT: Based on the story of a real-life folk hero, Chen Zhen, who was driven to avenge the death of his legendary kung fu teacher, who was killed while dueling a Japanese master. Set in Shanghai after the turn of the century. Bruce Lee as Chen takes on a rival Japanese martial arts school with his deadly kicks and punches, but it is only a matter of time before he falls at the hands of the enemy. In the end, Chen opts to die on his feet rather than give in on his knees, jumping defiantly straight toward the police, who gun him down midair.

Bruce Lee's second film hit an emotional nerve in Chinese audiences through its depiction of Japanese cruelty toward the Chinese, a wound that has yet to ever truly heal among many in both countries. In a scene forever etched in the minds of his countrymen, Lee sees a sign reading NO DOGS OR CHINESE above a door entrance. In a controlled fury, Lee leaps into the air, kicks the sign off the door, and smashes it to pieces with a final vicious kick before it can land on the ground. In slow motion, no less. Even if the film hadn't contained some of the most amazing kung fu fighting courtesy of Lee, it would still have been a classic for the sign scene alone.

Fist of Fury is not exactly showcase material for Chan, who appears only briefly. His big moment comes when he has the honor of being kicked through a wall by Bruce. Everyone has to start somewhere. Besides Jackie's involvement, *Fist of Fury* is notable for several other reasons.

First, it is often included as one of the top martial arts films of all time. It catapulted Bruce Lee to international stardom and introduced most Americans to a genre that was virtually unknown to them.

Second, it contains Lee's only screen kiss, courtesy of Nora Miao.

And lastly, despite its enormous success everywhere, there was, and probably still is, a quandary about the movie's correct title. Bruce Lee's first film was a Lo Wei production called *The Big Boss*. When released in American the movie was released under the title *Fists of Fury*. In the movie, Bruce works in a Bangkok factory and ends up fighting a horde of bad guys.

The movie was such a hit, Lo Wei and Bruce quickly did another and called it *Fist of Fury*. *Fist* singular. When it came time to release the film in the States, even Lo Wei realized it might be a bit confusing, so the movie was called *The Chinese Connection* in American theaters when first shown here. But over the years, there's been confusion anyway, with people referring to *The Chinese Connection* as either *Fist* or *Fists of Fury*, many not realizing they are actually two different films.

The muddled title situation continues to cause countless problems for people trying to buy video and laser disc copies. The best way to know for sure what film you have is to check the movie's release date if possible. *The Big Boss* was originally released in 1971; *Fist of Fury* was released in 1972.

CAST: Bruce Lee, Nora Miao, Tien Feng, James Tien, Jackie Chan (stunt extra)
DIRECTOR: Lo Wei
PRODUCER: Raymond Chow
WRITER: Lo Wei
FIGHT/ACTION/ DIRECTOR: Bruce Lee
PRODUCTION COMPANY: Golden Harvest
DISTRIBUTORS: Best Film & Video; CBS
U.S. RELEASE: 1973 (theatrical and video)
MANDARIN: Jing1 Wu3 Men2
A/K/A:
- *The Chinese Connection*

HAPKIDO (1972)

PLOT: After having invaded Korea, the Japanese have their sights set on invading China. Three Chinese friends who are attending school in Korea are taught Hapkido from a Chinese master who also happens to be living in Korea. Once they learn the new fighting skill, which requires equal parts strength and concentration, the students return to China and open their own school.

This does not amuse the students of a nearby Japanese-run school. After one of the three Chinese students is killed by members of the other school, the two remaining friends join force with another Hapkido instructor, and together they defeat the Japanese and destroy the rival school.

Generally considered to be Sammo Hung's first starring role, this movie also features a walk-on by Jackie, who was still depending on the kindness of strangers, and friends, for work.

Of Special Note: One of the villains was played by Korean fighter Huang In-sik, who made quite a few enemies on the set by kicking to hurt. The general feeling was that he was trying to show up the Chinese fighters. When Bruce Lee got wind of what was going on, he hired Huang for *Way of the Dragon.* During a pivotal fight scene, Lee out-kicked the Korean but stopped short of actually hurting him. Huang got the point, and the one-upsmanship stopped.

CAST: Sammo Hung, Angela Mao, Carter Wong, Wei Ping, Jackie
   Chan (extra)
DIRECTOR: Huang Feng
PRODUCER: Raymond Chow
WRITERS: Ho Jen; Huang Feng
PRODUCTION COMPANY: Golden Harvest
U.S. RELEASE: 1989 (video)

THE HEROINE (1973)

PLOT: A young woman travels to Peking to search for her brother, a collaborator who is helping the Japanese forces occupying the city. Once there, the woman turns out not to be the collaborator's sister, but a rebel freedom fighter who is on a mission to free another member of the resistance from jail.

The woman's identity is uncovered and she is killed, but only after she is able to help free the resistance leader.

During this time, Jackie was still being hired mostly as a fighting extra and stunt person, traveling between Hong Kong and Taiwan, where he made a series of bad B flicks. The extent of his contribution here is a fight with the female lead, Cheng Pei Pei, using the ever-popular "swingy arm" style.

Cheng is considered by many to be *the* first queen of kung fu flicks. She was also the first Asian actress to win the Golden Knight Award at the International Producers' Association confab. After a brief retirement in 1970 to get married and temporarily relocate to America, Cheng returned to Hong Kong and went to work for Golden Harvest, which is how she ended up on *The Heroine*, which was to be her comeback vehicle.

According to Bey Logan in *Hong Kong Action Cinema* it was during *The Heroine* shoot that Lo Wei claimed to have first recognized Chan's star potential when he was demonstrating the best way to die on film to one of the stunt extras. The same cannot be said of Cheng, who readily admits she never dreamed Chan would become the international superstar he is today.

An interesting footnote: Years later Cheng showed up in *Painted Faces*, the based-on-fact account of Master Yu Chan Yuan, Jackie's teacher at the Peking Opera School. Most recently, Cheng was busy with her own cable talk show called *Pei Pei's Time*.

Of Special Note: This film was essentially a remake of *Fist of Fury*. Lo Wei simply changed the lead character to a woman.

CAST: Cheng Pei Pei, James Tien, Jo Shishido, Jackie Chan
DIRECTOR: Lo Wei
FIGHT/ACTION DIRECTOR: Jackie Chan
PRODUCTION COMPANY: Golden Harvest
A/K/A:
- *Kung Fu Girl* (UK title)
- *Attack of the Kung Fu Girls*

ENTER THE DRAGON (1973)
"Lung Jaang Foo Dau"

PLOT: Bruce Lee classic in which he portrays a Shaolin temple teacher who avenges his sister's death at the hands of a gangster associated with a drug-running, white slave-trading operation. Lee infiltrates the gang and single-handedly destroys it.

This time, Chan gets to have his neck snapped by the rampaging Lee. Yet another installment in the dues department, but at least he got his neck snapped in the movie often called the most famous martial arts film of all time, and by the most famous movie star in Asia at the time. Being around Lee during his glory days must have added fuel to Chan's own burning ambition.

Like Lo Wei, Robert Clouse, director of *Enter the Dragon*, recognized Jackie's potential. Years later the director would have an opportunity to try and help Jackie realize his goal of being a true international star, when he hired Chan for *The Big Brawl*, his American film debut. Despite the movie's dismal performance at the box office in the States, Clouse was still convinced Jackie could be a Hollywood star. In the years following *The Big Brawl*, the director also wrote two movies specifically for Chan—*Blood Island* and *The Protector*. But neither effort succeeded in establishing Jackie as a major player on American shores. That would have to wait another twenty years.

A quick trivia quiz. What American martial arts star makes a cameo appearance in *Enter the Dragon?* Give yourself a pat on the back if you said Chuck Norris.

Of Special Note: Although hardly amazing in today's world of $8.50 ticket prices, *Enter the Dragon's* $100 million worldwide box office was unheard of for a chopsocky film. It was a record that wouldn't be broken until Jackie Chan did it years later.

CAST: Bruce Lee, Shek Tien, Yank Sze, Peter Archer, Sammo Hung, Bob Wall, John Saxon, Jackie Chan (extra)
DIRECTOR: Robert Clouse
PRODUCERS: Paul Heller, Fred Weintraub

WRITER: Michael Allin
FIGHT/ACTION DIRECTOR: Bruce Lee
PRODUCTION COMPANY: Warner Brothers
DISTRIBUTORS: Warner Brothers; Ocean Shores Video; NYUE
U.S. RELEASE: 1973 (theatrical and video)
MANDARIN: Long2 Zheng1 Hu3 Dou4
A/K/A:

- *The Deadly Three*

EAGLE SHADOW FIST (1973)

PLOT: Set in 1937. Chan portrays a member of a Peking Opera troupe who manages to escape from Japanese soldiers looking for Chinese rebels. The actor becomes a resistance fighter against the Japanese—and traitorous Chinese. After only a few skirmishes with the enemy, Chan's character is killed.

And Jackie probably couldn't wait for his character to die. This movie has little value beyond being a curiosity piece. It's one of the rare opportunities where you can see Chan act out a death scene.

Another movie Jackie fails to list on his official acting filmography.

CAST: Wang Ching, Lin Xiu, Jackie Chan
DIRECTOR: Zhu Wu
PRODUCER: Hoi Ling
WRITER: Su Lan
FIGHT/ACTION DIRECTOR: Jackie Chan
PRODUCTION COMPANY: Great Earth
DISTRIBUTOR: All Seasons Entertainment
U.S. RELEASE: 1986 (video)
A/K/A:

- *Not Scared to Die*

Jackie Chan and his parents

Jackie as one of the Seven Little
Fortunes performing troupe

Jackie, twelve years old

JACKIE 成龍 CHAN

Teenaged Jackie with his mother

Jackie on his twenty-fifth birthday

JACKIE

CHAN

Jackie makes war.

JACKIE 成龍
CHAN

Jackie makes peace.

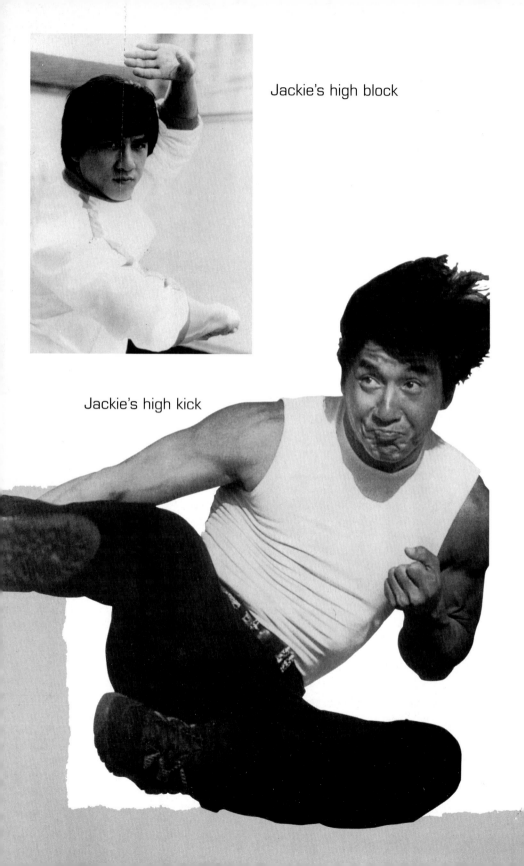

Jackie's high block

Jackie's high kick

JACKIE 成龍 CHAN

Chow Yun Fat

(Photo by Michael Rovin

Jet Li

Sonny Chiba

Bruce Lee

JACKIE 成龍
CHAN

Jackie makes an impression at Mann's Chinese Theater in Hollywood.

(Photos by Cynthia Woodard Perry)

Jackie meets his U.S. fan club
(Photos by Cynthia Woodard Perry)

JACKIE 成龍
CHAN

Jackie directs.

JACKY CHAN: LA MANO CHE UCCIDE

con **JACKY CHAN**

JAMES TIEN · SHIH TIEN · LI KUEN
YEN SI KUAN · Regia di **JACKY CHAN**
EASTMANCOLOR

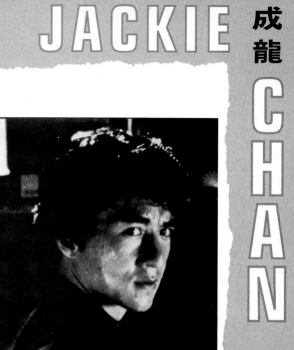

JACKIE 成龍
CHAN

GOLDEN LOTUS (1974)

CAST: Jackie Chan

THE HIMALAYAN (1975)

PLOT: Another story of revenge toward a ruthless leader. A man and a woman go to study kung fu under the guidance of a holy lama in Nepal. Despite the grueling training, they persevere and exact their revenge.

The best reason to track this movie down is to see Angela Mao in action and the early fight direction of a young Sammo Hung. Chan's appearance is forgettable except for another chance to see him pre-eye-opening surgery.

Mao was one of Golden Harvest's first stars. Interestingly, her childhood shares similarities with Jackie's. Born in 1950, she was enrolled in Taiwan's Fu Shing Academy when she was just five. There she learned acting, singing, and martial arts. When she was twelve, she went on a world tour and then joined the Hoi Kwan theatrical company the following year. She retired from acting in the late 1970s to get married.

CAST: Angela Mao, Chen Sing, Tan Tao Liang, Sammo Hung, Jackie Chan (bit role)
DIRECTOR: Huang Feng
PRODUCER: Raymond Chow
WRITER: I Kuang
FIGHT/ACTION DIRECTORS: Han Ying Chieh, Sammo Hung
PRODUCTION COMPANY: Golden Harvest
DISTRIBUTOR: NYUE
U.S. RELEASE: 1992 (video)

ALL IN THE FAMILY (1975)

PLOT: A family reunites to keep vigil over their dying patriarch during his final days in this turn-of-the-century sex farce.

Chan, of all people, plays a rogue rickshaw puller who spends most of his time in bed, seducing both a mother and her daughter.

This is the only film Chan has made that doesn't have a single fight or stunt sequence. It is also the only film where you can see Jackie, twice, buck naked in bed having sex with a woman. Perhaps that's the reason this film has all but disappeared from collective Hong Kong cinema memory in general and Jackie's in particular. Whether by accident or design, very few people are even aware of this film's existence. Including historians. Only one reference guide lists a director, Chu Mu, whose other credits are all for acting—which would make *All in the Family* his first and last directorial effort.

Of Special Note: This is another film made prior to Jackie's cosmetic surgery.

CAST: Linda Chu, Dean Shek Tien, Jackie Chan, James Tien, Sammo Hung
DIRECTOR: Chu Mu
PRODUCER: Raymond Chow
WRITER: Ken Suma
PRODUCTION COMPANY: Golden Harvest
DISTRIBUTOR: NYUE
U.S. RELEASE: 1992 (video)

HAND OF DEATH (1975)
"Siu Lam Moon"

PLOT: Dorian Tan and sidekick Chan are dispatched by a Shaolin temple abbot to protect a messenger from corrupt Manchus. Then they kill a murderous lord and his group of followers who are slaughtering people all across China.

Still going by the name Sing Lung, Jackie was given some room to shine in this early John Woo effort, thanks to Sammo

Hung's always creative fight choreography. Although it wasn't the breakthrough role he was looking for, this film has one of the more interesting pedigrees of Chan's early work.

Besides being written and directed by a still relatively unknown John Woo, it is the only time Woo and the "three brothers"—Chan, Yuen Biao, and Sammo Hung—worked together on a movie. Although the average moviegoer might not realize that fact: Sammo is sporting a wicked set of buck teeth, and Yuen is largely unrecognizable.

The "star" of *Hand of Death* was an excellent martial artist named Tan Tao Liang known for his lethal kicking ability. Tan was yet another in a long line who tried to be the next Bruce Lee, and for a while he used the moniker Bruce Liang. But after that experiment failed, he went back to being called Tan Tao Liang (Anglicized to Dorian Tan) and enjoyed a solid, if not necessarily spectacular, career during the 1970s.

CAST: Dorian Tan, Yuen Biao, Sammo Hung, Jackie Chan, James Tien
DIRECTOR: John Woo
PRODUCER: John Woo
WRITER: John Woo
FIGHT/ACTION DIRECTOR: Sammo Hung
PRODUCTION COMPANY: Golden Harvest
DISTRIBUTORS: SB Video; NYUE
U.S. RELEASE: 1988 (video)
MANDARIN: Shao3 Lin2 Men2
A/K/A:

- *Countdown in Kung Fu*
- *Shaolin Men*
- *Countdown in Death*

FIST OF DEATH (late 1970s)

PLOT: Two rivals meet for a showdown to see who's going to take over leadership of their respective gangs. But the fight ends up a stalemate, and as a result, the two rivals become friends. Later they join forces to defeat the gangs.

This is one movie that is better off staying one of Jackie's "lost" films.

CAST: Jackie Chan, Tong Lung
DISTRIBUTOR: Mogul
U.S. RELEASE: 1988 (video)

NEW FIST OF FURY (1976)

PLOT: A continuation of Bruce Lee's *Fist of Fury* epic, which once again pits Chinese against Japanese. In this go-round, Chan plays Chen Zhen's brother, who is a thief in Japanese-occupied Taiwan. The legend's sibling has no interest in learning kung fu—until he discovers a Japanese sympathizer has helped close down the local martial arts school and humiliated its master. The same traitor who beat Chan up when he refused to join the man's fighting school.

After the beautiful granddaughter of the master begs for his help—and after getting some sense beaten into him after being smacked around by some Japanese—an enraged Chan goes on the offensive. He enlists the people in the town to help reopen the school, studies diligently, and becomes a mean, lean fighting machine. He uses his new skills to kill a particularly offensive Japanese opponent. But in a rather startling twist, rather than having an upbeat ending of Chinese triumph, the movie ends with the thief and others from the school being shot and killed by Japanese gunmen in a disturbing massacre scene.

Apparently Lo Wei followed the old Hollywood philosophy: If you don't have an original idea, just retread old ones.

Jackie tries hard to follow in the formidable footsteps of Bruce Lee and as such is kept from showing any indication of his future potential. When compared to the original *Fist of*

Fury, this knockoff comes across as a poor second. The fights are satisfactory although nothing out of the ordinary. Chan gives imitating Bruce's style and emotional intensity the old college try, but he looks tense and uncomfortable on screen. It's obvious he knows the attempt is a failure.

New Fist of Fury was one of a series of movies Chan made in Taiwan while under contract with egotistical producer/director Lo Wei, a man of limited creative vision who takes credit for being the first to see Chan's star quality. Maybe so. But as their films together indicate, he didn't have a clue what to do with it. And trying to promote Jackie as Bruce reincarnate was a grave error.

Ironically, Lo Wei also took credit for discovering Bruce Lee and was listed as the director of the classic *Fist of Fury* as well as Lee's *The Big Boss*. However, more than a few people wonder if Bruce actually was the man calling the shots on those two "Lo Wei" movies. Especially after Chan later revealed that Lo Wei had a habit of napping during filming.

Of Special Note: Lo Wei was only one of several people who would eventually take credit for discovering Bruce Lee. As far as it can be sorted out, Lo's son David saw Bruce on a Hong Kong television show. Later, Raymond Chow claimed *he's* the one who saw said program. Whoever saw it, the result was Lo's wife, Liu Liang Hua, being sent to Los Angeles to have a chat with Bruce about signing up with Golden Harvest, which he eventually did.

CAST: Jackie Chan (listed as Jackie Chen in the credits), Chen Sing, Nora Miao, Chang King
DIRECTOR: Lo Wei
PRODUCER: Hsu Li Hwa
WRITER: Pan Lei
FIGHT/ACTION DIRECTOR: Han Ying Chieh
PRODUCTION COMPANY: HK
DISTRIBUTOR: All Seasons
U.S. RELEASE: 1985 (video)

A/K/A:

- *Xin Ching-Wu Men*

SHAOLIN WOODEN MEN (1976)

PLOT: Chan plays a mute named Su, who goes to a Shaolin temple where he meets several masters. One, an imprisoned thief named Fat Yu, agrees to teach Su kung fu and how to defeat the wooden sentries guarding the temple's exit—but only if the young man delivers a message to a friend on the outside. Su agrees, but before he can leave he must defeat the deadly wooden men obstacle devised by the Shaolin—something nobody has done before him.

After a brutal effort, Su finally makes it through the gauntlet and leaves the Shaolin. With his new skills, Su sets off to avenge his father's murder. While on his quest, he comes to the aid of Fat Yu, who has escaped and is being chased by someone from the Shaolin.

Believing he had done a good deed, Su goes on, only to discover that Fat Yu is actually the leader of an evil gang. Even worse, the thief is the one who killed Su's father, setting up a confrontation with the gangster with Su using the dreaded Lion's Road kung fu.

After Lo Wei realized Chan was not going to be picking up the mantle left by Bruce, he switched gears and cast Jackie as a stoic, silent hero—the character takes a vow of silence until he can avenge his father's death. It is too reminiscent of Shaw Brothers period pieces made famous—and done better—by Lau Kar-leung. Lo Wei was still trying to fit a square peg through a round hole. In the meantime, Chan was doing whatever he could to insert a little of his own personality into the roles and sneaked a few comic bits into an otherwise straighter-than-thou film.

Of Special Note: This movie was almost lost forever—the last known print had begun to deteriorate before a video copy was made of it. As a result, available copies are not of the greatest quality.

CAST: Jackie Chan, Kam Kan, Simon Yuen, Lung Chung-erh.
DIRECTOR: Lo Wei
PRODUCER: Hsu Li Hwa
WRITER: Chin Hsin
FIGHT/ACTION DIRECTORS: Jackie Chan, Li Ming Wen
PRODUCTION COMPANY: HK
DISTRIBUTOR: All Seasons
U.S. RELEASE: 1987 (video)
A/K/A:

- *36 Wooden Men*
- *Shaolin Chamber of Death*
- *Young Tiger's Revenge*

DANCE OF DEATH (1976)

PLOT: A comedy about a woman who learns kung fu from two rival masters, so she can avenge the death of her clan by killing the leader of the gang responsible for the murders.

Dance of Death stars Angela Mao, who in addition to being a top film star was also a black belt in Hapkido. As a result, Mao was known for her kicks and her natural athletic ability, which would have given Jackie a lot of room to be creative when designing her fight sequences.

CAST: Angela Mao, Shek Tien, Chin Pei
DIRECTOR: Chen Chi Hwa
PRODUCER: Yen Wu Tun
FIGHT ACTION/DIRECTOR: Jackie Chan
DISTRIBUTOR: Unicorn
U.S. RELEASE: 1986 (video)
A/K/A:

- *The Eternal Conflict*

TO KILL WITH INTRIGUE (1976)

PLOT: A woman sets out to destroy the family of the man who disfigured her face. With a mask covering her scars, the woman kills everyone—except Hsiao, the son, played by Chan, with whom she falls in love and by whom she gets pregnant. But to her surprise, the son rejects her so she leaves—not knowing he intentionally drove her away to protect her.

Eventually, Hsiao discovers his friend is really the leader of the evil Deadly Rain Clan, who has killed Hsiao's other friends. To avenge their deaths, he battles and defeats the two-faced friend.

Not your average Lo Wei/Jackie Chan collaboration, although the change of pace failed to change Jackie's film fortunes. Shot in Korea, the production was plagued by extremely cold weather conditions, causing equipment to freeze and morale to plummet.

By this time, Chan knew his career was never going to fly under Lo Wei, but there was little he could do except wait for a chance. While waiting, he devoted himself to learning as much as he could about the process of making films. Lesson number one: Frozen springs make for difficult trampoline work. Lesson number two: Try not to look like you're wearing a bad toupee. Either that was the world's worst hairpiece or Jackie was really having a bad hair *shoot*.

This film was obviously made before Jackie was too concerned with family-oriented films. Hence the bloody hand he chops off an opponent and then carries around like a trophy.

Of Special Note: According to *Oriental Cinema* magazine, the name of the movie girlfriend, Chin Chin, had to be changed in the Japanese version because *chin chin* is a Japanese slang term for penis.

CAST: Jackie Chan, Hsu Feng
DIRECTOR: Lo Wei

PRODUCER: Lo Wei
WRITER: Ku Lung
FIGHT/ACTION DIRECTORS: Chin Hsin, Chen Wen Lung
PRODUCTION COMPANY: Lo Wei Motion Picture Company
DISTRIBUTOR: Trans World Entertainment
U.S. RELEASE: 1985 (video)
A/K/A:

* *Jackie Chan Connection*

IRON-FISTED MONK (1977)

PLOT: Sammo plays a young man out to avenge the death of his uncle at the hands of the Manchus. He learns kung fu at the Shaolin, then leaves to confront and defeat his enemy.

Sammo cowrote the screenplay with Huang Feng, the man who directed Sammo in *Hapkido*. Not exactly a wildly new movie concept, but this film marks Sammo's directing debut. Other than that, and the fact that Jackie choreographed the fights, there's not much else going for this film.

CAST: Sammo Hung, Chen Sing, Dean Shek
DIRECTOR: Sammo Hung
WRITERS: Sammo Hung, Huang Feng
FIGHT/ACTION DIRECTORS: Sammo Hung, Jackie Chan
PRODUCTION COMPANY: Golden Harvest
DISTRIBUTORS: NYUE (Rainbow Video)
U.S. RELEASE: 1991 (video)

THE KILLER METEORS (1977)

PLOT: Chan plays a villainous warrior, Immortal Meteor, who is so feared that people who live near him bring him yearly offerings so he won't kill them. Which is fairly easy for him to do because he carries around a weapon that can apparently kill those who dare to look upon it.

But when the Meteor Man is given a stolen pearl by a

thief, he has a premonition that he will meet his doom at the hands of Killer Weapon, a lawman who wields a sword forged from a meteor.

With that thought having apparently slipped his mind, Immortal Meteor goes on a mission to kill the wife of his enemy. In the end, he finds himself duking it out with warriors in charge of guarding a poison antidote that he wants to obtain.

Needless to say, this is not one of the classics. Even hardcore Chan fans have a difficult time finding many saving graces about *The Killer Meteors*, the kind of film you would find on a drive-in triple bill. Playing last. Tougher still is figuring out what is really going on in the movie. There appear to be a lot of phantom plot lines that vanish without a trace.

Chan is visibly uncomfortable playing an evil warlord type, and the production values come complete with visible wire work. It is movies like *The Killer Meteors* that Americans thought of as typical "kung fu" movies—badly made period pieces with fake-looking fighting. These clumsily made works are no doubt why the genre has had such a hard time getting its foot in the mainstream U.S. market even after the genre evolved into top-notch filmmaking.

For Chan, *The Killer Meteors*, was merely another example of Lo Wei's staggering lack of vision. Or stubbornness. Early on in their collaborations, Chan suggested to Lo Wei that maybe they should try something a little more up Chan's personal alley, like tossing in some humor. *Intentional* humor, that is.

Lo Wei disdainfully rejected the idea as preposterous. Kung fu was serious business. After each flop, Chan pressed the director more and more but was always rebuked. No one was about to tell Lo Wei how to make a movie.

What's Cantonese for *diva?*

Of Special Note: Although made in 1976, it took almost two years for the film to be released. Gee, wonder why?

CAST: Jackie Chan, Jimmy Wang Yu, Yu Lin Lung, Kao Fei
DIRECTOR: Lo Wei
PRODUCER: Hsu Li Hwa
WRITER: Ku Lung
PRODUCTION COMPANY: HK
DISTRIBUTOR: Ocean Shores Video
U.S. RELEASE: 1988 (video)
A/K/A:

* *Jackie Chan vs. Wang Yu*

SNAKE AND CRANE ARTS OF SHAOLIN (1977)

PLOT: Eight masters get together and write a book, *The Eight Steps of the Snake and Crane,* which combines the best of their individual styles. Considered to be about the most dangerous style of kung fu known to man, the book goes missing after the masters are murdered.

Chan plays a warrior who later shows up with the book. Although he is believed to be the murderer of the masters, the warrior is really using the book as bait to find the real killer. Because all the clans want the secrets contained in the book, the warrior is made offers ranging from money to women to give up the book. When he refuses he is attacked but uses the Snake and Crane styles, making him nearly invincible.

In their desperation to possess the book, the clans end up fighting each other in a huge battle—during which the warrior escapes. By the time the fighting ends, the warrior has discovered who the killer is and finally reveals his real mission to those left standing. Not all of the masters had died. One survived despite drinking the poisoned water left by the killer. The warrior had found him on the brink of death and nursed him back to health. Together they hatched a plot to smoke out the killer, who turns out to be the leader of the Black Dragons.

In the final confrontation, the warrior defeats the leader of the Black Dragons and his henchmen by using the Snake style on one hand, the Crane on the other.

This film boasts one of the more complicated plots to be seen in a Chan film as well as fight sequences that are a cut above Chan's other efforts with Lo Wei—no doubt because Chan himself choreographed the martial arts sequences. Being in charge of the action allowed Chan to show off some flashy moves and styles, including the Plum Blossom Fist, one of the ancient Shaolin styles.

Particularly effective is the last fight, where Chan uses the combination of styles against sword-wielding thugs. Because of this, *Snake and Crane Arts of Shaolin* generally gets a thumbs-up from Chan fans as one of his better, if not best, period melodramas.

CAST: Jackie Chan, Nora Miao, Kam Kan
DIRECTOR: Chen Chi Hwa
PRODUCER: Hsu Li Hwa
FIGHT/ACTION DIRECTORS: Tu Wei Ho / Jackie Chan
PRODUCTION COMPANY: Lo Wei Motion Picture Company
DISTRIBUTOR: Alpha Film & Video
U.S. RELEASE: 1984 (video)

MAGNIFICENT BODYGUARD (1978)

PLOT: Chan plays a bodyguard who agrees to escort a woman's dying brother to a doctor who can save his life. But to get there they must pass through Stormy Hills, an area rife with bandits. After he rounds up a posse of fighters to accompany him on the dangerous journey, they set off.

Along the way the group encounters the self-proclaimed King of the Bandits who tries to stop them from passing through Stormy Hills. It's only after battling with the bandits that the bodyguard learns the truth—his "dying" passenger is actually the true King of the Bandits. The journey was merely a way for the real king to smoke out his impersonator.

In the end, the bodyguard helps the real king defeat the impostor.

Lo Wei's gimmick this time around was to film *Magnificent Bodyguard* in 3-D, so the movie is full of punches and kicks being thrown directly at the camera. It didn't help. Although the fight choreography is fine, with some good kicking action, it's apparent that wires are being used in some scenes. The final fight has its moments, but not enough to make the film a standout.

This is yet another Lo Wei cookie-cutter production that was quickly forgotten.

Of Special Note: In some versions, this movie uses theme music from *Star Wars* as its score.

CAST: Jackie Chan, James Tien, Bruce Liang
DIRECTOR: Lo Wei
PRODUCER: Hsu Li Hwa
WRITER: Ku Lung
FIGHT/ACTION DIRECTORS: Jackie Chan, Luk Chuen
PRODUCTION COMPANY: HK
DISTRIBUTOR: 21st Century
U.S. RELEASES: 1982 (theatrical); 1987 (video)

SNAKE IN THE EAGLE'S SHADOW (1978)
"She Xing Diao Shou"

PLOT: Set in nineteenth-century China. Jackie plays Chen Fu, a somewhat slow-witted goof who works in a local kung fu gym. Chen is taught the Snake Fist style by the last living master after the old man takes pity on him being constantly used as a human punching bag.

The head of the Eagle Clan, with his deadly Eagle Claw, has sworn to leave no Snake fighter alive, so when he sees Chen Fu using the style, he sets out to kill both him and the old master. Realizing the Snake Fist is no match for the Eagle Claw, Chen Fu finally triumphs using the Cat's Claw—a style he invented after watching a house cat defeat and kill a cobra.

In a delicious irony, Lo Wei had nothing to do with this hit movie, except for agreeing to let Jackie work for a rival production company, Seasonal Films. Even though he had Lo Wei's blessing, Jackie almost didn't get to make the picture. Executives who were quite aware of his previous work thought that hiring Jackie would be the film's kiss of death. But producer Ng See Yuen stuck by his gut instinct, and Chan was eventually hired.

Snake in the Eagle's Shadow is credited with laying the foundation for the kung fu comedy genre. Interestingly, it was Yuen's directional debut—which probably explains his willingness to break from the mold. Instead of archly intense performances, Yuen encouraged his actors to loosen up and directed them to show off their physical abilities rather than just their fighting style.

The only character who stayed overly intense was the villain, which accentuated the comedic elements that much more. There's an important difference between this film and Chan's *Half a Loaf of Kung Fu*. The latter was more spooflike whereas *Snake in the Eagle's Shadow* was a real comedy. It's a fine distinction, but the difference is what sowed the seeds for the cultivation of a distinct genre of kung fu movies.

A big part of the film's appeal other than the top-notch fighting sequences was the relationship between Chan and the old master—who just happened to be Yuen's real-life father. Because the film succeeded on a story level as well as having terrific choreography, it became a landmark movie that would establish the career of both Jackie and Yuen.

One last note. Although he doesn't receive screen credit, *Snake in the Eagle's Shadow* was based in part on a screenplay written by Chan.

Of Special Note: During the last fight, Huang kicked Jackie in the face and knocked out a capped tooth, which is visible when Jackie smiles at the end of the movie. Actor Roy Horan dislocated his shoulder while fighting Chan—but finished filming the scene despite having a useless arm.

CAST: Jackie Chan, Simon Yuen Siu Tien, Shek Tien, Huang Cheng-li

DIRECTOR: Yuen Woo Ping

PRODUCER: Chen Chaun

WRITER: Ng See Yuen—based on a screenplay by Chan

FIGHT/ACTION DIRECTOR: Yuen Ho Ping

PRODUCTION COMPANY: Seasonal

DISTRIBUTOR: World Home Video

U.S. RELEASES: 1983 (theatrical); 1988 (video)

MANDARIN: She2 Xing2 Diao1 Shou3

A/K/A:

- *The Eagle's Shadow*
- *Bruce vs. Snake in Eagle's Shadow*
- *Snaky Monkey*

HALF A LOAF OF KUNG FU (1978)

PLOT: Chan plays a character who doesn't know the first thing about fighting but pretends to—and suddenly finds himself in over his head. Desperate, he agrees to help guard a jade treasure in exchange for lessons from a kung fu master. Later, he and the group of bodyguards have to fight off a gang of bandits intent on stealing the jade, and despite being heavily outnumbered, they defeat the infidels.

Probably just to get Jackie off his back, Lo Wei finally gave in and allowed Jacking to make his kung fu comedy. Some of his later trademarks—the klutzy bumbler who's in over his head, the slapstick elements—can be seen here already, but because it was so unfamiliar, it was jarring. The humor tends to be all over the place, with bits like Chan eating spinach during a dream sequence while the theme music of "Popeye the Sailor Man" plays.

Lo Wei was not amused. He considered the final product "rubbish" and refused to release it. It wasn't until Chan had gone on to make a name for himself elsewhere with *Drunken Master* that Lo Wei released the film, which went on to do quite well at the box office. However, hardcore Chan fans tend to be split on whether it is a flawed transition film to be appreciated or just a big mess to be ignored.

CAST: Jackie Chan, James Tien, Lung Chung-erh, Kam Kan
DIRECTOR: Chan Chi Hwa
PRODUCERS: Hsu Li Haw/Lo Wei
WRITER: Tang Ming Chih
FIGHT/ACTION DIRECTOR: Jackie Chan
PRODUCTION COMPANY: HK
DISTRIBUTOR: All Seasons Entertainment
U.S. RELEASES: 1980 (theatrical); 1986 (video)

SPIRITUAL KUNG FU (1978)

PLOT: After knocking out a young student, played by Chan, a thief steals the Seven Fists book from the Shaolin temple library and gives it to his son, who is the clan heir apparent. The Seven Fists is a deadly kung fu style, and after learning it, the son uses it to begin a reign of terror against other clans. The only known style capable of neutralizing the Seven Fists is the Five Fists, but the book teaching the art has been lost for many years.

Then one night, a mysterious comet crashes to earth near the temple, arousing five ghosts who live in the library—"the" five ghosts. But not knowing who they are, Chan confronts the ghosts and tries to fight them and in the process finds the long-lost book.

The ghosts are the spirits of the five masters who had written the book. Together they teach Chan the Five Fists and he is able to defeat not only the marauding son but also the thief, who turns out to be a member of the temple itself.

This film shows Chan's continued maturation as a fight choreographer. The Five Fists—the Snake, Crane, Dragon, Leopard, and Tiger animal styles of Shaolin—allowed Chan to do some creative fight sequences. The training scenes also let him show off his abilities with a variety of weapons.

Coincidentally or not, Chan looks much less stiff as an actor, although it's still obvious costume melodrama is not his strength. And what costumes! The hula skirts worn by the red-haired aliens are particularly snazzy.

Perhaps because his last series of films had not set Hong Kong on fire, Lo Wei actually tried for a little razzle-dazzle in this one. To set the mystical tone of the movie, *Spiritual Kung Fu* opens with a shot of a comet hurtling through space. Although special effects had already become highly developed in American films such as *Alien* and *Star Wars*, the technology simply wasn't used in Chinese cinema so it was something unique to see.

The special effects were primitively done, achieved by somebody moving a sparkler against a painted backdrop of the night sky. Even so, it was an attempt by Lo Wei to add some creativity to a film. Despite B production values, there are cineasts who feel *Spiritual Kung Fu* is actually the director's best film, combining a decent plot, attention-grabbing fighting choreography, and an interesting visual style.

CAST: Jackie Chan, James Tien, Shih Tien
DIRECTOR: Lo Wei
PRODUCER: Lo Wei
FIGHT/ACTION DIRECTOR: Jackie Chan
PRODUCTION COMPANY: HK
DISTRIBUTORS: Trans World Entertainment; Ocean Shores Video
U.S. RELEASE: 1985 (video)
A/K/A:
- *Karate Ghostbuster*
- *Karate Bomber*

DRAGON FIST (1978)

PLOT: After Tang How-yuen's master, San-Thye, is murdered by Patience Clan leader Chung Chien Kuen, whose wife was once

San-Thye's lover, How-yuen swears to avenge his master's death. When Chung Chien Kuen's wife commits suicide out of shame over what her husband has done, the killer cuts his leg off in remorse for his actions.

Now that the killer is disabled, revenge is out of the question. Meanwhile, the evil Lord Wei poisons San-Thye's widow, Madam Chuang, forcing How-yuen to work as his henchman in exchange for medicine. Eventually, How-yuen and the Patience Clan join forces to defeat the Weis and to heal their old wounds. (Not so coincidentally, How-yuen is sweet on Chung Chien Kuen's martial arts daughter, Chio-ping.)

Jackie must have felt like a drowning man, especially after having enjoyed a small taste of success with *Spiritual Kung Fu*. *Dragon Fist* was yet another attempt by Lo Wei to mold Jackie in the likeness of Bruce Lee. The film was a box office bomb despite some very exciting fight scenes, including the final confrontation between Jackie (as How-yuen) and the Wei Clan thugs.

Chan understood why fans didn't see the film as anything special. It was a meandering retread of the overused revenge plot, and worse, the movie lacked even a hint of humor. He disowned the project and now knew beyond a doubt that Lo Wei would never make him a star, unless he permitted Jackie to direct a film himself.

CAST: Jackie Chan, Nora Miao, James Tien
DIRECTOR: Lo Wei
PRODUCER: Hsu Li Hwa
FIGHT/ACTION DIRECTOR: Jackie Chan

FEARLESS HYENA (1979)

PLOT: A comic period piece set during the Ching dynasty. Chan plays a young man named Lung who swears revenge after the murder of his grandfather—the last of the Hsin-yi fighters. Adding to Lung's sorrow and loss are feelings of guilt—he had accidentally led his grandfather's enemies to the old man's home and watched as they brutally killed him. And yes, this really is a comedy.

Under the tutelage of an old teacher, who also witnessed the grandfather's deadly fate, Lung learns Emotional kung fu. Using this fighting style, which draws its power from how the body reacts to laughter and tears, Lung defeats the killers.

Chan's first directorial effort was also his last complete film for Lo Wei. Seeing how Chan's career was suddenly taking off, Lo Wei finally decided that maybe it wasn't such a bad idea after all to let Jackie call the shots in a film. Finally, Chan could begin to make films the way *he* felt they should be made.

Jackie also took the opportunity to add a new element to his repertoire—dressing up in drag and then surprising his opponent when he uses his "breasts" as a weapon.

Now that he was calling the shots, Jackie was also free to adopt an acting style that can best be summed up as shameless mugging for the camera. But somehow between his boyish enthusiasm, cherub-shaped face, and obvious joy in what he was doing, it worked.

CAST: Jackie Chan, Yen Si Kwan, Li Kuan, James Tien, Shih Tien
DIRECTOR: Jackie Chan
PRODUCER: Hsu Li Hwa
WRITER: Jackie Chan
FIGHT/ACTION DIRECTOR: Jackie Chan
PRODUCTION COMPANY: Goodyear Films Limited
DISTRIBUTOR: All Seasons
U.S. RELEASE: 1979 (theatrical)

36 CRAZY FISTS (1979)
"Saam Sap Luk Mai Ying Kuen"

PLOT: After a man refuses to pay for protection, he's killed by Manchurian fighters. The man's son is saved by monks who take him to learn kung fu so the boy can avenge his father's death.

When he returns home, he beats up on some gangs, then takes on and defeats the leader of the Taoist gang.

By the way, this was a comedy.

Although he doesn't appear in the film, Chan did some fight and action choreography on this Taiwanese production. Unbeknownst to Jackie, the producers shot behind-the-scenes footage of Chan as he was working, which ended up being included in some of the released prints.

Going one step further, a distributor cobbled together a "The Making of . . ." documentary using the bootleg footage of Jackie. Knowing how mindful Chan is of being a role model for children, he must have just loved seeing himself smoking a cigarette for the duration of his time on screen.

CAST: Liu Chia Yung, Ku Feng, Chin Pei
DIRECTOR: Chen Chi Hua
PRODUCER: Chiang Kit
FIGHT/ACTION DIRECTOR: Jackie Chan
PRODUCTION COMPANY: HK Film & Video Assn.
DISTRIBUTORS: Ocean Shores Video; NYUE
MANDARIN: San1 Shi2 Liu4 Mi2 Xing2 Quan2
U.S RELEASE: 1989 (video)
A/K/A:
- *Blood Pact*
- *Master and the Boxer*

ODD COUPLE (1979)

PLOT: The two leads play dual roles as each other's teacher and student. As a student, Sammo learns from Liu how to fight with a sword; then they switch and Sammo teaches Liu how to use a spear. Together, they join forces to fight an opponent. When the two are injured, their students come to their rescue.

At least on paper, this comedy sounds an awful lot like *Dance of Death*, the Angela Mao film on which Jackie worked as the fight director. It even has some of the same actors in it. Just proves that Hollywood isn't the only place where if an idea was good the first time around, it is reused until the audience can't stand it anymore.

CAST: Liang Cha-jen, Sammo Hung, Liu Chia-yung, Shek Tien
DIRECTOR: Liu Chia-yung
PRODUCER: Karl Maka
FIGHT/ACTION DIRECTOR: Jackie Chan
PRODUCTION COMPANY: Gar Bo Films
DISTRIBUTOR: Unicorn
U.S. RELEASES: 1986 (theatrical); 1990 (video)

DRUNKEN MASTER (1979)
"Jui Keun"

PLOT: A comic retelling of the Wong Fei-hung legend that stars Chan as a happy-go-lucky young man named Freddie who is constantly getting into mischief. Finally his father has had enough of his son's antics and decides to teach him a lesson. Freddie runs away hoping to avoid his punishment of having to study with an old master—only to stumble right into the liquor-sodden master's house while being chased. In between drinks, the old man sets about trying to teach Freddie the Eight Drunk styles of fighting—which are best done when inebriated.

The rigorous training is too much, and Freddie quits. But when he gets the stuffing beat out of him by the villainous Thunderfoot, played by Huang Cheng-Li, the humiliation changes the young man. He returns to the master humbled and with a new determination to learn. This time, he endures the torturous training necessary to learn the styles—Snake, Tiger, Monkey, as well as the drunken styles—that will enable him to defeat Thunderfoot, who it turns out has been trying to force Freddie's family off their coal-rich land on behalf of a greedy neighbor. With his family's honor at stake, Freddie defeats Thunderfoot in a spectacular fight finale.

A Hong Kong classic, *Drunken Master* is generally agreed to be the first of the true "modern" kung fu comedies and one of the best ever made. Some would say *the* best—the climactic eighteen-minute fight between Chan and Huang Cheng-Li literally sets kung fu aficionados' hearts a-flutter. Chan's engaging personality combined with the film's carefully thought-out humor, the stunning physical strength and agility Jackie exhibits during the training scenes, and the exciting fight choreography has made *Drunken Master* the standard against which all other kung fu comedies would be judged for years to come.

Although Wong Fei-hung was a real historical person, he has taken on mythical proportions in Chinese culture. Born in 1847, Wong was famous for his martial arts ability in the Hung's Fist style. But he also made a name for himself through his philosophical beliefs of helping the weak and downtrodden. Wong died in 1924 at the age of seventy-seven.

Many, many films had been made about Wong, but none quite like this. The title *Drunken Master* comes from a style of fighting with moves that imitate a drunk's staggering gait and because it's believed a person will move less predictably and become less susceptible to pain as his blood alcohol level rises.

It almost hurts to watch Chan as he goes through some of the training scenes in the film. In one of the more mind-boggling scenes Chan hangs upside down with an empty bucket tied above his suspended feet, and two full buckets on the ground on either side of his head. His task is to fill the empty bucket with water, using only the tiny sake cups he has in each hand. To do this he must reach into the buckets near his head, do a sit-up, then dump the water into the bucket hanging overhead—all the while making sure the water doesn't slosh out of the cups

Another torture has him squatting for hours, balancing cups on his head and outstretched arms. And there's a burning ember beneath his haunches to keep him from relaxing his stance. What's most numbing is that many of the training techniques shown in the film are similar to ones Chan suffered through in real life during his childhood days at the Peking Opera, requiring equal parts mental toughness and almost superhuman physical endurance.

There are also some inventive scenes proving that anything can be a possible weapon in the right hands. In one scene, Chan uses a cucumber to fend off a swordsman. In another, the old master battles a roomful of opponents using his chopsticks and rice bowl. The sheer creativity of the fight scenes was something that caught people's attention.

When Lo Wei agreed to lend Jackie to Seasonal Films, he had no idea it would be the beginning of the end of their collaboration. Instead of being able to cash in on Jackie's rising star, he'd soon have to just admire it from afar. And when *Drunken Master* wound up being the second most successful film of the year, pulling in more than $8 million in Hong Kong—and breaking Bruce Lee's old box office record—their split was only a matter of time.

Proving that nepotism is not an American phenomenon, the actor playing the old master is Yuen Siu Tin—director Woo Ping's father.

CAST: Jackie Chan, Shek Tien, Yuen Ho Ping, Simon Yuen, Hsu Hsia, Lin Ying
DIRECTOR: Yuen Woo Ping
PRODUCER: Ng See Yuen
WRITER: Hsaio Lung
FIGHT/ACTION DIRECTORS: Yuen Ho Ping, Hsu Hsia
PRODUCTION COMPANY: Seasonal
DISTRIBUTOR: NYUE
U.S. RELEASES: 1979, 1989 (theatrical); 1989 (video)
MANDARIN: Zui4 Quan2
A/K/A:
- *Drunken Monkey in Tiger's Eye*
- *Eagle Claw, Snake Fist, Cat's Paw*

FEARLESS HYENA II (1980)
"Lung Tang Foo Yeuk"

PLOT: What plot there is centers around two brothers out to avenge their father's death caused by a feud between the rival Ying/Yang and Heaven and Earth clans.

Unbelievably, despite suffering through the agony of Lo Wei's filmmaking for years, Chan signed a new contract with the director, and *Fearless Hyena II* was to be the first film under this new agreement. But Chan shot only a few scenes before coming to his senses—or, to be more exact, finally took the advice of his manager—and jumped to the Golden Harvest ship, which was run by Raymond Chow.

After his cash cow moved on to greener pastures, Lo pieced together the scenes Chan had already shot, as well as the film's outtakes and new footage with a Chan look-alike, and hoped to cash in on Jackie's popularity. It didn't work.

In 1983, Chan filed a lawsuit to prevent Lo Wei from releasing this film but dropped it after it was ruled that Lo could do whatever he wanted with film he legally owned.

CAST: Jackie Chan, Shek Tien, James Tien, Hon Kwok Choi
DIRECTOR: Lo Wei
PRODUCTION COMPANY: Lo Wei Film Company
DISTRIBUTOR: Trans World Entertainment
U.S. RELEASE: 1980 (video)
MANDARIN: Long2 Teng3 Hu3 Yue4

THE YOUNG TIGER (1980)

PLOT: There is none to speak of.

This is simply a Jackie Chan compilation using clips from *Spiritual Kung Fu*, *Shaolin Wooden Men*, and who knows what else. Still feeling in a snit over being dumped by Chan and not content to simply put out a Triad hit on him, Lo Wei decided to squeeze the sponge dry. Hence, this mishmash of disjointed clips strung together in a way Lo Wei apparently thought could pass as a story.

The most interesting thing is how different Chan looks, since most of the footage is presurgery and predental work.

CAST: Jackie Chan, Meng Fei, and various costars
DIRECTOR: Wu Ma
PRODUCER: Lo Wei
A/K/A:
* *The Jackie Chan Story*

THE YOUNG MASTER (1980)
"Si Dai Chut Ma"

PLOT: Chan stars in yet another takeoff on the Wong Fei Hung legend, playing a lazy young "Dragon" who avoids any type of schooling if possible. But things get busy for him after he is mistaken by authorities for his "brother" Tiger, who in turn is wanted for a murder he didn't commit. While trying to clear his own name, Chan also works to prove Tiger's innocence by finding the real killer, named Master Kan.

This film, which is difficult to find, was Jackie's first for Raymond Chow's Golden Harvest Films. Enjoying the sensation of being the man truly in charge, Chan jumped feet first into production. It was a case where a little less enthusiasm may have been called for. He began shooting before there was a finished script, resulting in a flimsy story.

But who needs plot when you have such a creative director? And Chan took advantage of his new autonomy by taking the time he felt each scene needed. Like shooting over *three hundred* takes for a fighting sequence featuring a paper fan. But the fight sequences are masterly, with Jackie utilizing a variety of unusual props in the choreography including a Chinese workbench and a lariat. And the sequence where he takes on an opponent using only a folding fan—a bit of business he'd do again years later in *Drunken Master II*—is truly inventive.

As usual, Jackie relies heavily on the silly humor he so loves. Since it was such a hit in *Fearless Hyena*, Chan also does another drag sequence. And in keeping with Jackie's antisuperhuman persona, the final scene shows his character's body bandaged from head to toe, except for some fingers used to wave good-bye to the camera. Even though fans went wild over the imaginative fights, the lack of thought-out story line prevented this movie and others that followed from being overall classics à la *Drunken Master*.

One last point about the reference to Chan's brother in the plot line above. The word *brother* is in quotations because translations differ on whether the man Chan is trying to help is a blood relative brother or a friend. A close male friend is often referred to as a "brother."

Of Special Note: The man who composed the score for this film, Frankie Chan (no relation), years later would direct the car race action in *Thunderbolt*. A man of many talents, Frankie acts, directs—and was a champion body builder.

CAST: Jackie Chan, Shek Kin, Chiang Kam, Yuen Biao, Wei Pei
DIRECTOR: Jackie Chan
PRODUCER: Leonard Ho
WRITERS: Jackie Chan, Lau Tin-chi, Tung Lu, Tang King-sang
FIGHT/ACTION DIRECTOR: Jackie Chan
PRODUCTION COMPANY: Golden Harvest
DISTRIBUTOR: NYUE
U.S. RELEASE: 1989 (video)
MANDARIN: Shi1 Di4 Chu1 Ma1

THE BIG BRAWL (1980)

PLOT: This comedy set in the 1930s has Chan playing Jerry Kwan, an immigrant from China who has to protect his grandfather's restaurant from local gangsters. Wanting to teach the upstart a lesson, the gang boss kidnaps his brother's fiancée, then blackmails the young man into entering a bareknuckle boxing competition in Texas—unless he fights, he'll never see his prospective sister-in-law again. In the end, he not only has to beat his opponents but also has to battle members of a Chicago crime mob.

This film was the first attempt to create a Hollywood star vehicle for Chan. Despite already being Asia's number one box office star at the time, he was unknown in America. *The Big Brawl* needed a high "Wow!" factor to generate interest. But the action sequences, watered down by Chan standards, left U.S. audiences going "ho-hum" instead. It was difficult to see what the big deal was. The film bombed at the U.S. box office but was an international video success.

For Chan, it was an important film experience because it showed him how difficult his style of filmmaking would be in America, with studios exerting such tight control over productions. On the brighter side, while working on *The Big Brawl* Chan learned how to roller-skate, skateboard, and ski barefoot—skills he would incorporate into his future films.

CAST: Jackie Chan, Jose Ferrer, Mako, Kristine de Bell
DIRECTOR: Robert Clouse
PRODUCERS: Fred Weintraub, Terry Morse, Jr., Raymond Chow
WRITER: Robert Clouse
FIGHT/ACTION DIRECTOR: Pat Johnson
PRODUCTION COMPANY: Warner Bros.
DISTRIBUTOR: Warner Bros.
U.S. RELEASE: 1980
A/K/A:
- *Battle Creek Brawl*

CANNONBALL RUN (1981)

PLOT: A road/action picture that follows the exploits of contestants in an illegal cross-country race based on the real Cannonball Sea to Shining Sea race, which starts in Connecticut and ends in California.

Burt Reynolds plays an adventurer who decides to join the other contestants—a motley group of eccentrics, who will do anything to win, even cheat. Make that, especially cheat.

Jackie's big moment comes when the racers are confronted by nasty bikers. A brawl ensues, and during it, Chan mops the floor with *Easy Rider* Peter Fonda. Then they get back in their car and keep going.

It's difficult for some fans to watch this performance because Chan looks so out of his element. For American audiences, who had no frame of reference for Chan, the impression left is of a kung fu guy trying way too hard. To make things even worse, the filmmakers made Chan's character Japanese. But aren't they speaking Chinese?

Cannonball Run tried for an *Around the World in 80 Days* sensibility but lacked the charm. It's too bad the audiences didn't have as much fun as it appeared the actors were having. Perhaps too good of a time was being had by all. It was during the making this movie that stuntwoman Heidi von Beltz, then only twenty-four, was paralyzed from the earlobes down during a car stunt gone wrong.

Heidi was doing a fairly routine stunt in a car that was on a highway swerving through traffic. So routine that she didn't bother to strap herself into a safety harness. The first take went fine. Then, according to Heidi, the director decided he wanted the car to go faster. On the next take, when the driver tried to turn the wheel going at the higher speed, it failed to respond, and the car crashed head-on into a van.

It is a possibility all stunt people, especially one as daring as Chan, must live with. Little did Jackie know he would come close to losing it all in just a few short years when another "routine" stunt took a tragic turn.

A footnote on von Beltz. Defying the odds, Heidi has regained limited use of her arms and sensation in her legs. With the aid of special braces, she is working on taking small steps.

Of Special Note: Say what you will about this film, *Cannonball Run* grossed over $100 million in worldwide box office at a time when few films did. So you can't just blame the American audience for there being a sequel. This may be where Jackie got the idea to show outtakes at the end of his films. It was the most creative aspect of the *Cannonball* films.

CAST: Burt Reynolds, Farrah Fawcett, Dean Martin, Jackie Chan (cameo)
DIRECTOR: Hal Needham
PRODUCER: Albert Ruddy
WRITER: Brock Yates
PRODUCTION COMPANY: Twentieth Century-Fox
DISTRIBUTOR: Twentieth Century-Fox
U.S. RELEASE: 1982

DRUNKEN FIST BOXING (1981)

PLOT: A stranger comes to town and forcibly takes over the local restaurant and gambling room. One of his henchmen wants a young woman, Kam Fa, from the town to marry him. Unfortunately, she can't stand the sight of him, which causes the man to vow revenge.

It turns out that the stranger is an enemy of Kam Fa's master, who also teaches her brother Ah-chung. Joined by a friend also skilled in martial arts, the brother and sister confront the stranger and defeat him and his henchmen.

Anyone renting this movie thinking they are getting a Jackie Chan movie will be in for a surprise. Although he may be prominently displayed on the video jacket, his role is no more than a cameo in an otherwise poorly made movie. And not even a real cameo. His scenes are actually outtakes from *Drunken Master.*

However, as many other distributors the world over would come to realize, just having Chan's name on a video jacket guaranteed a certain number of sales—no matter the brevity of Chan's role or the cheesy production values or the lackluster fighting.

Costarring in the film is a character named Casanova Wong, who was a talented kickboxer but had no chance to become much more than a supporting player because he lacked looks, size, and acting talent. Villains and crisp-kicking fighters were his lot in film life.

CAST: Simon Yuen, Shih Tien, Casanova Wong, Yang Pan Pan, Yen Si Kuan, Jackie Chan (bit part)
DIRECTOR: Wei Hui Feng
PRODUCER: Shih Chao Chin
PRODUCTION COMPANY: Golden Tripod Film Corp.
DISTRIBUTOR: Ocean Shores Video
U.S. RELEASE: 1988 (video)
A/K/A:
- *The Story of Drunken Master*
- *Story of the Drunken Kung Fu*

FANTASY MISSION FORCE (1981)
"Mai Nei Dak Gung Dui"

PLOT: During World War II, a band of mercenary warriors sets out to rescue four generals—and stolen government money—being held captive by the Japanese. But they must get there before rival soldiers of fortune do. Complicating their mission are an assortment of creatures, including vampires, ghosts, and even a tribe of Amazon women. After the climactic battle scene, there aren't very many left on either side who lived to tell the tale.

It's easy to understand how production references and film histories might differ by a year or two about when a particular film was made, but *Fantasy Mission Force* takes inconsistency to new heights. Depending on where one looks, the film was made and released in either 1979, 1981, 1982, or 1984, so a little process of elimination is called for.

Since its U.S. release was 1982, a 1984 production year is obviously way off. The best clue may be Chan's hair, which is cut in the same bowl style he wore in *The Big Brawl*, which was unquestionably made in 1980. So it seems more likely *Fantasy Mission Force* was made in 1981 after he returned from America. Besides, who else but an American film hairdresser would give Jackie that kind of 'do?

Many Chan film references take the easy way out and don't bother to list it at all—including Jackie on his official résumé. Small wonder. To begin with, it is not a major Chan film. In fact, it's not much of a film, period. Allegedly, the only reason Jackie appeared in it at all was because the film's star, Jimmy Wang Yu, asked him. Lest we forget, Chan appeared before with Jimmy—in the eminently forgettable *The Killer Meteors*. Despite that experience—often referred to as the worst film Chan ever appeared in—Jackie couldn't refuse. As explained in Chapter 1, "The Personal Jackie Chan," of this book, he owed Wang Yu a favor.

However unpleasant or time wasting this experience may have been, at least it was over relatively quickly. His character appears only briefly, and even then, a double for his character is used in many of the scenes. Apparently, the idea was simply to be able to list Chan among the credits.

CAST: Chang Ling, Brigitte Lin, Sun Yuen, Jackie Chan
DIRECTOR: Chu Yen Ping
PRODUCER: Shen Hsiao Yi
DISTRIBUTOR: Trans World Entertainment
U.S. RELEASE: 1982 (video)
MANDARIN: Mi2 Ni3 Te4 Gong1 Dui4
A/K/A:
  • *The Dragon Attack* (Japanese title)

DRAGON LORD (1982)
"Lung Siu Ye"

PLOT: Wong Fei Hung redux. Chan returns as the young, lazy "Dragon" who would rather play hooky—gambling or flirting with women—than study. But things get busy for Dragon and his friend Cowboy when they inadvertently stumble across a plot to steal some Chinese treasures and smuggle them out of the country. Along with Cowboy, Dragon saves the day by preventing the thief, a former soldier gone bad, from making off with the goods.

It's amazing how similar this plot sounds to *Drunken Master II*. But it makes sense if you consider that this was Chan's first major Hong Kong production after returning from his ill-fated foray into American films. Working on familiar ground was a good way to get back into the Hong Kong swing of things. As usual, Chan fills the exposition gaps with enough amazing fight scenes and action—like when he backflips off a barn loft or plays a crazy game of shuttlecock—so that viewers will hopefully forget there's not much of a story attached.

In retrospect, this film contains signs that Chan was moving away from strict chopsocky fighting action—using hands and feet to do any of the traditional Shaolin styles—toward more acrobatic action that used a lot of movement across the screen.

It was a smart choice in more ways than one. Besides being a fresh approach, it also minimized the pressure on Chan's fighting skills. They're good when compared to many others, but he's never been the best pure fighter around. Still, his fighting was good enough to get Jackie nominated for Best Action Design by the Hong Kong Film Awards, which had begun handing out awards a year earlier, in 1981.

Of Special Note: Ever the perfectionist, Jackie did over 1,600 takes to get a shot that lasted about two seconds in the final cut.

CAST: Jackie Chan, Mars, Chang Chung, Tien Fun, Huang In-sik
DIRECTOR: Jackie Chan
PRODUCER: Leonard Ho
WRITER: Jackie Chan

FIGHT/ACTION DIRECTOR: Jackie Chan
PRODUCTION COMPANY: Golden Harvest
DISTRIBUTORS: Cinema Group, All Seasons
U.S. RELEASE: 1986 (video)
MANDARIN: Long2 Xiao3 Ye2
A/K/A:

- *Young Master in Love*

NINJA WARS (1982)

PLOT: A mystical tale begins with the kidnapping, rape, and death of a maiden. One of her kidnappers uses her tears to make an aphrodisiac for the woman he wants to marry. But the maiden's boyfriend puts a damper on his plan when he avenges the maiden's death.

The movie was based on a novel by Hutaro Yamada. Jackie chose to make a cameo in this film in order to work with Sonny Chiba, a well-known martial artist from Japan and the star of the popular Street Fighter films of the 1970s.

CAST: Henry Sanada, Noriko Watanabe, Sonny Chiba, Jackie Chan (cameo)
DIRECTOR: Mitsumisa Saito
PRODUCER: Masao Sato
WRITER: Ed Ogawa
PRODUCTION COMPANY: Haruki Kado Kawa/Toei
DISTRIBUTOR: ANE Home Video
U.S. RELEASE: 1988 (video)

WINNERS AND SINNERS (1983)
"Kei Mau Miu Gai Ng Fuk Sing"

PLOT: Determined to stay on the straight and narrow, five ex-cons set up a cleaning company. Chan plays the policeman trying to help them abide by the law. But they soon show up on trouble's doorstep when they discover a gang of counterfeiters working out of a building they've been hired to clean. Before they know it, the five former prisoners are caught in a war between rival gangs and suddenly discover the counterfeit money plates have been left in their van. Eventually the excons are forced to square off against the crooks with the expected heroic results.

What's interesting about this film is seeing Jackie once again agree to make what is basically a cameo appearance in someone else's film. However, that someone else is his long-time friend Sammo Hung, and in fact it was their shared history at the Peking Opera that Sammo plumbed to get the idea for *Winners and Sinners*.

Sammo was smart enough to snag Chan for a role and to give him some spectacular moments to shine, including one stunt where Chan roller-skates over a Volkswagen, and then after being towed behind a moving tractor trailer actually skates under the speeding truck. However, to achieve the effect seen on screen, stunt doubles were used.

The film also features Yuen Biao. Although he possesses jaw-dropping gymnastic ability, Yuen has never been able to break out of the others' shadows and establish himself individually as a strong headliner. His best solo efforts remain *Dreadnaught* (1988), *The Prodigal Son* (1988), *A Kid from Tibet* (1991), and *Kick Boxer* (1993). His most recent starring vehicle, *Dragon from Shaolin* (1996), is uninspired and excruciatingly dull.

Although nobody knew it at the time, *Winners and Sinners* was the first of the "Lucky Stars" movie franchise, in which a group of petty criminals raised at the same orphanage find themselves on the right side of the law helping another old childhood friend who's now a cop. The Lucky Stars moniker was inspired by the Japanese title for *Winners and Sinners*.

Although he has played second fiddle in most professional regards to Chan, Sammo is clearly an *auteur* in his own right, with a recognizable directorial style and film persona.

Richard Ng was nominated for Best Actor but lost out to Tony Leung.

CAST: Jackie Chan, Sammo Hung, Yuen Biao, Richard Ng, Ching Shung Lin
DIRECTOR: Sammo Hung
PRODUCER: Leonard Ho
WRITER: Sammo Hung
ACTION/FIGHT DIRECTOR: Chan Wui Ngai
ACTION DESIGN: Chan Wui Ngai, Yuen Biao, Lam Ching-Ying
PRODUCTION COMPANY: Golden Harvest
DISTRIBUTORS: Golden Harvest; Paragon; NYUE
U.S. RELEASES: 1983 (theatrical); 1992 (video)
MANDARIN: Qi2 Mou2 Miao4 Ji4 Wu3 Fu2 Xing1
AWARDS: Best Action Design 1983 H.K. Film Awards
A/K/A:
- *Five Lucky Stars* (Japanese release title)

PROJECT A (1983)
"A' Gai Waak"

PLOT: Set at the turn of the century, the story has Chan starring as Dragon Ma, a coast guard officer who is on a detail intended to rid the harbor of marauding pirates who have been terrorizing the harbor and nearby coastal communities of the China Sea.

After a barroom brawl with the local police, Dragon and his fellow sailors are horrified to learn that the coast guard has been disbanded in a cost-cutting move and they're being reassigned to work with the same police they just battled. But that's the least of it. There's a traitor in their midst. When he realizes the police aren't interested in capturing crooks, Dragon does it on his own and breaks up a smuggling ring.

Fed up with politics, Dragon quits and joins forces with a gambler played by Sammo Hung. With some help from a young police officer played by Yuen Biao, they infiltrate the pirate gang and blow them to smithereens.

Project A was the name of a real plan implemented by the Chinese coast guard to rid the harbor of pirates.

With this film, Chan finally succeeded in bringing his movies into the present century—he had also clearly left classical chopsocky films behind.

There's still plenty of martial artistry in *Project A*, but the kung fu is not presented as showcased set pieces anymore. (Jab-jab-punch-block-duck-kick). This film is a good example of how Chan began to make traditional combat secondary to the physically stunning stunt/action sequences. One of the classic scenes that represents this change in *Project A* is a bicycle chase through narrow streets that requires split-second timing and exquisite balance and strength.

The film is so geared toward action and stunts that there's spoken dialogue in less than 50 percent of the film. Who needs words when actions speak so eloquently?

This is also the film that includes the famous Harold Lloyd homage—Jackie dangling from the clock tower. Of course Lloyd wasn't daft enough to actually let go—Chan did. His free fall was slowed somewhat when he tore through two awnings on his way down, but it was the ground that brought him to a complete stop—when he landed on his head. And lest anyone suspect the stunt was a sleight-of-hand cinematic trick of editing, the scene was filmed in one continuous shot. Each of at least three takes.

Incidentally, and ironically, the title of that famous Harold Lloyd film where he hung from the clock face was *Safety Last*.

After playing the man who literally fell repeatedly to earth, *Project A* also offers an example of Jackie using a wire. Look carefully at the scene where Chan is outside and scrambles up a near-vertical wall. In the outtakes, there are several shots of him being unable to make it before he finally succeeds. But on the footage of him successfully running up the wall, it's as if an invisible hand grabbed the front of his shirt and pulled him up. Make that an invisible wire. Not even the greatest can always defy gravity.

Project A marks the beginning of another grand Chan tradition—showing audiences footage of missed stunts and/or injuries sustained while shooting the movie. That jarring sight of Jackie plummeting to the ground from the clock can be seen again several times during the end credits after the movie ends. In one take, the awnings don't rip as expected. Instead the top canvas acts as a rather nifty trampoline, bouncing Chan onto the ground, again headfirst.

The success of *Project A* can in part be credited to the presence of Sammo Hung—who some newspapers have called the fastest fat person alive—and to a lesser extent Yuen Biao. Sammo and Yuen balance out Jackie's death-defying approach to action movies because they always seem to be performing totally within their own impressive capabilities. Neither ever appears to be pushing the envelope the way Chan feels compelled to, turning movie stunts into a type of Extreme Sport.

Although Jackie is the one who parlayed his Peking Opera training into action movie superstardom, his two "brothers" are just as physically skilled—if not more so. But Chan touches a chord with audiences through his go-for-the-gusto philosophy. In this film for the first time he's a living, breathing Walter Mitty through whom we can live and dream vicariously.

And, occasionally, borrow. Jackie claims director Steven Spielberg fashioned Harrison Ford's *Indiana Jones and the Temple of Doom* motorcycle chase sequence after the bicycle stunts in *Project A*. Take a look and decide.

Of Special Note: Jackie handcuffed to a flagpole and escaping by shimmying to the top of the pole; the fight scene in the bar, where for the first time stuntmen are shown hitting the ground hard, giving the kung fu an air of realism not often seen before.

CAST: Jackie Chan, Sammo Hung, Yuen Biao, Chen Hui-min, Dick Wei, Maggie Cheung, Mars, Lau Siu-ming
DIRECTOR: Jackie Chan

PRODUCER: Leonard Ho
WRITER: Jackie Chan
FIGHT/ACTION DIRECTOR: Jackie Chan
ACTION DESIGN: Jackie Chan's Stuntman Association
PRODUCTION COMPANY: Golden Harvest
DISTRIBUTORS: American Imperial; NYUE
U.S. RELEASES: 1987 (theatrical); 1989 (video)
MANDARIN: ''A'' Ji4 Hua4
AWARDS: Best Action Design 1984 H.K. Film Awards
A/K/A:

- *Pirate Patrol*

TWO IN A BLACKBELT (1984)

CAST: Jackie Chan (cameo)

POM POM (1984)

PLOT: Two bumbling Hong Kong detectives are constantly butting heads with their boss, but in the end they always get their man—in spite of themselves.

This collaboration between John Shum and Richard Ng marked the beginning of the very popular *Pom Pom* movie series. Sammo, who produced the movie for his new banner, appears in a cameo, and Jackie roars through so quickly at the end as a motorcycle cop that if you have a coughing fit at the wrong moment, you'll miss him.

A year later, Chan and Sammo would have a falling out that resulted in the demise of the Lucky Stars series. The void was filled by the *Pom Pom* films.

CAST: John Shum, Sammo Hung, Richard Ng, Dick Wei, Mars, Jackie Chan (cameo)
DIRECTOR: Cheung Cheung Joe
PRODUCER: Sammo Hung
PRODUCTION COMPANY: Bo Ho Films

DISTRIBUTORS: NYUE (Rainbow Video)
U.S. RELEASE: 1992 (video)

WHEELS ON MEALS (1984)
"Faai Chaan Che"

PLOT: Chan plays Tom, who runs a food wagon in Barcelona, Spain. The father of Tom's partner, David (Yuen Biao), has fallen in love with Gloria, the mother of Sylvia, a beautiful young woman who happens to be a petty thief. What none of them knows is that Sylvia's the illegitimate daughter of a count and stands to inherit a fortune.

But not if her greedy uncle can help it. If Sylvia doesn't show up for a hearing, he will inherit the estate. The uncle sends hired thugs to kidnap Sylvia to make sure she doesn't appear.

Tom, who along with David has a crush on Sylvia, joins forces with a private eye buddy (Sammo Hung) hired to find the heiress before her uncle's henchmen do. In the end, Tom and his friends storm the uncle's castle and, armed with fencing foils, take on the evil uncle and save the girl.

In addition to some inventive action sequences, like the car chase that takes place in reverse, this film contains the fight that many claim is Chan's greatest ever—a climactic brawl with Benny "The Jet" Urquidez, who plays one of the uncle's goons. Benny was the undefeated kickboxing champ who himself was hero to a loyal following, and Golden Harvest, the production company, had flown him over from America just to appear in the movie.

While film fans were thrilled with the results, Jackie was less than taken with "The Jet." Apparently, Chan didn't like the fact that Benny was kicking him for real. (Curious, considering Chan often boasts about the realism of Hong Kong action movies as opposed to the simulated fights of American films. It must depend upon who's doing the kicking.) Whether fueled by animosity or competitiveness, the fight is a classic in part because of the many real punches thrown. At one point, Chan lands a solid left cross to Benny's head, followed by Urquidez getting in a flurry of body blows. Finally, after one hit too many, Jackie reportedly lost his cool and told Urquidez that if he didn't stop it he would never work in Hong Kong again.

Some have said that Benny wore a body protector under his shirt (he certainly *looks* padded) while Chan was totally unprotected, perhaps explaining why Jackie got irritated at "The Jet" for pummeling him.

Other clues that the fight scene became personal was the appearance of genuine frustration that led to wild leg swings and even some professional but uncharacteristic grappling. Clashing egos notwithstanding, thanks to the unforgettable fight with Urquidez and the camaraderie among the three brothers, *Wheels on Meals* was a huge box office success and another notch on Chan's star-power belt.

The film's success brought to light some curious quirks common to Chinese films that find their way to the West, like a multiple choice option for character's names. In articles promoting *Wheels on Meals*, Yuen Biao was referred to as Jimmy, even though the Americans working on the film were told to call him Bill.

Last, it might seem curious that the name of the film itself underwent a strange transformation, to *Wheels on Meals* from the original *Meals on Wheels*. There are two popular explanations for the switch. The first is that being a superstitious lot, the folks at Golden Harvest had done poorly at the box office around that time with films that began with the letter *M*, so they changed the title so it would begin with a *W*. The other explanation is that somewhere along the line, somebody got confused and accidentally inverted the words.

And while we're on the topic of confused, why does it appear at the film's end that Tom and David *both* get the girl, whatever her name may be?

CAST: Jackie Chan, Sammo Hung, Yuen Biao, Lola Forner, Richard Ng, Herb Edelman

DIRECTOR: Sammo Hung
PRODUCER: Leonard Ho
WRITER: Sammo Hung
FIGHT/ACTION DIRECTOR: Sammo Hung
PRODUCTION COMPANY: Golden Harvest
DISTRIBUTORS: Toho Towa; NYUE
U.S. RELEASES: 1985 (theatrical); 1989 (video)
MANDARIN: Kuai4 Can1 Che1
A/K/A:

- *Meals on Wheels*
- *Million Dollar Heiress*
- *Weapon X*
- *Spartan X* (Japanese release)

CANNONBALL RUN II (1984)

PLOT: More mayhem on another mad cross-country dash in a variety of vehicles. This time, though, the mob is on their tail.

Why would Jackie come back to the scene of an earlier crime? Who knows. While the film did nothing for Jackie's stature either in America or back at home, *Cannonball Run II* did earn Richard Kiel (the unforgettable James Bond villain "Jaws") quite an Asian following after he and Chan were paired up as partners in this sequel.

This time around, Jackie gets to show off his kung fu skills in two fights. The first one is a rematch with bikers hassling a family running a fruit stand. There's also a brawl at the end of the film.

CAST: Burt Reynolds, Sammy Davis Jr., Dom De Luise, Susan Anton, Jackie Chan (cameo)
DIRECTOR: Hal Needham
PRODUCER: Albert Ruddy
WRITERS: Harvey Miller, Hal Needham, Albert Ruddy
PRODUCTION COMPANY: Twentieth Century-Fox

DISTRIBUTOR: Twentieth Century-Fox
U.S. RELEASE: 1984

MY LUCKY STARS (1985)
"Fuk Sing Go Jiu"

PLOT: Chan and Yuen Biao play undercover Hong Kong CID officers, Muscles and Ricky, sent to Tokyo to apprehend a dirty cop named Blockhead who has stolen a fortune in diamonds and bust the criminal ring he's associated with there.

But their cover is blown, and after a confrontation with Blockhead's band of Japanese ninjas, Ricky is captured. All alone and having to hide out in fear for his life, Muscles has nowhere to turn for help except the Lucky Stars, a band of peaceful con artists he met in the orphanage where he was raised.

Led by Fastbuck, the Lucky Stars agree to help their old friend rescue Ricky and catch Blockhead after realizing they'll be trained by a beautiful policewoman, who will also accompany them to Japan. Once they reach Tokyo, the Lucky Stars find Muscles, and together they set off to rescue Ricky and bring Blockhead and his gang to justice.

Even though Jackie Chan is listed as its star and his popularity provides the name power that helped box office receipts both home and abroad, *My Lucky Stars* is another example of a Sammo Hung film—in spirit and in tone and in the substantial amount of martial arts included. In fact, as in *Winners and Sinners*, Chan's presence is limited, although he returns in time for the climactic fight. Sammo keeps the pace fast and furious with a Keystone Kop-esque slapstick wackiness.

Although Sammo was no stranger to shooting movies on location, he chose not to travel to Japan for *My Lucky Stars*, although he found a little touch of Nippon in his backyard at the Hong Kong Omni Plaza hotel, where many of the scenes were shot.

This film also marks the first-ever appearance by Japanese

bodybuilding champion Michiko Nishiwaki in a Hong Kong production—despite not speaking a word of Chinese on a crew where no one spoke a word of Japanese. But she understood how to throw punches and kicks, and her fight scene against Sibelle Hu is a particular favorite of those who like watching skillful kung fu women duke it out.

CAST: Jackie Chan, Richard Ng, Fung Shui Fan, Charlie Ching, Andy Lau, Sibelle Hu, Eric Tsang
DIRECTOR: Sammo Hung
PRODUCER: Leonard Ho
WRITER: Barry Wong
FIGHT/ACTION DIRECTORS: Sammo Hung, Yuen Biao, Yuen Wah
PRODUCTION COMPANY: Golden Harvest
DISTRIBUTORS: Golden Harvest; Paragon: Cinema Group; NYUE
U.S. RELEASES: 1985 (theatrical); 1992 (video)
MANDARIN: Fu2 Xing1 Gao1 Zhao4
A/K/A:
- *The Lucky Stars*

TWINKLE, TWINKLE LUCKY STARS (1985)
"Ha Yat Fuk Sing"

PLOT: To celebrate their part in capturing the drug lord from *My Lucky Stars*, the guys plan a lighthearted vacation to Thailand. But their R&R is cut short when a trio of hit men is dispatched to kill the drug lord before he incriminates others. Once again the Lucky Stars find themselves involved in a case with their police pal Muscles, played by Chan.

Muscles and his new partner are assigned to protect their prisoner until the killers are caught. They've already murdered one man, but not before he put incriminating evidence in the mail—making the woman, Yi Ching, who received the letter the new target for the hit men. To help out, the gang agree to let the woman move in with them. To help flush the assassins out, a policewoman poses as Yi and tricks the killers into the open, where the police are waiting for them, setting off a free-for-all. Muscles is wounded during the confrontation and has to sit on the sidelines and watch as his cohorts finally defeat and arrest the killers.

Another Lucky Stars adventure with a few changes this time around. First, Chan is paired with a new partner, played by newly emerging star Andy Lau, with Yuen Biao teamed with Sibelle Hu.

Adding to the fun are numerous cameo appearances by top drawer Hong Kong stars, including regular Chan costar Michelle Yeoh.

As usual, director Sammo Hung stages ingenious and exciting hand-to-hand fight scenes, including one where he uses two tennis rackets to take on a Japanese martial arts expert. And the movie opens with a splash when Chan, Yuen, and Lau go *mano y mano* with a boatload of crooks.

But one originally planned highlight was never filmed because Chan injured his back doing a stunt on another movie he was filming simultaneously with *Twinkle, Twinkle Lucky Stars*. Australian karate star Richard Norton was supposed to battle Chan twice. In the first fight, which made it into the movie, Norton gets the better of Jackie. The second square-off was to be in the film's final fight, but Chan's back injury put him out of commission, and he was unable to participate in the rematch. Although Chan fans were disappointed they didn't get to see him give Norton his comeuppance, the scene didn't suffer, as Sammo stepped in.

Fights and action aside, some moviegoers may be put off by the frat house-type humor, with a lot of jokes centered around the guys trying to get some action with any number of women.

This was to be the last Lucky Stars film. Shortly after production ended, Sammo and Jackie had a falling out and wouldn't resolve their differences for several years.

Of Special Note: Some bootleg videos of this film are titled *Police Woman Against Jackie Chan.*

CAST: Jackie Chan, Sammo Hung, Yuen Biao, Sibelle Hu, Richard Ng, Fung Shui Fan, Charlie Chin, Michiko Nishiwaki, Ching Ying, Dick Wei.

DIRECTOR: Sammo Hung

PRODUCER: Eric Tsang

WRITER: Barry Wong

FIGHT/ACTION DIRECTOR: Sammo Hung

PRODUCTION COMPANY: Golden Harvest; Bo Ho

DISTRIBUTORS: Golden Harvest; NYUE (Rainbow Video)

MANDARIN: Xia4 Ri4 Fu2 Xing1

U.S. RELEASES: 1985 (theatrical); 1992 (video)

A/K/A:

- *My Lucky Stars 2*
- *The Target*

THE PROTECTOR (1985)

PLOT: Chan stars as a New York City undercover detective named Billy Wong whose partner is murdered during a robbery. His new partner is played by Danny Aiello, and before they barely learn each other's name, they are knee deep in a kidnapping case.

The daughter of a wealthy man has been kidnapped, but the case is more complicated than expected. Authorities suspect the father is involved with a Hong Kong crime boss who deals in heroin. The partners go to Hong Kong and try to infiltrate the drug smuggling ring so they can bring down the gangster and save the kidnapped daughter.

In this standard American thriller/cop/action film, *The Protector*'s director, James Glickenhaus, intentionally underplayed Chan's performance. In essence, the director all but eliminated kung fu of any substance, leaving Chan with little to do but look uncomfortable. Well, actually Chan did try to do something—he tried to have Glickenhaus fired. But the director's contract was airtight, so all Chan could do was grimace and bear it.

It was a completely humiliating film experience for some-one with Jackie's talent—and ego. Ironically, as noted pre-viously, the screenplay for this film was written by a director who held Chan and his abilities in the highest esteem—Robert Clouse, who directed *Enter the Dragon* and was one of the first who recognized Chan's potential as a film star.

The dispute escalated into animosity on both sides. Un-known to Glickenhaus, though, after the movie ended, Chan reedited the Chinese release, removing the nudity and adding fight footage he shot himself, including a new ending. Al-though not one of Chan's best efforts, the film was a modest Hong Kong box office success.

Even so, it failed to live up to the high expectations Golden Harvest had for the film. Studio head Raymond Chow had hoped the film would help lure American production compa-nies to Hong Kong, but the plan backfired thanks to the disap-pointing final product.

The most important outcome of *The Protector* was that it provided Chan with the inspiration to create a movie cop hero in his own image, an idea he ultimately developed into *Police Story*.

Of Special Note: A stunt where Jackie crashes into a wooden house while involved in a speedboat chase.

CAST: Jackie Chan, Danny Aiello, Roy Chiao, Bill ''Superfoot'' Wallace, Victor Arnold
DIRECTOR: James Glickenhaus
PRODUCER: David Chan
WRITER: James Glickenhaus
FIGHT/ACTION DIRECTORS: Billy Lai; Stanley Chow
PRODUCTION COMPANY: Golden Harvest
DISTRIBUTORS: Warner Brothers; NYUE
U.S. RELEASE: 1986

POLICE STORY (1985)
"Ging Chaat Goo Si"

PLOT: Jackie plays Ka Kui (Kevin Chan in English-subtitled prints), a Hong Kong policeman whose life is turned upside down after he goes up against an outwardly upstanding businessman who in reality is a vicious crime lord. First, a drug bust intended to nail the gangster goes wrong and a small shanty town is razed during the ensuing battle between the cops and the crooks.

But the worst is yet to come. The crime lord is acquitted after the cop's evidence is tampered with by the gangster's girlfriend, who was supposed to be the prosecution's star witness. Once she helps get him off, the gangster does an about-face and orders her to be killed.

Ka saves her life but in the process finds himself framed for killing a fellow cop. In order to clear his name, he must find the real killer while running from the cops who want to arrest him and the gangsters who want to kill him. Helping Ka for personal reasons of her own is the former girlfriend—a situation that doesn't please Ka's longtime girlfriend May. But the gangster's moll comes through and amasses enough evidence to send the crime lord away for life.

The first of Chan's highly successful *Police Story* film franchise is a classic on many levels. With this film, Jackie fully modernized the kung fu genre and forever earned his place as top stunt hotdog of all time. The movie is a showcase of amazing feats of daring, not the least of which is Jackie sliding down a light bulb-wrapped three-story pole, with exploding fixtures showering electrical sparks and exploding bulb glass all around his face and body.

Actually, this stunt ended up being potentially more dangerous than even Jackie knew. It wasn't until after he finished the stunt that he discovered the film electrician had plugged the Christmas lights into a regular house current instead of using a weaker portable battery.

Equally chancy was the fight sequence staged inside—and outside—a fast-moving bus as it careened down a winding mountain road. To get on the bus, Jackie hooks an umbrella onto the back of the bus and hangs on while the vehicle flies down the street.

Jackie wasn't the only one nursing aches and pains. Maggie Cheung had the pleasure of being kicked down a staircase. Literally. Compared to that, the scene where she's plucked off a moving motorcycle must have seemed like a snap.

Depending on which version you are watching, Chan's character's name is either Chan Ga Kui, Ka-Kui, or plain old Kevin. Whatever you want to call him, just call him pleased— Chan lists this movie as his overall personal favorite.

Of Special Note: In the scene where Jackie is trying to stop the oncoming bus of fleeing criminals, the bus stopped short by mistake. Instead of landing behind Jackie as planned, the stuntmen crashed through the glass and landed in front of Chan, resulting in many injured stuntmen.

CAST: Jackie Chan, Brigitte Lin, Che Yuen, Bill Tung, Maggie Cheung
DIRECTOR: Jackie Chan
PRODUCER: Leonard Ho
WRITER: Edward Tang, Jackie Chan
FIGHT/ACTION DIRECTOR: Jackie Chan
ACTION DESIGN: Jackie Chan's Stuntman Association
PRODUCTION COMPANY: Paragon; Golden Way
DISTRIBUTORS: Golden Harvest; NYUE
U.S. RELEASES: 1985 (theatrical); 1992 (video)
MANDARIN: Jing3 Cha2 Gu4 Shi4
AWARDS: Best Picture, Action Design 1985 H.K. Film Awards.
A/K/A:

- *Jackie Chan's Police Force* (American version—dubbed)
- *Jackie Chan's Police Story*
- *Police Force*

FIRST MISSION (1985)
"Lung Dik Sam"

PLOT: Chan is a CID officer who has given up his dream of sailing around the world as a merchant seaman to stay home and care for his mentally disabled brother, Danny, played by

Sammo. Things take a deadly turn when the brother inadvertently becomes involved in a jewelry heist. Danny is kidnapped and held hostage by a local crime lord. Chan is told that to get his brother back alive he must turn over a police informant. Instead, Jackie and members from the force have a showdown with the gangster and his henchmen at a construction site, leading to a martial arts melee.

Despite the title, which sounds like another typical action flick, this surprisingly serious drama—one reviewer referred to it as *Rain Man* for the kung fu fan—was a change of pace for both Sammo and Chan. But for some fans it may be too much so. The film makes minimal use of martial arts, most of the action coming during the movie's opening and at the end in the traditional fight finale. And in keeping with his character's diminished mental capacity, Sammo has no fighting scenes at all.

However, whether because of the emotional story or not, Chan's final fight is highly regarded because of his intensity and precision and often cited as one of the best film fights he's ever done. As often noted, regardless of the movie's plot, Chan tends to look better in screen fights when he is directed by someone else and made to toe the line. In other words, there's less or none of Chan's incessant mugging.

Chan functions quite well with minimal action. A Golden Harvest executive was quoted as saying the film stood on its own merit as a drama and that they didn't want superfluous stunt work and kung fu detracting from the movie's heart. So those who care less about a tender family drama and more about bone-jarring fight scenes should watch the uncut Chinese version.

Of Special Note: The decision to keep the martial arts to a minimum prevented international audiences from seeing some spectacular fight choreography by Yuen Biao, including a battle set in a restaurant parking lot. Also cut was a hospital fight scene that featured some of Hong Kong's best-known martial arts actors.

CAST: Jackie Chan, Sammo Hung, Emily Chu, Man Hei, Liu Chia-yung, Wu Ma
DIRECTOR: Sammo Hung
PRODUCER: Jackie Chan
WRITER: Sammo Hung
FIGHT/ACTION DIRECTOR: Sammo Hung
PRODUCTION COMPANY: Golden Way
DISTRIBUTORS: Golden Harvest; NYUE
U.S. RELEASES: 1987 (theatrical); 1989 (video)
MANDARIN: Long2 De1 Xin1
AWARDS: Best Song 1985 H.K. Film Awards
A/K/A:

- *Heart of the Dragon*

ARMOUR OF GOD (1986)
"Lung Hing Foo Dai"

PLOT: Chan plays a former rock band singer turned adventurer for hire who finds antiques of value for wealthy clients or for dealers to auction off. Known as the Asian Hawk, Chan has just secured part of an exquisitely valuable religious artifact "Armor of God" for a collector. To believers, the Armor of God is the relic of an ancient battle between good and evil. To the antique collector and dealer, it's a priceless possession. For Chan, it's the beginning of a big headache.

Out of the blue, a former friend of the Hawk comes to him for help. The Hawk and Alan used to be in a band together, and now Alan is a famous pop star. But Alan is in trouble. His girlfriend—who years before just happened to be Hawk's gal until she dumped him for Alan—has just been kidnapped by a cult leader whose ransom demand isn't money. To return Alan's girlfriend the cultist wants the Armor of God pieces Chan has just gotten for the collector.

The leader of the evil cult needs the remaining pieces of

armor to fulfill an ancient prophecy—even though Good won that ancient battle, should the five remaining pieces of armor ever be destroyed, Evil will return and triumph.

Knowing that the cultists probably already possess the two remaining pieces of the Armor, Hawk makes a deal with the collector—let me borrow the three pieces you have, and I'll return with the entire set of five. The collector goes for it. The only catch is that the collector's daughter insists on coming along to protect the family interests. So does Alan. The three of them set out to find the Armor and defeat the cult leader and his followers.

Which they do. But in the process Hawk fails to recover the Armor, leaving the threat of a new dark age to hover at the film's end.

Although *Armour of God* was an unqualified success, ending up the third highest grossing Hong Kong film of the 1980s, the production suffered from numerous behind-the-scenes problems—the least of which was Jackie Chan's brush with death. Certainly for someone who had slid down a pole with live electrical wires exposed or hung on to a speeding bus, swinging on a tree limb probably seemed like a walk in the park. It was the slight lapse of care that almost caused Chan his life shortly after production had begun on the film in the former Yugoslavia.

On paper, the stunt was easy enough. Jackie needed to jump from a castle wall and grab the branch of a nearby tree. Because of the relative simplicity of the stunt, nothing was put under Chan to break a fall.

Jackie did the stunt once, felt good, then decided to do a little improvising, adding a turn as he jumped. He slipped. Although it was "only" a nineteen-foot drop, the ground underneath was littered with rocks. Chan landed on a sharp, jutting corner of rock, which drilled a hole through his scalp. The outtakes at the end of *Armour of God* show the accident in gruesome detail: Chan clipping, grabbing wildly for the branch, landing on the rocks, then just lying on the ground with blood pouring out of his ear, surrounded by horrified crewmen.

Chan was rushed to the nearest hospital, where he underwent emergency surgery to repair a ruptured inner ear. He also had a fractured skull. Production was put on ice while Chan recovered.

As for the movie itself, with its Asian Hawk character and supernatural elements, it is impossible not to notice the similarities in tone and plot between *Armour of God* and Steven Spielberg's *Indiana Jones* franchise. The question is, who borrowed from whom? At the end of the day, probably both. Although some would say it's more accurate to call *Armour of God* an homage to the *Indiana Jones* films.

Indiana Jones and the Temple of Doom was made in 1984, two years before *Armour of God*. However, Chan appears to be correct when he says that Spielberg "borrowed" Jackie's bicycle chase scene from 1983's *Project A* and reinvented it as a motorcycle chase sequence for *Indiana Jones*.

But what counts ultimately is the final project, and *Armour of God* stands tall on its own merits. That the film ever finished production was amazing enough, much less that it turned out as well as it did. Not that there aren't problems, the most noticeable being the lapses in continuity, mostly the result of Chan's return after his recuperation. Even after Jackie felt he was well enough to go back to work, the production couldn't resume. Doctors had shaved Jackie's head for the surgery, so in addition to his wounds having to heal, his hair needed to grow back. Which brings up another sore spot, so to speak. When he was hired as director, Eric Tsang had wanted to give Chan a new film look, so he had Jackie cut his hair short. Chan did it but really didn't like it. So when he came back after his accident, he decided to forgo the short 'do and go back to the longer look. In some publicity stills, Chan is shown with the short look, but in the film, his hair length fluctuates, making it easy to tell which scenes were shot preaccident and which after his return.

Once back on the set, Jackie acted as if he'd never been

away. Needing to get right back on that stunt horse, Chan created some doozies, including one where he free-falls off a mountain onto a hot air balloon floating by beneath him.

Because of the supernatural aspect, *Armour of God* assembles a surreal collection of characters including machine gun-toting monks and what appear to be transvestite Amazons. Originally there had been a planned fight with Cynthia Rothrock but she turned it down after being offered a more substantial role in the film *Righting Wrongs*—opposite little brother Yuen Biao.

Of Special Note: A fight in a cave with four Amazon women wearing stiletto heels and leather and another sequence where Jackie sleds down the side of a hill while being pursued by a tribe of pygmies.

CAST: Jackie Chan, Lola Forna, Rosamund Kwan, Allen Tam
DIRECTORS: Eric Tsang (dismissed), Jackie Chan
PRODUCERS: Leonard Ho, Ohua Lam
WRITER: Tang King Sang
FIGHT/ACTION DIRECTOR: Jackie Chan
ACTION DESIGN: Jackie Chan's Stuntman Association
PRODUCTION COMPANY: Golden Harvest; Harvest
MANDARIN: Long2 Xiong1 Hu3 Di4
DISTRIBUTORS: NYUE (Rainbow Video)
U.S. RELEASE: 1989 (video)

NAUGHTY BOYS (1986)
"Nau Gai Jaap Paai Gwan"

PLOT: Just after getting released from prison, an ex-con goes to retrieve the money he hid for his gang before they were convicted. When it turns up missing, he has to go on the run from his former cohorts, who believe he's trying to rip them off. He also has to save himself from whoever really took the money.

A forgettable film that came and went quickly. However, from the it's-a-small-world file, this was Ken Lo's first film for Golden Harvest. He has a small part toward the end where he fights well-known kung fu diva, Kara Hui Ying-hung. From this, he was cast in *Project A, Part II*. And it was during that film that Jackie asked Ken if he'd like to be his bodyguard. Lo said yes, became a member of Jackie's stuntmen, and looked after his new boss's personal security.

The other thing of interest about *Naughty Boys* is the widely held suspicion that Jack Chan directed this film using a pseudonym.

CAST: Kara Hui, Carina Lau, Clarence Ford, Mars
DIRECTOR: Wilson Chin
PRODUCER: Jackie Chan
PRODUCTION COMPANY: Golden Harvest
DISTRIBUTOR: NYUE
U.S. RELEASE: 1992 (video)
MANDARIN: Nui3 Ji4 Za2 Pai2 Jun1

DRAGONS FOREVER (1987)
"Fei Lung Maang Jeung"

PLOT: A Hong Kong chemical plant run by a local crime boss is feeling the heat from environmentalists and residents sick and tired of the company polluting their area and destroying the local fishing. When one farmer—who happens to be a pretty woman—threatens to take them to court, the company hires a lawyer played by Chan. Jackie's morally free-wheeling attorney breezily goes about his business of trying to buy off the farmer and her compatriot, a beautiful woman to whom Jackie is instantly attracted.

The women can't be bought, so Chan's next plan is to win over their trust so he can sabotage their plans, enlisting the help of a petty criminal, played by Sammo Hung. Instead of undermining them, Sammo becomes smitten with the farmer while the lawyer falls head over heels for the other lady.

Now Jackie is torn between his dangerous boss and his heart—until he discovers the truth—the chemical plant is really a narcotics refinery. No wonder the fish are dying. Jackie renounces the gang boss and decides to help his new love. Aided by Sammo and their mentally challenged burglar friend, played by third "brother" Yuen Biao, Chan takes on the crime lord and destroys his evil empire.

It was supposed to be a special occasion. The three brothers were back together again, but by the end of the film, the atmosphere was more like *Family Feud* than a fraternal love-fest. Depending on who was talking, the brothers reunited on *Dragons Forever* because: (1) it seemed like a sure box office hit that would be released for the Chinese New Year, or (2) Jackie wanted to help resuscitate Sammo's fizzling career and ebbing popularity.

The movie created a surprising strain among the men, considering they had worked together enough to know what to expect. But the tension was apparent all the way around. Sammo and Jackie allegedly argued over how the fight scenes should be done, and while they were drawing lines in the cinema sand, Yuen was off on the sidelines feeling left out and underappreciated.

As usually seemed to happen, Yuen was given the least amount of screen time to showcase his abilities. Arguably, however, his acrobatics on a catwalk are the film's highlight. Yuen has admitted in interviews that the situation made him realize he would forever be in Sammo's and Jackie's shadows unless he made his own films.

Imagine how Sammo felt. He actually made a name for himself before Jackie got his big break and is an extremely talented writer, director, producer, and fight choreographer. Yet he has stood by and watched Jackie become an international Asian film deity.

The resulting bad feelings seemed to have a karmic cost with fans. *Dragons Forever* was given a decent reception in

Hong Kong but was hardly the second coming of *Armour of God*. And in Japan, it was a downright bust.

Which in some ways was surprising; it's grand entertainment. The three brothers still have a good on-screen chemistry and fans enjoy seeing them together. Sammo directs a mean fight and Jackie throws caution—and good sense—to the wind in pushing the edge of the stunt envelope.

And in *Dragons Forever*, there are the expected number of stunts and fights, including Jackie's wild escape from a yachtload of villains and the long awaited rematch with Benny "The Jet" Urquidez, his worthy opponent from *Wheels on Meals*. There are also some standout fight scenes among the three little brothers.

Of Special Note: One of the villains is Yuen Wah, who was a fellow Peking Opera School brother of Jackie, Sammo, and Yuen.

CAST: Jackie Chan, Sammo Hung, Yuen Biao, Dick Wei, Pauline Yeung, Yuen Wah, Crystal Kwok
DIRECTOR: Sammo Hung
PRODUCER: Leonard Ho
PRODUCTION COMPANY: Winston Entertainment/Golden Way
DISTRIBUTORS: Golden Harvest; NYUE
U.S. RELEASE: 1989 (video)
MANDARIN: Fei1 Long2 Meng3 Jiang1
A/K/A:

- *Cyclone Z*
- *Three Brothers*

PROJECT A, PART II (1987)
" 'A' Gai Waak Juk Jaap"

PLOT: Once again it is turn-of-the-century China, and Chan returns as Dragon Ma. This time he's been assigned to run one of the police precincts—half the force is on the take, including the superintendent. Dragon purges the force of its dirty cops and cracks down on the local gangs and in return is named new superintendent.

Meanwhile, Dragon and his men are ordered to provide security at a party being thrown at the governor's house for the prince, who is in town on a mission to track down local rebels. During the party, a gang of thieves in cahoots with the former superintendent break into the governor's safe, steal a necklace, and manage to plant it on Dragon, who is subsequently arrested.

With Dragon out of the way, the crooked superintendent is reinstated. He hands Dragon over to the rebels, who are now in cahoots with the gang, and they throw him in the river bound in a burlap bag. He escapes. Making matters worse, he's also being chased by pirates still miffed that Dragon blew up their hideout and killed their leader in the first movie.

Things turn around after a group of rebels double-cross the others and sell the names of the rebels to the prince. Armed with the names of their enemies, Dragon and his coast guard buddies confront and defeat the criminals.

The sequel to *Project A* picks up pretty much where the original left off, although there are some significant differences this time around, most notably the absence of Sammo Hung and Yuen Biao. Even though Hung wasn't credited as the martial arts director in *Project A*, his influence was still obvious in the fight scenes, where his hand-to-hand choreography is second to none. As he tends to when directing, Chan opts for goofiness and is not terribly concerned with showing off fighting the way Sammo does. As a result, the emphasis tends to be on finding a way to be humorous as opposed to choreographing a meaty fight scene. But that's what Jackie fans usually want, and Chan makes sure they get their fix.

One sequence in particular is amazingly choreographed. In it, Maggie Cheung has to hide up to five different sets of people from one another in her small apartment. Chan says it took him a month to figure out the comings and goings of the various groups. And yes, it is an homage to the Marx Brothers, inspired by one of their movies.

From the point of view of production values, *Project A, Part II* is top-notch. To film this period-piece epic, Chan built a huge set on a lot formerly used by the Shaw Brothers, and he certainly got his money's worth. As do Jackie fans, who are treated to scenes that are more than just stunts—they're outrageous examples of plain old derring-do, particularly the Buster Keaton homage of the falling wall stunt. The original stunt, of a building falling down around Buster, was seen in the silent film *Steamboat Bill, Jr.* But Jackie does more than simply borrow the idea. He updates and improves on it. Instead of standing around while the walls cave in around him, Chan actually runs down the side of the building as it's collapsing. Not a facade, mind you, a real building, and the only opening is a pint-size window through which Jackie is left standing. A miscalculation of mere inches in any direction and he would have been the *late*, great Jackie Chan.

Another bit of business that stands out as an example of Jackie's delightfully bent way of thinking out a fight scene is when he stuffs a handful of hot peppers in his mouth. With his rubbery face contorting from the volcanic eruption going on inside his mouth, Chan chews then spits the fire-hot mixture of saliva and pepper juice onto his hands, then rubs them into his opponent's eyes. He also uses the bit as an excuse for some slapstick, trying to put out his oral fire by chugging gallons of water.

There's also a nifty confrontation on the bamboo scaffolding and a scene where Jackie is forced to fight while handcuffed to someone. Their hatchet-tossing shenanigans are brilliant.

And reminiscent of Chan's fall from the clock tower, one of the stuntmen working on this film tumbles from the second floor of a building, bounces off the top of a huge pot, then lands smack on his back. Unlike Jackie, however, he was hurt.

Of Special Note: A stunt where Jackie nearly escapes being squished by a grain grinder.

CAST: Jackie Chan, Maggie Cheung, David Lam, Rosamund Kwan, Carina Lau
DIRECTOR: Jackie Chan
PRODUCER: Leonard Ho
WRITER: Edward Tang
FIGHT/ACTION DIRECTOR: Jackie Chan
ACTION DESIGN: Jackie Chan's Stuntman Association
PRODUCTION COMPANY: Golden Harvest
DISTRIBUTOR: American Imperial; NYUE
U.S. RELEASES: 1987 (theatrical); 1989 (video)
MANDARIN: ''A'' Ji4 Hua4 Xu4 Ji2
AWARDS: Best Action Design 1987 H.K. Film Awards
AKA::

- *Project B*

ROUGE (1987)
"Yin Ji Kau"

PLOT: An Asian retelling of *Romeo and Juliet.* Anita Mui plays a 1930s Hong Kong courtesan who falls in love with a young master. When they are forbidden to marry, they commit suicide.

Fifty years later, the concubine's ghost returns, searching for her young master. Eventually she finds him and they reunite.

Obviously, there's not a lot of kung fu in this one. *Rouge* was well received critically and brought Mui home the Best Actress award.

Of Special Note: In many filmographies for Jackie, a movie titled *Rough* is included. *Rough* is obviously *Rouge* misspelled. What's most amazing is how many people didn't catch the mistake and contributed to the confusion by passing the incorrect information along. (You know who you are . . . don't you feel silly now?)

CAST: Anita Mui, Leslie Cheung, Alex Man
DIRECTOR: Stanley Kwan
PRODUCER: Jackie Chan
WRITERS: Li Pik Wah, Yau Tai On Ping
PRODUCTION COMPANY: Golden Way
MANDARIN: Yan1 Zhi1 Kou4
U.S. RELEASE: 1988 (theatrical)
AWARDS: Best Actress, Cinematography and Art Direction 1988 Golden Horse Awards; Best Picture, Screenplay, Editing, Music and Song 1988 H.K. Film Awards

POLICE STORY II (1988)
"Ging Chaat Goo Si Juk Jaap"

PLOT: Because of all the property damage he helped cause at the end of *Police Story*, Detective Ka Chan has been demoted back to a patrol officer as punishment for his "reckless disregard for proper procedures." Adding injury to insult, the mobster Ka arrested has been given a "compassionate pardon" from jail because he has only a short time to live. But terminal illness hasn't slowed the criminal down, and he immediately sets out to take revenge against Ka, beginning by terrorizing his girlfriend, May.

Meanwhile, gangsters threaten to start blowing up various buildings around town in an attempt to extort money from some corporate bigwigs. This prompts the force to promote Ka back to a detective and put him in charge of the detail assigned to finding the extortionists before they carry out their threats.

Things take a serious turn when Ka is abducted by the would-be *blastmeisters*. After they amuse themselves by conducting a little torture with fireballs, they strap a dynamite coat on him (*dynamite* being a noun, not an adjective) and send him off to get their extortion money. Quick-witted Ka figures out a way to defuse himself without destroying half of Hong Kong, then sets off after the crooks. Ka confronts the crooks in a huge fireworks warehouse, and after a battle royal, Ka escapes while the gangsters suffer a poetic end when they get blown to smithereens as the fireworks explode.

Add Maggie Cheung, who plays the long-suffering May, Ka's girlfriend with the patience of a saint, to the list of human crash-test dummies. Cheung was injured during the final fight scene after being flung down a chute that's supposed to dump her outside the building. It does—right onto her head.

Cheung gained so much speed tumbling down the chute she was unable to control her fall and wound up in the hospital nursing a damaged head. As a result, the script had to be adjusted for her absence. But wherever possible—long shots or ones where you see the back of "May's" head—a double was used.

Police Story II has a different tone from the original, concentrating more on action than dialogue—or plot, for that matter. It's the movie equivalent of an amusement park ride intended to keep Jackie action fans "ooh"-ing and "ahh"-ing. And his costars "ouch"-ing.

Of Special Note: Jackie crossing the street by jumping first on a bus going one way, then onto another going the opposite direction, then jumping through a glass-enclosed balcony; Chan fighting a group of opponents in a breathtaking use of playground equipment; an explosive remote-controlled toy car that almost makes Chan a soprano.

CAST: Jackie Chan, Maggie Cheung, Bill Tung, Lam Kwok-Hunge
DIRECTOR: Jackie Chan
PRODUCER: Leonard Ho
WRITERS: Jackie Chan, Edward Tang
FIGHT/ACTION DIRECTOR: Jackie Chan
ACTION DESIGN: Jackie Chan's Stuntmen Association
PRODUCTION COMPANY: Golden Way
DISTRIBUTOR: Golden Harvest
U.S. RELEASE: 1989 (video)

MANDARIN: Jing3 Cha2 Gu4 Shi4 Xu4 Ji2
AWARDS: Best Action Design 1988 H.K. Film Awards
A/K/A:

- *Police Force II*

THE INSPECTOR WEARS SKIRTS (1988)
"Ba Wong Fa"

PLOT: Kickboxer Cynthia Rothrock stars as a policewoman, and Sibelle Hu is an equally tough commander in charge of shaping police recruits into an elite team of female cops called the Top Squad.

Members of the Top Squad are challenged by their male SWAT counterparts to a martial arts contest that's as much of an excuse to flirt as it is to fight. Eventually, the rivalry is put aside as the two groups join forces to collar a vicious gang of thieves.

A Hong Kong version of the *Police Academy* films. The film is most notable because of Rothrock, an American woman who managed to make a name for herself in Hong Kong as a martial arts film star. The American martial arts tournament champion was discovered by Chan's old mentor, Ng See Yuen. But it was actually Sammo Hung who jump-started her film career. After seeing a feature about her on television, he cast her in the superb *Millionaires' Express* (1988) with himself and Yuen Biao.

Even though Rothrock had bowed out of Jackie's *Armour of God*, where he wanted her to play the number one villain, he was still impressed enough with her that he served as producer on *The Inspector Wears Skirts*.

And maybe more. There are some who believe that Wilson Chin, the credited director for this film and its sequel, is really Jackie using an alias. What gives this belief possible credence is that the only other credits "Wilson Chin" has is as the director of the Chan-produced *Naughty Boys* and another Cynthia

Rothrock film, *Prince of the Sun*. All were comedies, all made within a few years of one another.

Why would Jackie feel the need to resort to deception? Perhaps to avoid the inevitable scrutiny that follows any film he's creatively associated with. Although Jackie has earned fame and fortune with his stunt-oriented film persona, he has never been able to earn respect as a director the way, say, Sammo Hung has. By keeping his involvement quiet, he would have more room to experiment without having people looking over his shoulder.

If Chan truly did direct the two *Inspector* films, it would also explain why his normally prodigious production of film output seemed to dip noticeably in 1988–89.

CAST: Sibelle Hu, Cynthia Rothrock, Jeff Falcon, Billy Lau, Wei Yin Hung, Bill Tung
DIRECTOR: Wilson Chin
PRODUCER: Jackie Chan
WRITER: Cheng Kam Fu
PRODUCTION COMPANY: Golden Way
DISTRIBUTOR: NYUE (Rainbow Video)
U.S. RELEASE: 1988 (video)
MANDARIN: Ba4 Wang2 Hua1
A/K/A:
- *Top Squad*

THE INSPECTOR WEARS SKIRTS II (1989)
"San Yung Fei Foo Ba Wong Fa"

PLOT: Sibelle Hu returns as the Top Squad leader, who this time around falls in love with the leader of the corresponding male SWAT unit, played by Billy Lau. Their romance gets detoured when the thieves from the previous movie break out of jail but Hu and her Top Squad track down the thieves and bring them back to justice.

Like the original, the action sequences for this sequel were filmed on the same sets Chan used for *Project A*. Interestingly, some have even referred to *The Inspector Wears Skirts* as a female *Project A*.

Although Cynthia Rothrock was the main focus of the first film, Sibelle Hu gets a chance to strut her stuff without having to share the spotlight. Earlier in her career, Hu was considered a conventional actress, appearing in light comedies. Then she abruptly changed her image into that of "fighting babe" with these two films as well as *My Lucky Stars*.

But regardless of the genre, Hu has never set the film world afire with her dramatic skills and is now viewed as your basic exploitation film actress, including such epics as *Sleazy Dizzy*, *Bury Me High*, and *Angel Terminators 2*. But the lowlight of her career came in 1995 when she was "awarded" the Golden Banana—given for the Worst Actress of 1994.

CAST: Sibelle Hu, Billy Lau, Jeff Falcon
DIRECTOR: Wilson Chin
PRODUCER: Jackie Chan
PRODUCTION COMPANY: Golden Way
DISTRIBUTOR: NYUE
U.S. RELEASE: 1989 (video)
MANDARIN: Shen2 Yong3 Fei1 Hu3 Ba4 Wang2 Hua1
A/K/A:

*   *Top Squad 2*

MIRACLES: MR. CANTON AND LADY ROSE (1989)
"Kei Jik"

PLOT: Jackie is a country bumpkin who loses his life savings almost as soon as he gets off the bus in the big city, circa the 1930s. While wandering around he is given a "lucky" rose by a street vendor. Rose in hand and not knowing where to go, he falls in with the wrong crowd—a gang of crooks. To everyone's surprise, the dying leader names Chan his successor, which includes taking over a nightclub. His lucky fortune creates animosity between the newcomer and skeptical gang members, but he wins them over displaying his kung fu skills during a confrontation with a rival gang. After proving himself, Chan works to achieve his goal of keeping the peace between rival gangs.

That settled, the movie shifts focus to Chan befriending the woman who sells flowers on the street. Along with his nightclub-singer girlfriend, Chan attempts to help the flower lady, who finds herself in a jam. For years the woman had been writing misleading letters to her faroff daughter, pretending to be a wealthy career woman instead of a street vendor. Now the truth is about to be discovered because her daughter is coming for a visit with her snooty, wealthy prospective in-laws.

Chan and his new gang of cronies help the woman try and pull off her masquerade. In the end, the two plots—Chan helping the flower lady and his involvement with the gangs—converge during a melee between Jackie and some thugs at a rope factory.

It would be pretty difficult to deny that *Miracles* is a rather obvious remake of Frank Capra's last film, 1961's *Pocketful of Miracles*—itself a remake of Capra's own 1933 *Lady for a Day* (starring May Robson and Warren William) which in turn was based on the Damon Runyan story "Madame La Gimp."

Whatever else it is, *Miracles* is a departure for Chan, to say the least. However, the action scenes that are in the movie are inventive enough to mollify the otherwise confused Chan action fans, including a dizzying fight in the nightclub, another fight sequence in a market where Jackie utilizes rickshaws and produce. These scenes are a definitive example of how Chan's choreography is shaped by the environment in which he finds himself. Also visually stunning is the final fight in the rope factory with Jackie scampering up and down ropes and ladders like a possessed gymnast. Which, when you think about it, he is.

Even though he's well past an age when most people's reflexes fall somewhere well below fighter pilot level, Chan still shows remarkable hand-eye coordination. In one scene from the film, Jackie is fighting an opponent when he kicks a cup straight up then kicks it again on the way down, creating a weapon that downs another approaching enemy.

Jackie also has some fun with cameo appearances, including brother Yuen Biao's brief appearance as a homeless panhandler.

Alas, it seems like nobody appreciates plain old artistic dramas anymore. Even the exhibitors were critics, irked by the film's three-hour length. While most fans certainly didn't mind spending extra time with Jackie, a longer film meant fewer daily show times, which in turn meant less money in ticket sales per day. Even though they ultimately grimaced and bore it, they weren't happy about it. Jackie would try to make it up to them with his next movie. But in the meantime, *Miracles* was surgically reduced to the point where nobody was sure a copy of the original director's cut still existed anywhere.

Surprise—it does. When Chan was in America promoting *Rumble in the Bronx* he attended the USA Film Festival. There, lo and behold, what should appear but the original cut of *Mr. Canton*. Reportedly, Jackie shed a tear when he saw it.

For those who were especially taken with *Miracles*, find a copy of the *Incredibly Strange Film Show* with Jackie, which spotlights the *Miracles* production.

Chan says this film is his favorite directorial effort.

Of Special Note: A fight sequence on a curving staircase; Jackie riding a rickshaw down a flight of stairs.

CAST: Jackie Chan, Anita Mui, Wu Ma, Gloria Yip, Richard Ng, Bill Tung, Yuen Biao, Jackie Cheung
DIRECTOR: Jackie Chan
PRODUCER: Leonard Ho
FIGHT/ACTION DIRECTOR: Jackie Chan
ACTION DESIGN: Jackie Chan's Stuntman Association
PRODUCTION COMPANY: Golden Harvest
DISTRIBUTORS: Golden Harvest; NYUE

U.S. RELEASES: 1989 (theatrical); 1992 (video)
MANDARIN: Qi2 Ji1
AWARDS: Best Action Design 1989 H.K. Film Awards
A/K/A:

- *The Canton Godfather*
- *Black Dragon*
- *Miracle* (Japanese title)
- *Singapore Sling*

ISLAND OF FIRE (1990)

PLOT: A thriller set in 1999 China, two years after the Mainland has reclaimed Hong Kong. Strange things are happening
on the island. After a murderer is blown up, fingerprint analy-
sis identifies the killer as a man who had supposedly been executed in prison two years earlier.

Because his father-in-law has been murdered by a hitman,
a young police officer, played by Leung Kar Fei, goes undercover in a local prison to find who ordered the assassination
and why the killer who did it hadn't really been executed, even
though the prison said he had. To his shock and horror, he
discovers the prison system is a cesspool of corruption, run
by a crooked warden.

Inside the walls, it's hard to figure out who are the worst
criminals—the prisoners or the guards and warden running
the place. The officer is so outraged by what he sees, he kills
one of the prison officials and suddenly finds himself alone, on
the wrong side of the law. He's convicted, sentenced to die,
and sent back to the prison for real. But just before he's to
be killed, a prison guard spares his life in exchange for the dis-
graced officer becoming one of the "dead" hitmen. Turns out
the warden is faking the executions so he can recruit the
murderers into a gang that kills other criminals who have
managed to beat the system.

Among the others in this secret group of assassins is a
former pool champ, played by Jackie Chan. He's in prison because he accidentally killed the brother of a Triad gangster

while trying to get to the hospital to pay for the life-and-death operation his girlfriend needed. And why did the fashion model girlfriend need an operation in the first place? Because she'd been sliced and diced by one of Chan's billiards opponents who was miffed at losing money in a tourney. And what was he using to pay for the procedure? Money he had hurriedly won in a card game after the attack.

Once in prison, the warden arranged for Chan to square off against a Triad representative in a fight to the death. Jackie won but refused to kill his opponent, so both men were channeled into the hit squad as a team. Pairing up with the former cop and another prisoner is a chronic escapee, played by Sammo Hung. The four are sent together on a hit, but all except the cop are killed.

In the end, the redeemed cop has the warden arrested.

This is another atypical Jackie Chan movie. Why would people like Chan, Sammo, Andy Lau, and the others appear in an overheated, far-fetched melodrama? There are a number of theories that have been bandied about and most involve the Triads in one way or another.

The producer of the flick was Jimmy Wang Yu, who, as has been previously mentioned in Chapter 1, was said to have very close movie ties to the Triads in Taiwan, where this film was shot. The most widely circulated explanation is that Yu, who saw this film as a comeback vehicle, called in some favors and the A-list actors tagged by him to "donate" their time agreed, as a favor for being protected, as it were, from the darker elements of the Triads.

There are those who feel Chan had already paid back his debt to Wang Yu and considered this mere coercion. If an unsettling story that has made the rounds is true, coercion would be putting it mildly. Supposedly, Chan agreed to donate his time and energies only after some persuasion involving a gun near the proximity of his head. True or not, the underlying sense remains that this was a project that Chan would have avoided doing if he could. He couldn't, but later he did the next best thing: Chan bought the film's Hong Kong rights and permanently shelved it.

Ironically, the film is not universally panned. As a prison drama it has its share of approving fans. But as a "Jackie Chan film" *Island of Fire* fails on several counts. Besides its notable lack of stunts and Jackie's signature action inventiveness, Chan's on-screen time is limited. While that no doubt relieved Jackie, it left his fans feeling cheated, especially since the film had hyped Chan's presence.

Of Special Note: This movie is often found on videos with the title *The Prisoner* "starring" Jackie Chan—even though he's only in it briefly.

CAST: Jackie Chan, Sammo Hung, Tony Leung, Jimmy Wang Yu, Andy Lau
DIRECTOR: Chu Yen-ping
PRODUCERS: Jimmy Wang Yu, Ka Chuen Hsiung
WRITERS: Fu Lee, Yen Yun Chiao
PRODUCTION COMPANY: Golden Harvest
DISTRIBUTOR: NYUE
U.S. RELEASES: 1991 (theatrical); 1992 (video)
A/K/A:
- *Island on Fire*
- *The Prisoner* (UK title)
- *Burning Island*
- *When Dragons Meet*

THE DEADLIEST ART (1990)

A compilation film that uses movie clips and interviews to give an overview of the martial arts action genre. Narrated by John Saxon, the lion's share of the film concentrates on the three brothers—Jackie Chan, Sammo Hung, and Yuen Biao.

The producer of this documentary is Fred Weintraub, who earned his martial arts stripes by producing Bruce Lee's *Enter the Dragon*, Chan's *The Big Brawl*, and other films of the genre, both dramatic and documentary.

CAST: Cynthia Rothrock, Yuen Biao, Sammo Hung, Bruce Lee, many others.
DIRECTOR: Sandra Weintraub
PRODUCER: Fred Weintraub

STAGE DOOR JOHNNY (1991)
"Mo Toi Ji Mooi"

PLOT: A period drama set in 1930s Shanghai where a troupe of female Chinese performers confronts and defeats a menacing Triad gang.

Set during the same era as *Miracles*, this film was its opposite in tone and success. *Stage Door Johnny* was an unremarkable movie that was seen by few people in Hong Kong and even fewer elsewhere in the world.

CAST: Anita Mui, Hui Ying-hung, Chan Yuk Lin, Lai Yin San, Wu Ma
DIRECTOR: Wu Ma
PRODUCER: Jackie Chan
PRODUCTION COMPANY: Golden Way
MANDARIN: Wu3 Tai Jie3 Zi3 Mei3
DISTRIBUTOR: NYUE

THE KID FROM TIBET (1991)

PLOT: Yuen Biao plays a young monk who studies under a Tibetan high dalai lama. Because he possesses magic powers, the monk is assigned to thwart an evil sorcerer from obtaining the cap of an urn. When the top and bottom are united, the urn has special powers the wizard wants to use for dark purposes.

This was Yuen Biao's directorial debut, which is no doubt why Jackie agreed to do a walk-through.

CAST: Yuen Biao, Jackie Chan (cameo)
DIRECTOR: Yuen Biao

DISTRIBUTOR: NYUE

U.S. RELEASE: 1992 (video)

ARMOUR OF GOD II: OPERATION CONDOR (1991)
"Fei Ying Gai Wak"

PLOT: Jackie Chan returns as the globe-trotting buccaneer for hire. Instead of being called the Asian Hawk, he's now known as Condor. But he's still working for the same antique dealer/collector who dispatches him to locate a mother lode of gold bars hidden in the Sahara desert during World War II by Nazi soldiers. This time Condor is accompanied by three women—a scholar, the granddaughter of one of the German soldiers involved in hiding the gold, and a street vendor.

But the past meets the present when Hawk finds the gold in a secret German underground fortress used as a research center left over from the war. In the finale, Condor must battle an old Nazi and his gang of goons who also want the gold for their personal retirement fund.

At the time it was made, *Operation Condor* was the most expensive Hong Kong film ever made and was an even bigger epic behind the scenes than it was on film.

It is estimated the movie cost over HK$80 million to make and took almost a year from preproduction to being ready for release. Hong Kong is a tiny island, so the cost of the film made it impossible to turn a profit at home—it desperately needed brisk ticket sales abroad. Which it got. Even so, it was not one of Chan's more profitable productions and the press was becoming irritatingly vocal in its observation that Chan spent money as if he had a hole in his pocket.

The final legacy of *Operation Condor*'s scope and cost was that it made Jackie rethink his dictum of assuming complete directorial chores. His pictures were only getting bigger and more complex with each outing, and just developing and designing the stunts was a full-time job, much less overseeing the other aspects of directing a film.

Although the film has some memorable action scenes, Chan has been criticized by some for what he failed to accomplish in this ambitious effort. The production traveled from Asia to locations in Africa and Europe over a grueling eight months, and the wear and tear appear to have truncated some of Chan's usual tireless energy. With such panoramic backdrops, Chan fans expected equally expansive action. Make no mistake—the action they got was unique and spell-binding. But fans may have been expecting more, considering the overall scope and ambition of the film's production.

As for what is there, the most memorable part of the movie for many is the fight in the wind tunnel. Jackie and his opponent appear to defy gravity as they hang on for actual dear life while battling it out.

Which brings up a little thorn in Chan's side. Jackie has publicly vented his pique at what he perceives to be an unmistakable similarity between *Operation Condor*'s wind tunnel finale and the climactic scene in *Mission: Impossible* where Tom Cruise is hanging for dear life on a bullet train, its high speed creating the effect of hurricane force winds.

Of course, there are some glaring differences. Cruise's ordeal was mostly courtesy of special effects, whereas Chan would have looked like a swatted fly had he lost his grip or had the wires broken while he was facing down a wind machine, and he would have been slammed into the wall behind him.

Of Special Note: In a film chock-full of action, some of the standouts include one where Jackie rolls down a hill in what looks to be a giant beach ball; rides a motorcycle off a pier then jumps off in midair to land on a net suspended by a crane; in keeping with *Armour of God* tradition, he falls thirty feet trying to climb into a Nazi bunker.

CAST: Jackie Chan, "Dodo" Cheng Yu Ling, Eva Cobo de Garcia, Vincent Lyn
DIRECTOR: Jackie Chan

PRODUCER: Leonard Ho
WRITER: Jackie Chan
FIGHT/ACTION DIRECTOR: Jackie Chan
ACTION DESIGN: Jackie Chan's Stuntman Association
PRODUCTION COMPANY: Golden Way
DISTRIBUTORS: Golden Harvest; NYUE
U.S. RELEASES: 1991 (theatrical); 1992 (video)
MANDARIN: Fei1 Ying1 Ji4 Hua4
A/K/A:
- *Operation Eagle* (Japanese release)
- *Project Eagle*

ACTRESS (1992)
"Yuen Ling Yuk"

PLOT: A docudrama about actress Ruan Ling Yu, China's first true movie star. The film combines actual footage of Runa, re-creations of lost films, interviews with friends and associates, and dramatizations of her life to create a riveting portrait of a fast-living woman who died before she hit thirty.

Maggie Cheung received raves for her performance in this critically acclaimed film—not to mention a Hong Kong Film Award for Best Actress in this Chan-produced film.

CAST: Maggie Cheung, Tony Leung, Waise Lee, Carina Lau
DIRECTOR: Stanley Kwan
PRODUCER: Jackie Chan
WRITER: Yau Tai On Ping
PRODUCTION COMPANY: Golden Way
MANDARIN: Ruan Lingyu (Ruan 3 Ling2 Yu4)
AWARDS: Hong Kong Film Award Best Actress to Maggie Cheung

TWIN DRAGONS (1992)
"Seung Lung Wooi"

PLOT: Jackie plays twins separated at birth whose lives follow very different paths. Minutes after being born, a wounded gangster being treated in the hospital's emergency room gets away from his police guard and takes one of the newborns as hostage. The criminal gets away and the baby is never found. The remaining brother, American-raised John Ma, is doted on and eventually becomes a well-known conductor—with absolutely no interest in the fighting arts.

The missing brother, Boomer, is alive—if not altogether well. The baby is found by a kind-hearted woman just this side of the law. Raised in a rough neighborhood full of gangsters, the boy learns to fight. Now grown, he works as a mechanic, although he's currently in a jam. Gangsters have kidnapped his friend Tarzan and are holding him hostage to force Boomer to drive a getaway car for a planned heist.

Meanwhile, John Ma is in Hong Kong to conduct a concert. Neither brother knows he has a twin, so when they meet by chance while eating with their respective girlfriends at the same restaurant, the hijinks begin. Especially since their encounter unleashes a long-dormant psychic connection, which enables one twin to experience what the other is going through.

The brothers end up switching places when some gang members mistake John Ma for the mechanic, forcing him to drive their getaway car, leaving grease monkey Boomer to fill in and conduct the orchestra. Their psychic empathy continues to cause madcap mayhem, causing one brother to react to stimuli the other sibling is experiencing in a completely different situation.

Eventually, the brothers find themselves side by side battling gangsters in a final confrontation at an automobile testing facility.

Apparently inspired by Jean-Claude Van Damme's *Double Impact*—or maybe *Trading Places*, since this movie is intentionally funny. Done as a benefit for the Hong Kong Director's Guild so they could build their own headquarters, the film features dozens of cameos by Honk Kong's most noted *auteurs* including John Woo and Kirk Wong doing their bit for the union. Jackie has also said one of the reasons he did *Twin Dragons* was to have the chance to get familiar with some of these newfangled special effects techniques.

Special effects or not, Jackie Chan gives his audience exactly what they come to a Jackie Chan movie for—humor, some fighting, and incredible stunts. Automobiles play a big part in the stunts this time around. In one scene Jackie runs across a speeding car with he and the car going in opposite directions. During the finale, he vaults himself through car windows while battling the gangsters.

Even though *Twin Dragons* was a hit with Jackie fans and the world at large, Chan was less than enthused with the project. He complained there were too many cooks in the kitchen, that Tsui's and Ringo's differing vision made him feel like a human yo-yo. Maybe that's why Jackie decided to show them how a real action star does it. Which goes to show that sometimes the best work comes out of adverse conditions. Because of the circumstances of the production, *Twin Dragons* doesn't have the usual outtakes at the film's end.

In case you were wondering, despite the aggravation, bruises, and minuscule pay, the Hong Kong directors are still waiting for their headquarters to be built.

Of Special Note: A series of stunts that take place in the car factory. First, Jackie rolls away from a car dropped from a hydraulic lift. Then the villains release another car from a ramp and Jackie has to flip upward, then runs over the car.

CAST: Jackie Chan, Maggie Cheung, Wang Lung, David Chiang, Anthony Chan
DIRECTOR: Tsui Hark, Ringo Lam
PRODUCER: Teddy Robin Kwan
FIGHT/ACTION DIRECTOR: Jackie Chan
ACTION DESIGN: Jackie Chan's Stunman Association
PRODUCTION COMPANY: Golden Harvest
DISTRIBUTOR: Tai Seng
U.S. RELEASE: 1992 (theatrical)
MANDARIN: Shuang1 Long2 Hui4

A/K/A:

- *Double Dragons*
- *Brother vs. Brother*
- *When Dragons Collide*
- *Duel of Dragons*

SUPERCOP (1992)
"Ging Chaat Goo Si III: Chiu Kap Ging Chaat"

PLOT: Hong Kong detective Ka Kui is given the unenviable, not to mention unusual, assignment of going undercover to break an imprisoned gangster out of jail. Once free, the plan is to have Panther lead Ka to a mighty drug lord, who happens to be Panther's brother Chaibat. Although risky, the Hong Kong authorities are desperate and will do almost anything to stop the unchecked flow of heroin into the island from the Golden Triangle.

Before leaving, he casually signs over his life insurance policy to his girlfriend, May, who has no idea he's going off on a near-suicide mission. She thinks he's going off to a routine training camp, even though his first stop really is at a training camp, run by his new boss, Hana Yang. She is the Chinese chief of security and will pose as Ka's sister. Once inside the compound, Chan befriends Panther, whom he takes along during a jail break. To show his gratitude, Panther invites them to join his brother's gang, then leads Ka and Hana to a jungle compound hidden near the Thailand and Cambodian border, where they'll hide out for a while. Now firmly entrenched, Ka and Hana are chosen to go with Panther to the sale of the year's opium crop.

Along the way, the movie hits a somber note when Chan and Yang are forced to shoot fellow cops in order not to blow their cover. Eventually, they meet Chaibat—but before they can collar him, they get swept up in an unexpected operation. Chaibat's wife is being held by authorities, and it is she who knows the Swiss bank account number where the drug lord has tucked away his money. No dummy, she has refused to tell her husband what the number is until he frees her.

Things begin to get complicated when Ka runs into May at a hotel in Malaysia. Naturally, she thinks he's cheating on her, and for her own safety he can't tell her the truth. But before he can fix the situation, May accidentally blows his cover. The gangsters take May hostage and force Ka and Yang to help free Chaibat's wife.

Eventually, Ka and Yang get away and engage in an extended battle with gangsters through the streets and in the sky of Kuala Lumpur while trying to prevent Chaibat's wife from getting away. After a climactic confrontation on a train, the good guys win.

Supercop is like watching a James Bond film, only with *real* death-defying stunts. Typically, the plot tends to be convoluted and downright distracting at times, but once you learn to ignore what the plot is supposed to be, *Supercop* keeps your attention out of sheer disbelief at the stuntwork.

The action starts out relatively low-key, with Chan showing off some agility during the scene when he first meets Yeoh at the training facility. After breaking out of prison, Chan shows his inventiveness with a sequence involving mine carts on a hill. But it's the stunts and hardcore action that fuel this film.

One of the more hair-raising scenes has Jackie jumping from a ten-story building onto a swinging rope ladder suspended from a helicopter flying by. To make sure the audience understands just what's happening, the camera pulls back to show Jackie flying through the air literally thousands of feet off the ground.

And contrary to the popular notion that no action scene in a Chan film is undercranked (shot at fewer frames per second so that when played at normal projection speed the action appears faster than it really was), the sequence where Jackie and the other actor hang on a cable between two mountains to escape from the prison is *way* sped up. However, director

Stanley Tong said safety necessitated the cheating. The distance between the mountains was about a thousand feet, and it was raining. Tong insisted the cable be moved very slowly because had it broken, the actors may very well have been killed.

Speaking of putting one's life on the line . . . In Michelle Yeoh, Chan has found a worthy partner. In one scene, she falls off a van and smashes against the windshield of the car behind her. In another scene she leaps her motorcycle onto the top of a moving train. This stunt was so dangerous that even Jackie didn't want Michelle to do it. But Yeoh trusted director Stanley Tong, so she went for it. It was difficult and took several tries to get. In the outtakes Yeoh can be seen flying off the bike over the side of the train time after time—with only cardboard boxes on the ground to break her fall.

The stuntman who worked out the logistics did a test run and broke his leg when he hit the track. He's lucky—had he landed on his head, he'd have been paralyzed or dead.

Then there's poor Maggie Cheung. When we last left Maggie, she had been hospitalized after being hurt during a scene in *Police Story II*. Well, the trooper was back for *Supercop* and . . . we last see her being carted off after being tossed from a helicopter and bouncing off a car roof.

Jackie had his share of bruises, too. While filming the climactic fight finale, Chan was clipped by a helicopter passing by as he hung off the side of the train. During the stunt where Chan is hanging off the helicopter, he got hit so hard in one take he was almost knocked unconscious—while flying high in the sky.

And if you think the havoc of working with the helicopter and train was tough on the actors, the locals didn't have it so easy, either. Anytime the crew was filming those sequences and tying up the tracks, all the other trains in that neck of Malaysia had to come to a halt, creating horrific traffic jams.

With all this action, you would think the Hong Kong audience must have gone wild, no? That's right—no. *Supercop* ended up being a startling disappointment in Hong Kong, although it was a huge hit in Taiwan. In fact, it was the highest grossing film in Taiwanese history. And it was well received in other international markets. So what was up with the Hong Kongers?

One theory is that moviegoers were getting weary of police thrillers in general, no matter how spectacular or insane the stunts. Interestingly, there was a minor resurgence of good old-fashioned chopsocky kung fu around the time *Supercop* was released. Which just goes to show that even the most loyal audience can be fickle.

Some fans weren't happy that director Stanley Tong toned down Jackie's on-screen mania several notches and allowed Yeoh to really shine—not a common occurrence for any of Chan's costars. Jackie himself displayed little enthusiasm for the film. Maybe some of his feelings were caused by production headaches. After the budget debacle on *Operation Condor*, Jackie assured the moneymen that he would be more financially responsible this time around. Despite his promise, *Supercop* went over budget, partly because of the time Chan frittered away deciding how he wanted the movie to end.

As he tends to, Jackie went into a project without the idea firmly plotted out on paper. While such an open-ended style gives creativity plenty of elbow room, it's also a lousy way to conduct the business end of moviemaking. Which is one reason Chan is so leery of strutting his stuff in an American production filmed in Hollywood.

Even the biggest stars take a backseat to studio accountants.

Thanks to the favorable reception to *Rumble in the Bronx*, which was made years after *Supercop* but released first in America, Miramax rereleased *Supercop* after making some changes. First they changed the cop's name from Chen Chia Chu, or Golden Horse, to Kevin. Then instead of subtitles, the new American version was dubbed, a smart choice, since it's difficult to follow the action while your eyes are trying to read the often illegible words at the bottom of the screen.

Lastly, Miramax inserted a new title sequence along with a

different soundtrack that includes Top 40 faves like "What's Love Got to Do with It" and "Stayin' Alive." But the oddest touch had to be Tom Jones's cover of "Kung Fu Fighting."

CAST: Jackie Chan, Yuen Wah, Kin Tsang, Michelle Yeoh, Maggie Cheung, Bill Tung
DIRECTOR: Stanley Tong
EXECUTIVE PRODUCERS: Leonard Ho, Jackie Chan
PRODUCERS: Willie Chan, Edward Tang
WRITERS: Edward Tang, Fibe Ma, Lee Wai Yee
FIGHT/ACTION DIRECTOR: Stanley Tong
PRODUCTION COMPANY: Golden Harvest
DISTRIBUTOR: Miramax Films
U.S. RELEASE: 1992 (theatrical); 1996 (dubbed rerelease)
MANDARIN: Jing3 Cha2 Gu4 Shi4 III: Chao1 Ji2 Jing3 Cha2
AWARDS: Jackie won Taiwan's Golden Horse Award for Best Actor
A/K/A:

- *Police Story III*
- *Supercop: Police Story III*

CITY HUNTER (1992)
"Sing Si Lip Yan"

PLOT: Chan is Ryu Saeba (Kyu Seabo in some translations), a skirt-chasing, mercenary private detective. Now that his partner has been murdered, Ryu is working on his own—except for his pretty assistant, Kaori, the one woman he can't touch. Ryu promised his dying partner he would both take care of Kaori and never, ever seduce her. A fact he chooses not to tell the young woman.

Kaori, on the other hand, dreams of little else and can't understand why Ryu acts as if she's a sexless blob. Upset at his lack of interest, Kaori decides to take a cruise with a friend to try and purge Ryu from her heart.

Meanwhile, the P.I. is hired by a millionaire newspaper magnate to find his runaway daughter (named Shizuko or Kiyoko, depending on the version one screens). Even though it's his birthday, Ryu gets to work and tracks the wayward daughter to the same ship his assistant is on. Unknown to Ryu or anyone else, a band of terrorists are also on board preparing to take over the liner once it's at sea. Ryu stows away, then comes out of hiding to try and locate the daughter. He also wants to score some food—he hasn't eaten and is starving.

Just as he collars the runaway, the terrorists commandeer the ship. Led by "Mad Mac," an American military man gone bad, and his ninja henchmen, their plan is to rob the passengers, kidnap the wealthiest, and take them to Thailand, then hold them for ransom. Now while trying to keep a handle on the daughter, Ryu must also try to thwart the crooks' plans. And keep a rival female private eye named Saeko out of his way—a P.I. who is secretly in love with Ryu.

After a series of battles throughout the ship, Ryu foils the terrorists' plot and shows his true feelings to Kaori by pummeling the slimeball who tried to rape her. He also shows Kaori his fashion sense—he fights while dressed in drag.

Dressing in drag is particularly hilarious to Asian audiences. It plays flat in the United States (as do the many cross-eyed crooks in so many Hong Kong films). What some here may find a little less amusing are the slew of gay-bashing jokes permeating the original version of *City Hunter* that were subsequently edited out of the video version that came to the States. (They're still in the laser disc import, however.) What most Americans would consider politically incorrect humor—or just plain bad taste—can be perceived as funny in other cultures.

This is where Chan has an edge. His humor comes more from physical slapstick than jokes where the humor springs in large part from cultural factors and familiarity. While jokes that insult certain ethnic minorities might be sidesplitters in Hong Kong, they would cause tension and possibly worse if played to a general American audience. (The blackface sequence in the Sammo Hung/Yuen Biao film *Don't Give a Damn* is a perfect example.) It's a pitfall Chan tends to avoid, which is why his movies play as well in Peoria as they do in Shanghai. *City Hunter* was one of the few times a Jackie Chan film contained material that was removed because it would not have been well received elsewhere.

That aside, the first thing that really jumps out at you about *City Hunter*—besides Jackie's frocks—are the colors. Filmed in the bright, vivid primary colors à la the classic *Batman* television series, the movie succeeds in making the audience feel like they're watching a living cartoon. Which they're supposed to, since *City Hunter* is based on a popular Japanese comic/anime and video game character who womanizes his way through his crime-fighting life.

Although he's supposed to be playing a Lothario, Jackie lightens the character by playing him less as a wolfish, testosterone-driven playboy than a libidinous schoolboy. But plot and character are really secondary to the action, which begins with a skateboard chase scene that has Jackie "jumping" over a car coming at him head-on and landing back on the skateboard after he clears the car.

The reason *jumping* is in quotation marks is that if you look closely you'll see there's an unmistakable cut in the sequence where the scene has been edited mid-stunt. This is not a criticism. Springing off a skateboard over a speeding car and then landing on the skateboard as it emerges from under the car almost defies human body physics. It's noted only because Chan as well as his fans always seem loath to admit there might be one or two things he's incapable of doing without killing himself. There's no argument that Jackie does 99 percent of his stunts himself without any tricks or assistance, but every now and then either time constraints or the laws of physics require a little help.

Speaking of stunt aids, *City Hunter* also features wire work, which was coordinated by Ching Siu Tung. But that doesn't take away from the assortment of fight sequences that move the story along. Among the more memorable scenes is one where Bruce Lee helps Jackie defeat his opponents. The fight takes place in the ship's screening room where a Bruce Lee movie is playing. At first Ryu is on the losing end of the duel—until he uses the movie as his guide. By watching the film and imitating whatever kick or punch Lee does, Ryu is able to defeat the burly gangsters.

The scene probably talked about most often comes near the end. In it, Jackie is fighting an American foe when they suddenly turn into characters from the "Streetfighter 2" video arcade game. The Yank becomes Ken while Chan transforms into the Japanese sumo E. Honda—and female kickboxer Chun Li.

After the film was completed, Jackie dismissed the film, which has an *Under Siege* flavor to it, as a lesser effort. Whether he realizes it or not, Jackie tends to downplay any film that he didn't direct himself. This is obviously a man who has a very hard time sharing the stage with someone else's vision. Even though he knows taking on that responsibility is just too much with everything else he does, Chan still has a hard time letting go. Or giving other people the credit they perhaps deserve. But you don't get to be one of the most popular cinema stars in the world by having low self-esteem and minimal ego.

What's most surprising is that even though Jackie knows the demands of making a film, he stretched himself paper thin during the *City Hunter* shoot by working on stunts for another movie—*Crime Story*—simultaneously. But for some reason Jackie was on a mission to get more movies in the theaters after having released "only" three films between 1989 and 1991.

Of Special Note: Jackie break-dances during a fight sequence.

CAST: Jackie Chan, Joey Wang, Richard Norton, Chingmy Yau, Gary Daniels, Leon Lai, Kumiko Goto, Ken Low.
DIRECTOR: Wong Jing
PRODUCER: Chua Lam

FIGHT/ACTION DIRECTOR: Ching Siu Tung
PRODUCTION COMPANY: Paragon; Golden Harvest
DISTRIBUTOR: Paragon
U.S. RELEASE: 1993 (theatrical)
MANDARIN: Cheng2 Shi4 Lie4 Ren2

CRIME STORY (1993)
"Chung On Jo"

PLOT: An intense, dark drama has Jackie starring as Eddie Chan, a high-ranking Hong Kong police detective who is first seen during a psychiatric session with a pretty therapist. Eddie's issue is his inability to put a past shoot-out with terrorists behind him emotionally. Their deaths weigh on him, but he doesn't have much time to dwell on his emotional state. Eddie is assigned to a new case—a real estate magnate is convinced there's a plot to kidnap him afoot and wants protection.

Unfortunately, the businessman is indeed kidnapped and being held for a $60 million ransom. Mobilizing their forces, the police put together a special task force made up of many officers, including Detective Hung, who has volunteered for the assignment and who is made Eddie's partner. Unknown to Eddie and the others, the kidnapping plot was actually masterminded by Hung. Tired of scraping by as a lowly paid public servant, the once-good cop decided to cross the line to the other side. Along with some wealthy partners in crime, he carries out the kidnapping and from his inside vantage point keeps an eye on how close the police are getting.

An early confrontation during the investigation leads to a fellow officer getting shot. Eddie rushes him to the hospital in hopes of saving his life. But it's too late, the cop dies, and something inside Eddie shuts off. Not even his psychiatrist, who shows up at the hospital, can get through to him. Instead of reaching out to her, he rejects her offer of comfort. He decides to become an island.

It's not until the investigation leads Eddie to Taiwan that

he begins to suspect something rotten is going on with his new partner. As he manages to hunt down suspects and gets ever closer to solving the case, he must keep a wary eye on Hung without letting on he suspects him. Finally, Hung makes a move and tries to kill Chan. He fails, and Eddie collars him but is never able to bring him in. During a literally explosive climactic sequence in a burning building, Hung is mortally wounded. But before dying, the detective tells Eddie where the magnate is being hidden. He also tells Eddie that everyone in the force thinks he's crazy. Eddie says that's just the way he is.

After being rescued by the police, the businessman leaves Hong Kong to start over in a new country, leaving Eddie behind, still dealing with his demons.

This film is one of several Hong Kong true-crime movies that made a splash in the early 1990s like the creepy *Dr. Lamb*. *Crime Story* was based on the real-life kidnapping of a Hong Kong billionaire named Wong Tak Fai. Fittingly, the production has a kind of documentary feel to it as well as a dark atmosphere. Not as dark as John Woo, but a far cry from *City Hunter*.

Crime Story was an unusual choice for Jackie, but it was another effort on his part to expand his range. His first films of the 1990s can all be said to be changes of pace for Chan in one way or another. The results were a mixed bag. On the one hand *Crime Story* earned Jackie respect as a serious actor. He won Taipei's Best Actor award, called the Golden Horse, in 1994 for his performance in this film.

But Jackie fans were shell-shocked. Although they love seeing their hero doing pretty much anything on screen, this was not the Jackie they'd come to know and love. No silly situations, no shameless mugging for the camera, no endearing smiles and twinkling eyes. Instead they got a dead serious, very grown-up character who might not crack a single smile through the entire film.

What they do get is some of Jackie's best martial artistry

this side of a Sammo Hung–directed film. Also there is action with buildings burning and blowing up and some intense car chases in which an exasperated Jackie actually rights his over-turned vehicle. But there always seems to be this trade-off for Jackie fans—the more plot, the fewer of Jackie's antics. One reason why there tends to be so much fighting and action and so many stunts in most of Chan's movies is that the movement is filling the gaps where plot exposition normally would be.

Perhaps the one thing that made it clear this was not a typical Jackie film was the absence of outtakes shown over the closing credits. It's also interesting to note that *Crime Story* was originally developed for Jet Li, but that deal fell apart when Li and Golden Harvest had a falling out. And speaking of falling out, Chan admits he got rid of director Kirk Wong before the filming ended but kept Kirk's name on as director.

It should not be expected that Jackie will forsake action films anytime soon for serious drama. As Sylvester Stallone and other action stars have found out, core fans really don't want you to grow as an artiste if it means moving too far afield from what made you a star—and their idol—in the first place. But unlike Stallone and other American actors whose film production is limited by the workings of Hollywood studios, Chan can do a *Crime Story* for himself and within a matter of months have a another film in the theaters that gives Jackie fans their fix. The question is, how long can he physically keep that kind of schedule up?

Crime Story was originally scheduled for an August 1996 release in America, but Miramax pulled it. As of this printing, the release date had not been rescheduled.

CAST: Jackie Chan, Kent Cheng, Ken Low
DIRECTOR: Kirk Wong
PRODUCER: Chua Lam
WRITER: Chan Man Keung
FIGHT/ACTION DIRECTOR: Jackie Chan
AWARDS: Taipei's 1994 Golden Horse Award for Best Actor; Best Action Design, Best Editing H.K. Film Awards
MANDARIN: Zhong4 An4 Zu3

A/K/A:

- *Police Story IV*
- *Serious Crimes Squad*

PROJECT S (1993)
"Chiu Kap Gai Waak"

PLOT: Michelle Yeoh is back as the intense Mainland cop. This time, she is called back to Hong Kong to help try and stem a recent crime wave. What she doesn't know is that the ringleader of the thieves is her own boyfriend, a disgruntled Chinese soldier who wants to get rich quick.

Along with his cohorts, he plans to rob the Bank of Hong Kong, but the "supercopess" is there to thwart the caper.

Yeoh proves her smooth moves in *Supercop* were no fluke as she capably headlines this rather tense dramatic action film. Unencumbered with the absence of Jackie on this film, director Stanley Tong weaves a solid narrative and uses synch sound to boot—that is, sound recorded during the filming, not after—something that just up until recently Jackie was always dead set against. Since the dialogue is going to be dubbed into Mandarin and whatever else anyway, Chan's attitude is, why bother with synch sound?

Speaking of Jackie, he was up to his old cross-dressing tricks. In a cameo that is so out of place as to look like an outtake from *City Hunter*, Jackie appears in a jewelry story robbery sequence as an undercover cop—in drag, doing shtick that has no bearing on the plot. But since he was the producer, he could do whatever he wanted.

The bit took two days to film. On the positive side, he worked for free.

CAST: Michelle Yeoh, Michael Wong, Emil Chow, Dick Wei, Yu Rong Guang
DIRECTOR: Stanley Tong

PRODUCER: Jackie Chan
PRODUCTION COMPANY: Golden Way
U.S. RELEASES: 1993 (theatrical); 1994 (video)
MANDARIN: Chao1 Ji2 Ji4 Hua4
A/K/A:

- *Once a Cop*
- *Supercop 2*
- *Police Story IV*

DRUNKEN MASTER II (1994)
"Jui Keun II"

PLOT: Another story inspired by the Wong Fei-hung legend. The film picks up shortly after the original film left off, showing "Dragon" as a young man who is a bit more free-wheeling and easy than his father would care to see. The movie opens with the young Dragon, dojo brother Cowboy, and Dragon's fa- ther—a martial arts instructor and healer—on a train heading back home. Dragon is carrying a box that contains a ginseng root that was bought for one of his father's clients. To sneak it past customs, Dragon hides it in someone else's luggage.

When he and Cowboy go to the baggage compartment to retrieve the root, they find a thief rifling through the piece of luggage that holds their container. As it turns out, Dragon's ginseng box is identical to the box the thief is looking for. When Dragon checks on his root, he discovers there's been a switch. The box in his hands holds a priceless treasure, an im- perial jade seal. He goes after the mysterious thief, but the man gets away.

Later, Dragon learns that the old thief is actually a patriot trying to keep priceless national treasures out of the hands of smugglers. The plot is masterminded by members of the Brit- ish Consulate, who plan to steal valuable Chinese artifacts and smuggle them to England. Dragon joins forces with the old man, who is eventually killed by the smugglers' henchmen.

Enraged at his compatriot's death, Dragon takes on the smugglers themselves and after a series of confrontations,

eventually faces the smugglers' head henchman in a fiery refinery and defeats him using the ultimate form of Drunken
Fighting.

There's mixed feeling out there in the Chan fan world
about *Drunken Master II*. While nobody can deny that some of
the fight sequences must be seen to be believed, not everyone
agrees on where the movie ranks on Jackie's all-time list.
Some place it at or near the top, others feel it's all right but
nothing to enshrine. It probably depends on how one feels in
general about old-time period kung fu films.

Unlike *Supercop* or other modern-day action films, *Drunken
Master II* is a throwback to the films of Chan's early career,
which placed more emphasis on fighting-related action than
on stunt-fueled action. And the fights are something special.
Jackie uses his unique ability to turn anything into a weapon
and to use his environment to dictate the action. In one scene,
Jackie and the old patriot are battling dozens and dozens of Ax
Gang members. When they're finally trapped upstairs against
seemingly hopeless odds, Chan uses a pole of bamboo with a
shredded end to slice and dice his enemies. In another scene,
while fighting, Jackie tosses his mother's purse in the air,
ducks a blow, catches the purse, puts it against his opponent's
forehead, hits him, then catches the purse before it falls.

Similarly, there are several times when Chan throws wine
bottles in the air as he fights so they won't be broken, then
catches them before they hit the ground after giving an opponent a flurry of punches and/or kicks. For those of us who
have yet to master juggling three oranges even once, the timing involved is unimaginable.

Then there's the climactic battle at the movie's end with
Chan's real-life bodyguard Ken Low, which took nearly four
months to shoot. At one point, Chan falls onto a bed of hot
coals, and while on his back, he scoots across the embers. Feeling that his reaction to the searing coals wasn't realistic
enough, Jackie repeated the stunt. One can't help but wonder
at what point perfectionism crosses the line into recklessness.

In an example of the audience needing to suspend disbelief, Chan's stepmother in the movie is played by Anita Mui, and his father is played by Ti Lung, a man old enough to be Jackie's . . . slightly older brother.

From a film criticism standpoint, *Drunken Master II* suffers from some poor editing and character continuity. True, so do most of Jackie's movies, but here it is perhaps more noticeable because the film underwent some serious behind-the-camera problems.

As he is prone to do, Chan clashed with the style of the director—celebrated kung fu filmmaker Lau Kar-leung, who began making martial arts films when Jackie was a never-heard-of doing extra work on films. Lau comes from a family firmly entrenched in both kung fu and Hong Kong cinema history. Translated, this means Lau has his own ideas of how things should be done. *Drunken Master II* was developed to be another collaborative benefit effort, this time for the Hong Kong Stuntman Association. On the one hand it was a curious choice for a project because the recent resurgence in kung fu movies was already dying down. But it gave Jackie a chance to revisit a character that had been very good to him. And Lau Kar-leung knew his kung fu fighting.

The bigger question was why Jackie would agree to be in a situation reminiscent of *Twin Dragons*, which he subsequently complained had been hurt by the directors' vision not being in sync with his.

Chan later said he believed he had made clear his position on what the style of the film should be. And at first, things went along well enough. Lau and Chan appear together in an early fight scene that takes place *under* the train, an amazing spectacle of timing and choreography. But before long their collaboration began to unravel. Lau was dogged to make sure the fighting was real kung fu and not what he considered watered-down "action fighting." It forced Chan to buckle down and work at making sure his kung fu was technically correct—and he hated it. It went against his grain, and not surprisingly he felt constricted.

But when Lau also wanted the fighting "enhanced" just a bit, Jackie made a stand. "I felt Lau's style was too much of the old school. I wanted to shoot in the style that the audience wants to see." In other words, with dazzling acrobatics sandwiched between traditional martial arts moves. Frankly, it all works brilliantly.

Then there was the matter of Andy Lau, who is now a star in his own right. Originally, Andy Lau was supposed to have a substantial role as one of the Chinese traitors helping the foreign smugglers. But as it turned out, his role was cut to little more than a cameo.

The rifts added to the existing tension caused by the tight schedule under which they were working. *Drunken Master II* needed to be released in time for the Chinese New Year 1994, and there wasn't the time to haggle. So, Jackie fired Lau and took over the directing reins—although Jackie let Lau keep the credit for himself.

It didn't do much to soothe Lau's wounded pride. Soon after, Lau hired the snubbed Andy Lau to costar in *Drunken Master III* (Willie Kwai—a/k/a Willie Chi—starred as a very athletic Wong Fei-hung). Interestingly, it's probably much more of a true sequel to the original *Drunken Master* than Jackie's *II* version. In it, he tells the story of a teenage Wong Fei-hung, and although not a blockbuster, it was credited for showcasing martial arts the old-fashioned way, just how Lau likes it. The climactic fight, which begins inside a confessional and ends in a wine cellar, is a doozy.

In more recent times, Lau Kar-leung has been away from the movie scene due to health concerns, relocating to Singapore to recuperate from stomach cancer surgery and the follow-up treatment.

Despite the personality conflicts and pressure to finish the project on time, *Drunken Master II* worked and was a huge hit at the Hong Kong box office. It also featured one of the best and liveliest musical scores in a Chan film. It was the second-highest grossing film of 1994 behind *Return of the God of Gamblers*.

Which brings up one last issue—the very final shot of the film. During the finale, Dragon runs out of wine, so he starts swinging methanol, otherwise known as wood alcohol. While it jump-starts Dragon's Drunken fighting ability, it also has some serious side effects. Like turning him into a mental vegetable. The final image of the movie shows Dragon, cross-eyed with his tongue half hanging out, looking the very picture of mental deterioration. Insensitive? Obviously. Immature? Sure. Vintage Jackie Chan? Absolutely.

Of Special Note: Chan says this is his overall favorite film. It's ours, too.

CAST: Jackie Chan, Ti Lung, Anita Mui, Ken Low, Lo Wei Kong
DIRECTOR: Lau Kar-leung (Jackie Chan)
FIGHT/ACTION DIRECTOR: Jackie Chan
ACTION DESIGN: Jackie Chan's Stuntman Association
PRODUCTION COMPANY: Golden Harvest
DISTRIBUTOR: Paragon Films
U.S. RELEASE: 1994
AWARDS: Best Action Design 1994 H.K. Film Awards

CINEMA OF VENGEANCE (1994)

A British documentary examining the history of Hong Kong's kung fu and action movies. More comprehensive than 1990s *The Deadliest Art*, this documentary includes rare footage and interviews with a wide variety of actors and directors. Instead of concentrating on the Jackie Chan era, this film is a historical retrospective of the genre.

CAST: Jackie Chan, Simon Yam, Ti Lung, Yukari Oshima, Sophia Crawford, Lau Kar-leung
DIRECTOR: Toby Russel

RUMBLE IN THE BRONX (1995)
"Hong Faan Kui"

PLOT: In yet another incarnation of a Hong Kong cop, Chan stars as Keung, who is visiting the United States to oversee

the sale of his uncle's convenience store, located in the brutally violent section of the Bronx known as Fort Apache. Once
the store is sold, the uncle takes off on his honeymoon, leaving the new owner, Elaine, to fend for herself. Feeling responsible, Keung decides to stick around for a while and help Elaine
get settled in.

Immediately, the trouble begins. First, a bunch of extortionists take most of Elaine's profits as their "fee" for being
the local "protectors." Then a punk biker gang terrorizes
Elaine, shoplifting willy-nilly in the store. This forces Keung to
step in and assert himself. Later, the bikers retaliate by attacking him with beer bottles in an alley.

As it happens, one of the bikers has somehow come into
possession of a package of stolen diamonds worth millions,
which happens to belong to the mob. Not knowing what to do
with the stash, the biker hides the jewels in the seat cushion
of a wheelchair belonging to a Chinese kid who just so happens
to be the brother of a biker chick.

Having tracked down their diamonds, the mob stakes out
the biker chick's apartment. Once again, it's Keung to the
rescue, and he battles it out with the mobsters. The climactic
chase features a hovercraft chase through the streets of the
city with Jackie pursuing behind the wheel of a Lamborghini.
Eventually, Jackie gets on board the vehicle and uses it to run
down the chief villain. Though Elaine's store was destroyed by
the thugs, Keung ends up with the stolen diamonds.

Jackie originally got the idea for this film back in 1980,
when he came to America to film *The Big Brawl*.

"After I did that picture, I studied English, and that's when
I thought of doing a story where I come to America as a student and tangle with a local gang. But when I finally got back
to Hong Kong and tried to sell the idea to Raymond Chow, he
told me no. He said I was never on schedule and always over
budget and that they wouldn't let me do my kind of film in
America. So I had to wait until now."

Since he's not the age of a college student anymore he made

himself a visiting cop. If the plot summary seems a big disjointed, there is good reason. In a career that has seen plenty
of examples of plot-thin movies, *Rumble in the Bronx* ranks
among the more disjointed Jackie film in terms of maintaining
a marginally cohesive story line. The movie jumps from one
plot device to another. These are present only to provide a reason to launch into another action sequence—of which there
are many.

Speaking of inconsistencies, when did New York City
sprout mountains? In this production, Vancouver subbed for
New York, and while it's not unusual for Canadian locations
to fill in for American locales, most filmmakers tend to shoot
away from geographical landmarks that might give the game
away. What happened here was that midway through the
shoot, Chan decided it was just too much trouble to keep up
the illusion.

"We even hired people to paint graffiti on the walls," Chan
has said. "But then we had to hire other people to paint over
when we were done for the day. It was just too difficult. So we
just forget about it."

Jackie was a man possessed during this shoot. He didn't
even let a broken ankle stop him. He broke his ankle when
jumping from a bridge onto a hovercraft speeding by underneath. For the last twenty days of the shoot, Chan worked
in a cleverly hidden cast painted to look like a tennis shoe,
undeterred by what had to be a painful injury. He even water-
skied "barefoot," fracture be damned.

Jackie's foot wasn't the only casualty during filming. Two
stuntwomen and actress Françoise Yip broke their legs riding
motorcycles during the course of filming. Welcome to the
world of living dangerously, Jackie style. And yes, Yip was
back working despite the injury. Even director Stanley Tong
took lumps—he insisted on trying out every stunt, although
usually using a wire.

Jackie had tried to get his unbroken foot in the American
movie door twice before and failed miserably each time, so he
wasn't about to let a fractured ankle stand in his way. If he

didn't succeed this time, there very well might not be another time. That was why he also went for the brass ring in the action department:

See Jackie leap from the roof of a garage onto the next building's fire escape twenty feet away (three times from different angles with no mat below).

Cringe as Jackie narrowly misses being unmanned when he drops through a car sunroof just as a motorcycle passes overhead.

Watch open-mouthed as Jackie fights villains with everyday household appliances like a refrigerator and a shopping cart.

Once again, opinions of the film from Jackie fans range from one extreme to another. The consensus was: *Rumble in the Bronx* was not the best film to be his American redebut—not even close. Those familiar with his body of work would have much preferred their man be showcased in something like *Drunken Master II* or *Police Story* or *Supercop*. But even American audiences forgot about plot and character development when faced with a human superman. No fear. No stuntman. No equal.

Rumble in the Bronx might not have been Chan's best film, but it was the number one film at the Hong Kong box office in 1995, and it was good enough to finally get him the name recognition he'd been desperately looking for in the United States. The scene where Chan appears in some tight skivvies probably didn't hurt either—more than one moviegoer reported hearing cat calls from appreciative women.

And the continuity problems certainly didn't affect the movie's box office tallies—*Rumble in the Bronx* opened number one, pulling in almost $10 million in its first week in the United States. Not bad, considering it cost only $15 million to make. A bargain basement price in Hollywood terms, where the *average* movie today costs from $36 to $54 million.

More telling about this film's popularity in Asia is that it was number two at the box office for the year, second only to *Jurassic Park*.

Of Special Note: A scene where Jackie scales the parking garage wall, making rock climbers look like slackers.

CAST: Jackie Chan, Anita Mui, Bill Tung, Françoise Yip
DIRECTOR: Stanley Tong
PRODUCER: Barbie Tung
WRITER: Edward Tang
FIGHT/ACTION DIRECTORS: Jackie Chan, Sammo Hung
ACTION DESIGN: Jackie Chan's Stuntman Association; Sammo Hung's Stuntman Association
PRODUCTION COMPANY: Golden Harvest
DISTRIBUTOR: New Line Cinema
U.S. RELEASE: 1995 (theatrical); 1996 (video)
MANDARIN: Hong2 Fan1 Qu1
AWARDS: Best Action Design 1996 H.K. Film Awards

THUNDERBOLT (1995)
"Pik Lik Foh"

PLOT: In his usual role as an underdog, Chan plays an auto mechanic named Jackie who returns to Hong Kong after losing his job at a Mitsubishi factory in Japan for taking a "crash-proof" prototype he developed out for an unauthorized test drive. Now back home, he works for a police task force trying to crack down on illegal racing, which has caused many fatalities. The police rely on Jackie's ability to identify illegally souped-up cars just by their sound.

One night, Jackie happens to be out towing away cars when a professional race car driver-hitman (now there's a very 1990s kind of dual career) named Cougar, whose favorite pastime is illegal racing, zooms by. Jackie jumps in his car and takes on Cougar in a wild car race-chase through town, ultimately outdriving Mr. Killer. Afterward, Cougar is arrested by an Interpol agent. Now Cougar is out for revenge, especially once he's back out on the street, courtesy of his corrupt lawyer.

Using a crane, Cougar destroys Jackie's home and kidnaps

his two sisters. The ransom: a grudge match between Cougar and Jackie at a racetrack in Japan. While following the breaking story of Jackie's troubles, a pretty Hong Kong reporter develops a crush on him and becomes personally involved. Along with his police buddies, she helps finance a racing car for him so he can go to Japan and rescue his sisters.

In Japan, Jackie finds out fast that Cougar plays dirty. After he posts terrific trial times, Cougar's henchmen trash his car, leaving him without a vehicle for the race. At the last minute, though, Jackie's old Mitsubishi boss comes to the rescue and has his workers modify a car for Jackie to use in the race.

The race itself is brutal, with members of Cougar's team intentionally causing accidents, hoping to wipe Jackie out. But Jackie is a superior driver, and always manages to outmaneuver whatever they throw at him, staying right on Cougar's tail. Frustrated, furious, and fearful he's going to lose the race, Cougar resorts to his last option, smashing his car directly into Jackie's. Guess who wins?

Even Jackie fans have to admit that *Thunderbolt* hits an all-time low as far as quality of plot. There *is* no plot, really. There is simply dialogue that fills the space between the next series of stunts.

By now, it's clear that minimal story development should be an expected element of most Jackie Chan films. They are meant to entertain, not stimulate thought. Jackie himself admits that the story is put in after the stunts and action scenes are played out. And that's more than fine.

But a "moving picture" needs at least a semicohesive semblance of plot to maintain the pretense of being a "film." Otherwise, why not simply edit together a series of filmed stunts and action sequences and release it as *The Big Reel of Stunts and Car Crashes* or *Stunt-o-Rama* or whatever. Then only those interested in watching stunt people perform will be satisfied while those hoping to see something more like a movie can spend their money elsewhere.

Many Hong Kong reviewers were scathing in their reviews of this film, lashing out at both the cost and lack of depth.

Of course, these discussions are irrelevant to Chan fans, who would show up regardless of what was on the screen, as evidenced by *Thunderbolt* breaking an opening day box office record by taking in over HK$4 million. The film would go on to break all existing Honk Kong records.

But big ticket sales aside, even Jackie doesn't look like he's having a whole lot of fun in this one, playing the revenge-obsessed mechanic-turned-driver. But there may be good reason for that. *Thunderbolt* has more violence, less humor, and fewer physical stunts than a typical Jackie Chan action movie. And plenty more car crashes.

With a budget close to US$30 million (HK$200 million) *Thunderbolt* is the most expensive Hong Kong film ever made. (It breaks a record he set with *Operation Condor*.) The cars destroyed during the filming alone cost over US$2 million, including the cost of shipping them to Hong Kong from Japan. Ironically, the original Gordon Chan script was supposed to be a small, intimate film about the lives of illegal race car drivers. Instead the story was gutted to make room for action shots.

As far as the film's action sequences are concerned, some of the racing footage is sped up to the point where it looks like the drivers are manning rocket cars. Some might call it heightened reality, others bad filmmaking. Ultimately, the viewers will decide for themselves.

On the positive side, a fight in a video game arcade is nicely done with some clever use of trampolines and acrobatics. Unfortunately, it's ruined too often with quick cuts. Jackie fans like to see him do a stunt from start to finish. Most of the action in the film is of the four-wheeled variety with one particularly nasty shot of a race car crashing through a tower at the track. There were so many stunt drivers injured that the producers express their apologies in the credits.

Originally, hot star Carrie Ng was supposed to appear in *Thunderbolt*, but her part was edited out from the final cut. It's a good bet she didn't lose any sleep over it. Relative Hong

Kong cinema newcomer Anita Yuen, however, was left in. The twenty-four-year-old former Miss Hong Kong is considered a definite up-and-comer in the movie biz, having won the Best Actress Hong Kong Film Award in 1994 for her performance in *C'est La Vie Mon Cheri*. There's also some dish circulating that some of the more established actresses, like Maggie Cheung, think young Anita is having stardom handed to her without having to suffer through bad B movies like the rest of them did.

But Jackie seems to like her, so it wouldn't be surprising to see her pop up in future Chan films. The only problem is that Jackie seems very reticent to actually participate in an on-screen romance unless it's juvenile or completely devoid of chemistry. In the *Police Story* films, if you didn't know that Maggie Cheung's character was supposed to be his longtime girlfriend, they could almost pass for brother and sister.

In the United States, *Thunderbolt* was not released in America's Chinese neighborhoods the way all his other films had been. It was a conscious business decision on Chan's part. Hoping to keep increasing his film presence in the United States, he decided to wait and gave *Thunderbolt* a general wide release via his American distributor.

Of Special Note: The stunt sequence when Jackie is inside a huge container suspended from a crane. The container is going to be used to demolish a garage next to the crane. Before it can, Jackie jumps out onto the garage's second floor, dives over a balcony, somersaults in the air, then lands—flat on his back—as the wall above him is destroyed.

CAST: Jackie Chan, Anita Yuen, Michael Wong, Ken Low, Chor Yuen, Thorsten Nickel
DIRECTOR: Gordon Chan
PRODUCER: Leonard Ho
WRITERS: Gordon Chan, Chan Hing Ka, Kwok Wai Chung
FIGHT/ACTION DIRECTORS: Jackie Chan, Sammo Hung, Frankie Chan

216   Jeff Rovin and Kathy Tracy

ACTION DESIGN: Jackie Chan's Stuntman Association; Sammo
   Hung's Stuntman Association
CAR STUNT DIRECTOR: Frankie Chan
PRODUCTION COMPANY: Golden Harvest
DISTRIBUTOR: Miramax (International); New Line Cinema (U.S.)
U.S. RELEASE: scheduled 1997
MANDARIN: Pi1 Li4 Huo3

FIRST STRIKE (1996)
"Ging Chaat Goo Si IV: Zhi 1 Gaan Daan Yam Mo"

PLOT: This time Jackie's Hong Kong Supercop Ka is enlisted by
the CIA to go undercover and help investigate an international
arms smuggling gang. The suspect is a Russian showgirl
whose partner is a former Australian CIA agent of Chinese de-
scent turned big-time weapons dealer.

The smugglers eventually sniff Jackie out, resulting in a
frigid confrontation on a snowy Ukraine mountainside. After a
hair-raising snowmobile/snowboard chase scene, Jackie is rescued and sets out again to find the smuggler who has stolen
a nuclear warhead and taken it back to Australia.

Once he arrives Down Under, Jackie tries to get the ex-
CIA agent's sister to help him and even visits her father in
the hospital. But other evil forces looking to get their hands
on the warhead kill the father, framing Jackie. So now he has
to clear his name as well as find the weapon.

One of the confrontations takes place inside an aquarium
shark exhibit, with the man-eaters helping the Hong Kong cop
take care of a few bad guys. Eventually Jackie retrieves the
warhead, preventing nuclear destruction, and clears his name.

First Strike has some of the best production values of any
Chan vehicle. It's a very crisp-looking film. The story itself is
a bit convoluted, but it doesn't take too many illogical turns.

The locations where the film was shot—Russia and Australia—give Jackie's imagination some new stimuli for stunt creation. Using the expansive backdrop of the Russian Ural

Mountains, Chan choreographs a chase across the snow that would make George Lazenby queasy. On snowboard and snowmobile, Chan outruns a small army of smugglers, flying down the mountainside, careening perilously close to a sheer drop-off. Just as the bad guys are closing in, a helicopter suddenly comes into view from the bottom of the screen. Jackie sails off the mountainside and grabs onto the whirlybird's runner as several henchmen plummet to their deaths. His hat is demolished by the rotor. (Actually it's demolished by a small charge set inside the seal-face hat. Jackie was close to the rotor blades but not *that* close.)

Although not a stunt, Jackie shows his physical toughness in another way. For quite a bit of the Russian footage, shot outside in what is clearly very cold weather, Chan isn't wearing a coat. All he has on is a shirt. During the end credits he flashes the camera to show viewers he's not protected by any insulated underwear.

When the action moves from the snow and mountains to the Southern Hemisphere and Australia, Chan uses an aquarium as the setting for two different sequences that must have left a lot of stuntmen waterlogged beyond recognition.

First, Jackie stages a fight while swimming underwater in the shark tank—and it's obvious those are real sharks circling around. He touches one in the closing credit outtakes.

Later in the scene, on the observation side of the tank, one of the men chasing Jackie shoots a bullet through the tank's safety glass, shattering it and releasing a monsoon of water.

But the most amazing water stunt is a brief sequence that happens so fast that if you aren't watching the movie on a laser disc or video where you can replay the frames, you might think you didn't really see what you think you did. During a scene where Jackie is being chased by some bad guys, he eludes them by running across a swimming pool.

Let's rewind and look at that in slow motion.

Chan leaps from one side of the pool, uses a small float in the pool as a stepping stone, and lands feet first on the other side of the pool. There's only a minor slip as he springs off the float that perhaps gets his shoes a bit wet. Not bad, considering the rest of us would be under eight feet of water.

And one of the more creative sequences on land takes place in Chinatown during a parade. Jackie ends up fighting a six-foot-ten Russian KGB agent while walking on stilts.

But no day at the Jackie Chan office is complete without a medical report, and *First Strike* had its share of mishaps. During a startling fight scene in which he uses a ladder to defend himself, Chan got bruises, scrapes, and assorted crunched fingers, but the most serious injury came during another action sequence when Jackie got hit in the head and seriously injured his nose. Even so, he was back at work the next day. A local Australian newspaper reporting on the mishap referred to Jackie as "heaven's favorite."

Maggie Cheung, however, certainly wasn't on Jackie's top ten list. For the first time, Jackie's *Police Story* cop girlfriend, May, is nowhere to be found. A good old-fashioned salary dispute is the reason. Since *First Strike* was shot almost entirely on location, Chan wanted to use Cheung for only two days of work. He claims that she wanted to get paid as if she had worked for weeks; Jackie decided it was too much money. Who knows how Maggie felt about the impasse, but her insurance company had to be thrilled.

For some reason, the production company had a difficult time deciding on a "sub-name" for this fourth *Police Story* installment. Before *First Strike* was settled on, the film was variously called *Simple Mission*, *Story of CIA*, and the oddest, *Piece of Cake*. Interestingly, Jackie didn't like the *First Strike* choice, thinking it was "too Van Damme."

No matter what they called it, any *Police Story* sequel can expect to do good business, and *First Strike* was no exception. The movie broke weekend box office receipts when it opened in Hong Kong and was on line with *Rumble in the Bronx*'s overall ticket sales.

CAST: Jackie Chan, Jackson Lou, Annie Wu, Bill Tung, Yuri Petrov, Terry Woo

PRODUCER: Barbie Tung
DIRECTOR: Stanley Tong
WRITERS: Stanley Tong, Nick Tramontane
FIGHT/ACTION DIRECTORS: Stanley Tong, Jackie Chan
ACTION DESIGN: Jackie Chan's Stuntman Association
PRODUCTION COMPANY: Golden Harvest
DISTRIBUTOR: New Line Cinema
U.S. RELEASE: 1997
MANDARIN: Jing3 Cha2 Shi4 IV Ji Jian3 Dan1 Ren1 Wu4
A/K/A:

- *Police Story IV*

A NICE GUY (1996)

PLOT: Set in Australia. Jackie plays a popular chef with his own television show. One day, his life is thrown into chaos when he finds a strange tape mixed in with his cooking tape. It is a video of one gang leader murdering the leader of a rival gang. Naturally, the mobster wants the tape back, and Jackie suddenly finds himself on the run.

This is the first time Jackie has made a film entirely in English. *The Big Brawl* and *The Protector* were not *his* films—in those he was simply an actor for hire.

Taking over the directing reins is Sammo Hung, who for the first time in his long career has a big-time budget to work with. And he's going to town with it. Among the action sequences in *A Nice Guy* is one where Jackie drives the world's largest monster truck through several buildings. There's also a tightly choreographed fighting scene that takes place inside a van.

Sammo's reunion with Jackie comes after Chan's repeated collaborations with Stanley Tong, who directed *Supercop*, *First Strike*, and *Rumble in the Bronx*. According to an interview with Chan, Sammo's star has diminished to the point where he's been all but shut out of acting and was having a hard time finding directing work as well. Jackie says that he was advised against having Sammo direct but insisted—although he does add that Hung "cannot act in the movie."

Chan goes on to explain that there is a tradition in Hong Kong that you mustn't associate with people who've had a run of bad luck. (American translation in movie terms: box office bombs.) You're supposed to wait until they change their luck before going to them again. Sounds like a catch-22. How is someone supposed to turn it around if nobody lets them work anymore?

So there's as much riding on *A Nice Guy* for Sammo as there is for Jackie. Actually, probably more, since Jackie already has the ideas for his next two films lined up. At least as of this moment, he plans to do them with Stanley Tong. The first is a fireman saga, the other is a western.

A western actually has a lot of good possibilities, considering the Chinese influence and assistance in settling parts of the American West. Beyond that, it would be fitting for him to do a western. It could be argued that the American West, with its rich history and mythology, is an ideal metaphor for Jackie Chan. Here is a man who forged his own road and against great odds carved out a unique niche. Regardless of the imitators who have come and gone, Jackie continues to ride tall in his own celluloid saddle, marching to the sound of a slightly different drummer.

Of Special Note: A stunt where Jackie jumps from a building and grabs on to the end of a giant crane, which swings him across a river.

CAST: Jackie Chan, Richard Norton, Gabrielle Fitzpatrick, Karen Mclymont, Peter Lindsay
DIRECTOR: Sammo Hung
WRITER: Edward Tang
PRODUCTION COMPANY: Golden Harvest
DISTRIBUTOR: New Line Cinema

AN ALAN SMITHEE FILM (1997)

PLOT: A black comedy that satirizes the often back-stabbing business of making Hollywood movies. The title refers to the fake name inserted in movie credits when a disgruntled director refuses to let his name be used.

This is not your father's Jackie Chan film. For the first time in memory, Chan will star in a nonaction film. That's right, no kicks or punches, just Joe Eszterhas-written dialogue. He is, of course, best known for writing *Showgirls*.

Chan's first inclination was to turn down the film, until his old friend Sylvester Stallone intervened and persuaded him to accept.

Even though he's just one member of a large ensemble cast, comprised mostly of celebrities playing themselves, Jackie has said in interviews with the press that he realizes he's entering uncharted territory and he's admittedly nervous about it.

"I don't want the audience to enter the theater thinking, 'Let's see Jackie doing a stunt!' I don't like that. I want the audience to go to see a Jackie Chan movie that can include action, drama, humor, comedy, stunt, or action. *Everything*. Even if there are no stunts or no action, it's still a Jackie Chan movie. that's what I want to do. I want to be seen as more than just a stuntman. I want people to think of me as an actor, too.

"I'm slowly changing. Of course, as time goes on I have to do some movies without action. If the audience doesn't like to see me in that kind of movie, then I'll fail on that level and that's something I'm really scared of. I'm really scared. But I want to change audience thinking about me a little bit."

CAST: Jackie Chan, Sylvester Stallone, Eric Idle, Coolio, Whoopi Goldberg
DIRECTOR: Arthur Hiller
WRITER: Joe Eszterhas
PRODUCERS: Joe Eszterhas, Ben Myron, Andrew Vajna

Incredibly Strange Picture Show: Jackie Chan

A documentary series that currently airs periodically on cable's Discovery Channel first aired in 1989, long before most people had ever heard of Jackie Chan. Despite his near-total anonymity in America, his desire to be accepted here was obvious. In the installment on Jackie, the star made the following statement:

"I want to be in the history books. Bruce Lee, number one. John Wayne, number two. And Jackie Chan, number three."

To say that he's almost killed himself trying to fulfill this goal would be figuratively and literally true.

It's also interesting to note that in the program Chan also predicted he'd be able to continue his action-film career for only three, maybe four years. Of course, he gives himself the same timetable now. A more logical guess is that he'll keep doing it until his body literally commands him to stop.

成
龍   MYSTERY MOVIES   成
龍

Below are listed some mystery movies—titles that do not appear to be distinct, unique Jackie Chan films.

They are either compilations put together to make a quick buck or alternative titles that have worked their way into some Chan filmographies. Most telling is that none of the following films shows up on Jackie's official acting filmography.

Granted, Chan did a lot of clinkers in the 1970s that he and everybody else would just as soon forget, but he was a star in the 1980s, the decade listed for many of these mystery movies. Beyond that, there's a curious lack of information about most of these films.

Until somebody can actually produce a physical copy of,

say, *Gold Hunter* that proves conclusively it is a new film and not just an alternate title of a different film, then *Gold Hunter* and the others will remain in the mystery movie category.

Remember, all it takes is one slip for a film title to become "fact." As reported previously, many filmographies include a Chan-produced film called *Rough*, when in fact the name of the film is *Rouge*. Just a typo or quirky translation and *voila*—a mystery movie.

Another possibility is that some of these films were considered small, "arty" films. And if such a production doesn't become a hit, it is quite possible it falls through the cracks.

But until copies of the movies in question pop up, or a printed article from a local newspaper or magazine is found, it'll be impossible to be sure one way or the other, and the movies below will continue to exist only on lists, treading water in mystery movie limbo.

MARVELOUS FISTS (1982)

PLOT: ????

By 1982 Chan's career was on the rise, so it's a good bet any costume drama released on video in 1982 was yet another attempt by someone to cash in on his newfound stardom. It's entirely possible *Marvelous Fists* is an alternate title for *The Young Tiger*, the compilation put together by Lo Wei and originally released in 1980.

It's also possible this is another title for the reworked *Master with Cracked Fingers*.

JACKIE CHAN'S BLOODPACT (????)

PLOT: Jackie fights a bunch of people.

A retread of *The Young Tiger?*

THE INVINCIBLE FIGHTER—THE JACKIE CHAN STORY
(1996)

PLOT: Jackie fights a bunch of people.

A definite retread of *The Young Tiger*, with new Cantonese narration dubbed over. Delightfully incoherent subtitles for those with way too much time on their hands.

GOLD HUNTER (1985)
"Lo Sue Gaai"

PLOT: ????

In many Chan filmographies, Jackie is listed as a producer for this title. Also named are two cast members—Wu Ma and Liu Chia-yung. These two veteran actors have worked together a few times in their careers, first in the 1974 release *Seven Soldiers of Kung Fu*, Sammo Hung's *Eastern Condors*, and on Jackie's *My Lucky Stars* and *First Mission*. Beyond all that, both men are accomplished directors in the industry. However, nowhere is there to be found a plot summary of this movie.

Of the films mentioned above, *First Mission* is the only one Jackie produced. The literal translation of the Cantonese title—*Old Rat Street*—doesn't really cause a light bulb to go off, either, so therein lies the mystery.

LISTED CAST: Wu Ma, Liu Chia-yung
LISTED PRODUCER: Jackie Chan
MANDARIN: Lao3 Shu3 Jie1

HIGHWAY (????)

PLOT: ????

LISTED PRODUCER: Jackie Chan

RED LIPS (????)
"Ma Bo Chong Baat Gwaan"

PLOT: ????

Some lists misspell this film's name as *Read Lips*. Jackie has never played a deaf character, although his real-life hearing is certainly impaired.

LISTED CAST: Frankie Chan, Suet Lei
LISTED PRODUCER: Jackie Chan
MANDARIN: Zi1 Bao3 Chuang3 Ba1 Guan1

ENCHANTING NIGHT (197?)

PLOT: ????

This filmography phantom was supposedly produced by Jackie sometime in the 1970s. Producers were reluctant to hire him to act in films, much less run the whole show.

As with *Gold Hunter* and *Red Lips*, cast members are listed but no plot line is given, meaning the filmographers have not actually seen the movie. Interestingly, the film stars Ray Lui and Angile Leung, both relatively well-known Hong Kong actors, so it seems odd this would be so obscure.

Most logical explanation: There was a producer named Jackie Chan who isn't "our" Jackie.

CAST: Kung Chi-yan, Ray Lui, Angile Leung

IS IT OR ISN'T IT?

Here's a movie that does appear to be a distinct film, although it is not included on any filmography.

REAL KUNG FU OF SHAOLIN—PART I (19??)

PLOT: An evil leader and his henchmen run amok, looting and pillaging. When one of the villagers refuses to turn over his shop, he's murdered. The shopkeeper's wife sends her young son to the Shaolin for his safety and so he can learn kung fu to avenge the death of his father.

When he's an adult, he decides it's time to leave, but he can't until he proves his ability by sword, pole, and hand fighting. That done, he heads back home where he immediately stirs up trouble. After he kills a villain, the bad guys take over his uncle's restaurant and kill his mother.

Now he has to avenge the death of his father—and mother. Which he does.

When checking under Jackie's real Cantonese name, Sing Lung, this curious entry emerges from the shadows. The plot sounds suspiciously similar to *Master with Cracked Fingers*, the 1971 disaster that was shelved until Chan became popular years later. But then again, it also sounds suspiciously like *Shaolin Wooden Men*. Most of the kung fu costume dramas had nearly identical plots, so the similarity in and of itself means nothing—other than that screenwriters didn't get paid for originality.

It is known that early in his career Jackie was a journeyman, picking up whatever film work he could wherever he could get it, both in Hong Kong and Taiwan. Also, during the time of his nasty little fallout with Lo Wei when he fled Hong Kong out of fear for his life, Jackie made some films in Taiwan just to keep busy.

What's most curious about *Real Kung Fu of Shaolin—Part 1* is that except for actor Yang Lung—who also appeared in *Flying Claw Fights 14 Demons* and *13 Evil Bandits*—this is the only film credit for everyone else listed, actors as well as the producer and director. It's that old Sherlock Holmes wisdom— what's curious is what the dog didn't do. In this case it's what the cast didn't do, and apparently they didn't make any other films. Their careers began and ended with *Real Kung Fu*.

Highly unlikely.

More likely is that for some reason they were all using pseudonyms. And though Sing Lung *is* Jackie's real name, he never used it in a film. Unlike now, when Chan has avid fans who can tell you how many pairs of shoes he goes through in a year, back then most people just didn't care enough to know every detail about Jackie. He could use his real name and most probably nobody would be the wiser.

Perhaps the film was made as a "favor" to a local Triad and nobody wanted to be identified with the film while it was shooting. Or maybe, just for fun, everyone decided to use their Cantonese names so nobody would know who the actors were.

So far, a copy of this video has proved elusive. Until one is tracked down, it'll be uncertain whether this particular Sing Lung is our Sing Lung.

CAST: Sing Lung (Jackie Chan?), Kong Lai Lai, Yung Lu Sam, Yang Lung
DIRECTOR: Ko Yeung
PRODUCER: Yeung Hing Chi
PRESENTED BY: Yeung Hing Sang
SUPERVISOR: Yeung Hing Wan
FIGHT/ACTION DIRECTOR: Zaung Sea Yang
DISTRIBUTOR: Ocean Shores Video
U.S. RELEASE: 1986 (video)

THE
11 *Fighting*
成 JACKIE CHAN
龍

Although you really don't need to be a martial arts master to enjoy Jackie's early kung fu films, knowing a few basics about the history of the discipline and having some familiarity with fighting styles and terminology may help in understanding what the heck is going on in the movie. Heaven knows subtitles can't be trusted to clarify the action.

This chapter is divided into three sections: a brief history of kung fu, a glossary of frequently heard terms or names, and a description of the styles most relevant to Jackie's movies. In other words, since he didn't star in a film called *Tai Chi Champ*, we won't be delving into the intricacies of that discipline, although Drunken Fighting will be fleshed out. Unless noted otherwise, all the styles listed are Chinese.

And just to clarify:

Karate is the generic, umbrella term for **Japanese** martial arts. The literal translation is "empty hand."

Kung fu is the generic, umbrella term for **Chinese** martial arts. Its literal translation means "a skill achieved after long practice." And in truth, the fighting styles below cannot be learned quickly—they are intricate, complex disciplines.

The history of kung fu is a detailed story that is getting only a brief retelling here. There are literally hundreds of styles, but only those most relevant to Jackie's movies are being singled out.

THE HISTORY OF KUNG FU

According to legend, kung fu was developed at the Song Shan Shaolin Temple in Hunan Province during the Northern Wei dynasty about five hundred years after Christ. As opposed to the Hong Kong film industry, which can't even keep track of what year a movie was made, China still has county records from A.D. 464 that state the first chief monk at the temple was named Batuo.

Around A.D. 527 a Buddhist monk named Master Pu Ti Da Mo came to Canton, China, and from there made his way to the temple. But not knowing who this stranger was, the monks denied Da Mo admittance, so he toddled off to the first cave he could find and settled in to meditate.

After many years of solitude, he emerged from the cave and wrote two books: *Yi Jin Jing* and *Xi Sui Jin*. The *Yi Jin Jing* explained how to improve the monks' physical health and their strength. The *Xi Sui Jin* taught the monks how to nourish and empower the brain using *ch'i*, which might be simply described as the force of life. The *Xi Sui Jin* discipline was very difficult to learn, so its training methods were passed down secretly to only a select few over the years.

The Shaolin monks were ready to accept Do Ma by the time he emerged from the cave. They were impressed with his teachings and his abilities, which were so strong that the power of his stare was said to have bored a hole through the cave wall.

Martial arts, called Wu Shu, had already been around in China for several centuries by this time, but under the Shaolin monks, and via Da Mo, they evolved into a unique and definitive style.

Not only did the monks gain physical strength through their new discipline, but their ability to concentrate on their meditations increased as well. As time went on, the monks began developing even more exercises, using animal attack and defense postures as models. The Shaolin temple was said to be divided into thirty-five different chambers, each one specializing in a different fighting skill.

As news of the monks' new martial art spread, students converged on the temple in hopes of learning the discipline, called kung fu. Many who came would fail, and only those with the right combination of mental toughness and physical ability would succeed.

It is important to understand that Wu Shu in any form was more than just fighting skills to the people of China—it was truly a way of life. As one saying goes regarding a related martial arts form, "One is or one becomes Gong Fu—it is not something one does." Besides the physical component, it encompasses a philosophy in the "art" of living, and that philosophy is based heavily on teachings from Daoism (Taoism) and Confucianism as well as Buddhism.

Throughout the history of Shaolin, life there was intentionally Spartan. The hardships were intended to strengthen the spirit while toughening the body. Teachers told their disciples that they should never be afraid of the pain they would surely endure during training. Whether injured or ill or sweltering in heat or freezing in cold, they must train—day after day, week after week, decade by decade, in order to master Shaolin kung fu.

Those who persevered came away with supra-human abilities that in actuality made them the original lethal weapons. But aren't Buddhists supposed to be pacifists? Yes, and kung fu doesn't contradict that. To the Buddhist way of thinking, kung fu leads to a better understanding of violence and, as a result, a better understanding of how to *avoid* conflict. Their students were never the attackers, nor did they use their skills to the maximum. Instead they were taught to use the minimum skills necessary in any given situation.

However, it is true that the more violent an assault against them is, the greater the response to it. The bottom line is: Buddhists are not really being violent. They are simply refusing to accept the harm directed at them, and instead they turn it back to the aggressor.

The monks quickly realized that along with these powerful skills came the danger of misuse. Leery of divulging their secrets to any students with malicious intent, the monks developed a set of strict rules for admittance: Lies would not be tolerated, disobedience was punishable by banishment, those who learned kung fu promised to obey the laws of the land and assist people whenever possible. Those who failed to comply were to be pursued by the temple priests and executed.

Da Mo died in the Shaolin temple in A.D. 536 and was buried on Xiong Er mountain. But his legacy continued to live and thrive. Chinese emperors encouraged Shaolin monks to train their own "soldiers." In a way, it was necessary because it enabled the monks to protect the valuable Shaolin land from the packs of roving bandits terrorizing the countryside. Thieves quickly learned to give the temple a wide berth because of these warrior monks, called Seng Bing.

Sometime during the Sung dynasty (A.D. 960–1279) a Seng Bing named Qiu Yue Chan Shi wrote a book, *The Essence of Five Fists*, which discussed the training methods and applications of the Dragon, Tiger, Snake, Panther, and Crane styles. It's a good thing he did, because then came the dark days.

When the Manchus came to power, beginning what was known as the Ching dynasty, they worried that the Hans would rebel, using their martial arts skills. To prevent this feared uprising, martial arts training was outlawed for almost five hundred years, from 1644 until 1911.

To preserve the knowledge, Shaolin techniques were passed to laymen outside the temple. Martial arts training actually continued at the temple, but in closely guarded secrecy. Instead of thousands of Seng Bing proudly defending their land, there were only a few hundred secretly trained Seng Bing left by the turn of the century with nothing left to guard but their knowledge.

Outside the temple, as kung fu spread throughout the country, northern and southern sects emerged. Very generally speaking, the southerners emphasized hand techniques and the northerners stressed kicking and leg techniques. Both utilized a variety of weapons. Traditionally, individual families—or clans—passed their own special style down through successive generations. This is why there are so many different styles today.

When the Ching dynasty finally fell in 1912, martial arts made a comeback. But in 1928, a catastrophe occurred—the Shaolin temple was destroyed during the Chinese Civil War. The fire lasted forty days, and all the main buildings burnt to the ground, along with their precious contents—priceless books and records about the Shaolin martial arts.

Now the temple secrets could only be gleaned and passed down via that handful of secretly trained Seng Bing. And in fact, many masters were brought together for just that purpose by the Chinese government, which recognized the value of this ancient art.

In the 1950s, the government refurbished the temple at Hunan. In recent years it has become a bit of a tourist trap, with snack shops dotting the landscape and tours of the premises available. It amuses some Chinese whenever they see a Coca-Cola sign—a translation of the soft drink's name is "bite a wax tadpole." Wonder if Pepsi knows that?

Others are not so good-humored about the holy temple being turned into an amusement attraction. They point out that although Wu Shu is taught currently at the temple, Shaolin kung fu is not. It is insulting to many purists that some of the so-called monks work at the concession stands when not teaching Wu Shu.

It's a tricky issue. Although the Communist Chinese government takes credit for bringing back kung fu, there are those who believe they are also trying to keep a lid on it by making it available—but not *too* available. A recent article on the subject puts it this way:

> The Chinese government, it should be remembered, is communist and doesn't want a religious group generating any ideas that don't conform to the party line.

The fact is, the last of the genuine Shaolin practitioners fled the country or were killed during the civil wars of 1900–1931. They've come almost full circle—those who are left are passing their precious knowledge down to a select few, generation by generation.

FIGHTING STYLES

Chinese martial arts include over 1,500 different styles; a style meaning it has unique training methods and techniques and approaches to fighting. In ye olden days, students were told which particular style they would learn. Nowadays, people gravitate toward a style that fits their physical abilities and personalities.

Kung fu styles are divided into three different basic types:

- Shaolin styles—those developed by the monks at the Shaolin temple.
- Shaolin-derived styles—those developed from the Shaolin styles away from the temple.
- Family styles—those associated with a particular family or clan. Also called *pai*.

As previously stated, southern martial arts schools tend to concentrate on hand fighting and northern schools emphasize kicking, but naturally there are many exceptions on both sides.

The Shaolin styles, often featured in Jackie's films of the 1970s, were developed to train the student in a particular discipline. For example, the Crane style was meant to teach control and character and emphasized quick footwork.

Styles may be referred to as either "high and low" or "soft and hard." *High* and *soft* refer to a style having a larger mental or internal component, whereas *low* and *hard* styles are more reliant on pure physical abilities. Remember, these are very simplified descriptions.

The kung fu ideal is to have the mind and body perfectly complementing each other. For example, some martial arts instructors will have novice students do the following exercise:

The student will hold his arm out and try to prevent a second student from bending it. Usually, the student can only keep his arm from being pushed upward for a short time. Then the teacher will instruct the student to close his eyes and do a visualization—maybe that he is staring straight ahead until he can see the back of his own head or to fixate on a spot directly below his navel. Then the second student tries to bend the arm again. Often, the first student is able to resist much better.

The point being that a certain kind of concentration enhances physical strength and ability. Of course, the basis for Shaolin concentration wasn't visualization, it was the ability to harness *ch'i.* The internal and external go hand in hand and strengthen each other. If you can master the concentration *and* learn the physical skills of kung fu you will be virtually an indomitable fighter.

The catch-22 is that many of the styles are impossible to master *without* supreme concentration. That's why in *Shaolin Wooden Men*, the mute Jackie portrays had to stay at the temple until he was good enough to leave.

Remember, when we speak of style, we're referring to advanced learning techniques. The basics of kung fu and all other martial arts—kicking, punching, blocking, and adopting stances—must be acquired first before one can move on to perfect any style. Because the basics are necessarily dependent on physical strength and ability, they are considered "low" systems. In other words, one doesn't need any kind of spiritual enlightenment to do well in any garden variety martial arts class.

But when it comes to the elevated levels depicted in kung fu films, that's where the men and women are separated from the boys and girls, so to speak. And those are the styles listed below, many of which are featured in Jackie's kung fu films. The others are styles that frequently pop up in period kung fu movies in general.

Dragon

The epitome of styles, which was designed to enhance alertness and concentration and develop the spirit, with an efficiency of movement. At its most advanced level, muscle strength is replaced by *ch'i* in the Dragon style. Here's an example of what that means: A Tiger stylist would break a rock by sheer force and physical technique, while a Dragon stylist would shatter it by *ch'i* projection.

That's one mighty powerful style. Needless to say, this is a level not frequently seen. Except in old-time kung fu movies where the people can also fly.

Crane

A traditional Shaolin style that was taught to instill character, spirit, and control, it required light, quick footwork. The Crane style employs a one-legged stance—hence the crane designation—which requires an abundance of concentration. The attacking movements mimic the evasive body language of a bird.

Legend has it that the style was developed after a monk happened to see an ape fighting with a crane. He assumed the ape would rip the bird to shreds, but in fact the graceful bird had the upper hand. By flapping its wings and poking and darting quickly with its beak, the crane finally made the ape give up and run away.

The Crane style is believed to develop the "essence," and it features long-range kicks and a hand-fighting pose that "parrots" the crane's beak, so to speak.

Snake

Considered a particularly deadly fighting style that isn't all that difficult to master. Relatively speaking. The hallmarks of this style are deep breathing and a concentration on the fingers, which are used to stab at the face, throat, and groin of an opponent. Ouch. The movements, reminiscent of a coiling snake, are fluid and are intended to develop internal energy as well as mental, physical, and emotional balance.

Like the Praying Mantis, Snake style mostly forgoes any blocking moves.

Also, Snake style should not be confused with the Cobra style, which occasionally shows up in films. Cobra practitioners strike quickly at either the eyes or throat, then hang on until the opponent is dead. Charming thought.

Curiously, despite the fascination with this style in films, it was rarely taught. In recent times, Snake Fist was adopted and fostered by the Chen family, so it's now known as the Chen Snake Fist.

Tiger

Considered to be the opposite of the crane, the Tiger is a brutal defensive style that employs powerful kicks and vicious clawing motions that are meant to rip apart any unprotected area of skin.

This style's main feature is the Tiger Claw, a hand pose that is also used for defense against a weapon. In that case, the Tiger fighter grabs the weapon between his hands and crushes it in a powerful grip.

Not surprisingly, the Tiger style helps develop muscle and tendons, which help produce the short, powerful movements this style is known for.

Praying Mantis

A style based on the deliberate movements of the praying mantis, one of the fiercest killers in the insect kingdom. Seriously.

What's interesting is that today we know how brutal a creature the praying mantis is, thanks to technology such as super high-speed film and specially developed camera lenses. But how did the masters hundreds of years ago figure it out? Apparently by sitting there all day watching the little creature.

Called Tong Long, this style has both northern and southern schools, but the one seen most often in movies is the northern version. This style relies almost solely on hand movements, with very little footwork. It's identified by the virtual lack of any blocking techniques, instead adopting the old "yield in order to conquer" philosophy.

Or, as some of us put it, live to fight another day.

This style was believed to instill determination in the student.

Choi Li Fut

A lot of the fighting seen in *Drunken Master II* was of this style, which features punches and weapons work. It was based on a posture called the riding horse stance because when in it, the student appears to be riding a horse. A very short horse.

The movements are stiff and choppy, depending mostly on muscle power. Originally, Choi Li Fut only featured three kicks, but in modern times more have been adopted into the style.

According to legend, Choi Li Fut was developed to be used specifically on the many houseboats of southern China, where fighting would require balance. How the style got its name is an interesting story.

The Choi Li Fut style was developed in 1836 by Chan Heung, who had begun studying martial arts when he was seven years old. By the time he was seventeen, he was sent to study with his uncle's senior classmate from the Shaolin temple, Li Yau-san.

After four years, the boy was so advanced Li suggested Chan seek out a Shaolin monk named Choy Fok. At first, Choy would agree only to mentor the boy in Buddhism, but eventually he relented, and for eight years, Choy taught Chan both kung fu and the way of Buddhism.

When Chan returned home, he was twenty-nine. After refining all he had learned, he formally established it as a new system of kung fu. He called it Choy Li Fut to honor his two teachers—Choy Fok and Li Yau-san. *Fu* is the Chinese word for Buddhism and was used to honor the Shaolin roots of his new system.

Choy Li Fut is rarely practiced outside China, but on the Mainland it continues to be one of the most popular styles of kung fu.

Wing Chun

A style from southern China that Bruce Lee studied before developing his Jeet Kune Do style. Legend has it Wing Chun was developed by a Buddhist after seeing a snake fighting with a crane. It was a reaction to the more prevalent Shaolin styles, and the point was to enable a smaller, less accomplished fighter to beat a larger opponent—this is why it was considered a woman's skill.

Wing Chun is considered a full high system because of its efficiency of movement and use of *ch'i*.

Hung Gar

A subsystem of Tiger style, it was used by Wong Fei-hung and is considered to be directly passed down from the Shaolin Temple. Hung Gar uses hand fighting and weapons, with the object being, in essence, to break bones or otherwise destroy the opponent's "structure." We're talking eyes, blood vessels, etc.

Drunken

Although "Drunken Fighting" has been popularized in two of Jackie's movies, it's technically not a specific style the way, say, Eagle Claw is. Instead, the Drunken system is a subsystem known for lurching body movements that are intended to exhaust an opponent. The blows generate little force and are directed with apparent randomness at exposed areas. Its designation refers to the way the body movements mimic someone who's soused. Now, pretending to be staggering drunk is much harder than to *get* staggering drunk, making this deceivingly difficult to learn. Drunken fighting requires exceptional flexibility and strength.

As for the Drunken Monkey style made famous by Chan, Monkey style is considered a lower style.

Jeet Kune Do

An "art" developed by Bruce Lee. Although often called a style, notes left by Lee indicate he did not intend it to be a new style. Whatever one chooses to call it, Bruce incorporated elements from a number of styles—Tai Chi, Ju Jitsu, and most notably Wing Chun into fashioning Jeet Kune Do, which means "intercepting the fist."

Perhaps its most notable characteristic is flexibility, allowing the fighter to make adaptations that fit whatever circumstance they're in.

The American term for this is improvisation.

Apparently, there's a lot of bickering back and forth among Jeet Kune Do proponents about what JKD (as they refer to it) is *really* all about. Fortunately for Jackie fans, their hero would rather be jumping off buildings than arguing over semantics.

Chan quite openly acknowledges he's not a proponent of any particular school or style—except the school of entertaining. He uses whatever style will work best in whatever scene he's filming. His personal style is a smorgasbord of Wing Chun and Hapkido mixed with other less definable elements.

Maybe that instinctive ability to improvise is what bonds Jackie Chan and Bruce Lee, the two men who are most responsible for bringing not only action films but knowledge and appreciation of martial arts to the world.

GLOSSARY

Butterfly knife. A knife used in kung fu fighting, specific to southern China.

Ch'i. A vitally important concept, *ch'i* is the vital life force in the body. It's derived from the Chinese word for breath, *qi*.

Ching dynasty. Ruled China from 1644 until 1912. The Ching dynasty took power after overthrowing the Ming dynasty.

Dan dao. A Chinese sword with a curved blade.

Double hook swords. Ancient kung fu weapon with a curved blade seen frequently in kung fu movies of the 1950s and 1960s.

Hapkido. Korean style emphasizing kicking and grappling.

Katana. The long Japanese sword associated with the samurai.

Kwan. A long pole, used by the Shaolin monks for kung fu.

Kwan dao. A long pole with a blade attached to it.

Manchus. The common name for the Ching rulers. The Manchus' ancestral home is in northeast China, above North Korea and east of Mongolia. In most kung fu films, the Manchus are the evil villains. Ironically, it was a Ming general who turned to the Manchus for help to quell a local disturbance. After the Manchus' retook Beijing from a rebel leader, they refused to relinquish their control. Instead, supported by foreign interests, they eventually took complete control of China. That's why they are considered outlaws.

Ming dynasty. Ruled from 1368 until the Manchu takeover in 1644. These rulers were supported by the average Chinese, who waged a futile fight to restore the ousted rulers. The reason they were so supported is that they were purely Chinese—the regime before them had been the Mongols, the one after the Manchus. Also, under the Ming rulers, China enjoyed economic and social stability.

Nunchaku. Two short wooden sticks attacked by a chain. Bruce Lee used them frequently in his movies, whipping them around so fast they look like a blur.

Riding Horse Stance or simply **Horse Stance.** The torturous deep-squatting position Jackie assumed in *Drunken Master*. Used to develop leg strength and balance.

Sai. A dagger with a curved hilt. This weapon was used a lot by Richard Norton, Jackie Chan's nemesis in *Twinkle, Twinkle Lucky Stars*, who returns as a villain in *A Nice Guy*.

Style. A particular school of martial practice with its own unique training methods, techniques, and approach on attack and defense.

Wong Fei-hung. A legendary Chinese folk hero about whom literally hundreds of films have been made. Chan's *Drunken Master* films were based on Wong's legend. Born in 1847, Wong became famous for his kung fu skills as well as his commitment to social issues and helping the downtrodden.

12
THE *Peerless*

成龍 JACKIE CHAN

O ne can't help but wonder if there would be a Jackie Chan as we know him today had Bruce Lee lived. Would the development of action cinema have been molded more by Lee's intense fighting and haunting charisma, or would Jackie's mania for preposterous stunts and creatively agile fight choreography have won out?

Obviously, we'll never know, although it's clear Jackie owes a debt of gratitude to Lee and other visionaries who blazed trails before him. The fact is, without a Bruce there probably wouldn't be a Jackie. And without a Lau Kar-leung, there probably wouldn't have been a Bruce. And who knows where any of these guys would be if Wong Fei-hung had never been born.

What is known is that Jackie has been imitated but never duplicated. It would be hard to argue against the notion that Jackie Chan is the best known martial arts/action movie star in the world. There are other Hong Kong actors and actresses who are stars, but none can match Chan's worldwide box office power or fan idolatry. Even when compared to American action films, Chan's movies—in Asia—routinely outperform anything Stallone, Arnold, Van Damme, or Cruise throw his way.

At this point in time, Jackie Chan is simply without peer.

However, just because he's on top doesn't mean he's alone

on the mountain. Hong Kong action cinema is awash with talented men and women who throw their hearts, souls, and bodies into their work. But many wouldn't be there if it wasn't for Jackie, who helped make comedy kung fu a genre to be respected and then almost single-handedly set the standard for action film fighting and stunt work.

Below are some of the men and women past and present who, along with Jackie, have made the Hong Kong movie industry the third largest in the world, behind only America and India.

Run Run and Runme Shaw—founders of Shaw Brothers Studio

Although their names now evoke images of "old-fashioned" movies, the Shaw Brothers Studio, Hong Kong's oldest, paved the way for Hong Kong's action cinema as we know it today.

Run Run and Runme Shaw began working as theater owners, which led them to expand to the business of making movies—it was more financially efficient to make their own movies to show in their theaters than to rent movies from others. Run Run quickly took to filmmaking and was actually the first filmmaker to produce a Hong Kong movie with sound.

In the 1960s, Shaw Brothers had no particular cinematic agenda, producing whatever struck their fancy—historical dramas, documentaries, romances, comedies, and an occasional kung fu film. But Run Run had noticed the popularity of the martial arts flicks, and so in 1970 he decided the studio should concentrate its energies on that genre.

In the beginning there were hero kung fu films, called *wu xia pian*. These are the ones where fighters possessed supernatural powers—they could fly, shoot death beams from their eyes, and otherwise resembled your typical Saturday morning cartoon superhero.

Then came along more realistic martial arts movies, which were dubbed *gung fu pian*—kung fu films. Shaw Brothers smartly combined the two genres to create *guo shu pian*—new hero films—where there was plenty of kung fu but little or no mystical powers. It was with this genre that Shaw Brothers hit the jackpot and found its niche, cranking out a prodigious amount of kung fu and swordsman films that made the studio a recognized brand name the world over.

In many ways, Run Run and Runme were the Roger Cormans of China—they gave many future stars and renowned directors their first jobs, allowing them the opportunity to learn the ropes by working on a multitude of productions in a few-frills environment. Shaw Brothers offered acting classes as well as kung fu training for would-be action stars who had no previous martial arts experience. At times the schedules were so grueling that the actors actually lived on the lot.

One of the darker legacies of Shaw Brothers concerns their part in organized crime's infiltration into the Hong Kong film industry. Determined to protect their investments, Shaw Brothers forbade their contract players to work on films for any other production companies, even outside Hong Kong. Considering the actors were barely able to scrape by on the low salaries paid by Shaw Brothers, this was not a popular rule. But if anyone dared to work elsewhere, the studio would sue to get the wayward performer back in line.

Needing to find another source of income but lacking the ability to do much besides work in films, many of the Shaw Brothers contract players became active in the Triads, Hong Kong's powerful crime syndicate. That was all the entrée the mobsters needed. Since then, the Triads have become a constant element, and still unsolved problem, in Hong Kong filmmaking.

Shaw Brothers' decline in the late 1970s coincided with Golden Harvest's rise in fortune. The two studios represented the old and new wave of Hong Kong kung fu/action cinema, and by the mid-1980s, Shaw Brothers converted itself to a television production facility while Golden Harvest, with a stable of stars led by Jackie Chan and Sammo Hung, got busy conquering the world.

Currently, Shaw Brothers is inactive, but in the wake of the worldwide surge of interest in Hong Kong films, there are rumors that Shaw Brothers may be ready to stage a comeback.

Chang Cheh
(b. 1933, Shanghai)

The forerunner of John Woo, Chang Cheh was one of the more prolific directors at Shaw Brothers, at one point churning out in excess of seventy films in a five-year period.

Chang didn't start out to be a director—his first jobs were as a movie critic and a songwriter. But Chang was eventually bit by the movie bug and began his film career in 1962 as a screenwriter for a Shanghai production company. A year later he was approached by Run Run Shaw to direct a film for his new studio, and Chang agreed. The film was *Tiger Boy* and launched the career of Jimmy Wang Yu.

Needless to say, Chang's prodigious film output made it impossible to maintain any kind of consistent quality, so the caliber of his work fluctuates wildly, from cookie-cutter dreck to creatively innovative masterpieces. But as in the early days of Hollywood, Shaw Brothers was more concerned with quantity than quality, because at that time, the public's appetite was insatiable and not particularly picky. After he joined Shaw Brothers, he started directing "swordplay" flicks, including the now-famous *One-Armed Swordman*, which created a sensation when released in 1967 because of its unrestrained violence.

Prior to Chang, the fighting in kung fu movies was more mannered, but Chang Cheh upped the testosterone level considerably. It's not surprising to learn that Chang was a mentor of John Woo, who worked with the venerable director when he was starting out.

One of Chang's innovations was to have a "team" of actors playing the same role in a series of films. This would become a common movie staple adopted by most filmmakers including Jackie Chan, who consistently revisits his *Police Story* character. But nobody in Hong Kong had done it before Chang.

After his first group of actors became famous and moved on, the director debuted his "second team" in the film *The Five Venoms*—Kuo Chui, Chian Sheng, Sun Chien, Lo Meng, and Lu Feng.

Although Chang's place in the list of great directors is argued over because of the inconsistency of his work, one thing is beyond doubt: Chang Cheh had a knack for spotting talent—Lau Kar-leung, Ti Lung, Alexander Fu Sheng, David Chiang, John Woo, the Five Venoms actors, Wu Ma, Yuen Woo Ping—and as a result, he launched more careers than probably any other director before or since.

Selected Chang Cheh Filmography

Trail of the Broken Blade (1966)
The Assassin (1967)
Golden Swallow (1969)
Vengeance (1970)
Duel of Fists (1970)
The Boxer from Shantung (1971)
Disciples of Shaolin (1977)
The Five Venoms (1979)
Killer Army (1980)
Masked Avengers (1981)

Cheng Pei Pei
(b. 1949, Shanghai)

Cheng is notable as being the first, and basically only, female kung fu star for Shaw Brothers. After leaving behind a career as a ballerina, Pei Pei joined the Actors' Training Course at the studio in 1963 and that same year made her feature film debut in *The Magic Lamp*—playing a man.

In 1964, Pei Pei became the first Asian actress to win the Golden Knight Award at the International Independent Producers' Association, honoring her performance in *The Rock*. Thrilled by her growing popularity, Shaw Brothers began to market her as the "rival" to Golden Harvest star Angela Mao. It was a publicity ploy reminiscent of Hollywood in the 1940s when one studio would put an actress under contract to compete with another studios' star, like when Jayne Mansfield was tagged to be the answer to Marilyn Monroe.

Unfortunately for Shaw Brothers, Cheng was not happy with the roles she was being given and her interest in movie-making began to wane. She continued making films at Shaw Brothers until 1970, when she got married, officially retired, and moved to America.

Two years later she returned to Hong Kong, officially unretired, and went back to work, eventually making the crossover to television. Her most notable project in recent years was *Painted Faces*, the dramatized story of Jackie Chan's childhood experience at the Peking Opera.

Selected Cheng Pei Pei Filmography

The Magic Lamp (1963)
The Rock (1964)
Come Drink with Me (1965)
Golden Swallow (1968)
The Lady Hermit (1971)
None but the Brave (1973)
Painted Faces (1988)
Kung Fu Mistress (1994)

Alexander Fu Sheng
(b. 1954, d. 1983)

Known for his boyish charm, Fu Sheng was on his way to becoming one of Hong Kong's biggest stars, with seemingly limitless potential. A superb acrobat and martial artist, Fu Sheng was a favorite of both Chang Cheh and Lau Kar-leung.

Even in his first film roles, which were little more than bit parts, Fu Sheng's charisma was apparent, and it wasn't long before he was a young man on the rise. In 1973 he landed his first starring role, which was in *Police Force*, and after that he never looked back. With each successive film, his popularity grew in leaps and bounds.

Then, at the peak of his popularity, the actor suffered a horrible accident while filming a movie, breaking both his legs. Although many wondered if he could come back from such a debilitating injury, Fu Sheng returned to work a year later in top form and his career picked up where it had left off.

In 1982, Alexander appeared in what many to this day call the quintessential martial arts movie, *Legendary Weapons of Kung Fu*, which tells the story of how the various kung fu schools banded together during the Boxer Rebellion to fight a weapon that may spell their doom—the gun.

Fu Sheng and director Liu Chia-liang received universal acclaim for their efforts in this film. Alexander's future looked blindingly bright—then in 1983 tragedy struck. One night after dinner, Fu Sheng was being driven home by his brother when their car went out of control while navigating a curve, crashing full force into a cement wall. Although still alive when paramedics rushed him to the hospital, Alexander Fu Sheng was pronounced dead several hours later. He was twenty-nine years old.

A footnote to the story proves Hollywood's not the only place with its fair share of ghost stories: Fu Sheng's spirit is believed by many to still haunt the Shaw Brothers' back lot.

Selected Alexander Fu Sheng Filmography

Boxer from Shantung (1972)
Police Force (1973)
Disciples of Death (1974)
Na Cha, The Great (1974)

The Invincible One (1975)
Chinatown Kid (1977)
Brave Archer III (1979)
Return of the Sentimental Swordsman (1980)
Master of Disaster (1981)
Legendary Weapons of Kung Fu (1982)

Huang Cheng-li

Before he became a familiar face to moviegoers, Korean-born Huang Cheng-li spent the early part of his life doing little except studying martial arts. He used his extensive training to make a living in the early 1970s by teaching boxing and kung fu to Korean troops stationed in Vietnam.

His expertise in fighting got the notice of producer Ng See Yuen, who hired Huang to play the evil Silver Fox in the 1976 film *Secret Rivals*. The movie became a hit, and Huang Cheng-li found himself a new career. He moved to Taiwan and continued finding film work. Considered to possess some of the best kicking skills around, Huang Cheng-li made a career out of being the villain. He also managed to tick off Jackie Chan not once but twice by kicking him a wee bit too hard in the head, first in *Snake in the Eagle's Shadow*, then in *Drunken Master*.

Huang moved up the studio ladder and was allowed to direct himself in the Korean-made *Hitman in the Hand of Buddha*, which generated surprisingly good box office, although it was never released in Hong Kong. After a string of flops, Huang's star faded, and he eventually went back to Korea. Currently, he makes his home in Seoul, where he manages a hotel and runs a golf tee manufacturing company.

Selected Huang Cheng-li Filmography

Secret Rivals (1976)
Secret Rivals II (1977)

Tiger over Wall (1979)
Magnificent Warriors (1984)
Shanghai Express (1987)
Street Warriors (1990)

Bruce Lee
(b. 1940, San Francisco, d. 1973)

Bruce Lee's movie persona conveyed the essence of intensity and an aura of mysterious depth. He didn't have blood coursing through his veins, he had magma.

The son of famous Hong Kong actor Lee Hoi Chuen, Bruce was born in the United States and always considered himself an American first, even though he grew up in Hong Kong.

Like Chan, Bruce began his career as an actor, but the similarities end there. Lee lived at home with his parents, and becoming an actor was more an act of following in his father's footsteps rather than the escape vehicle it was for Jackie.

Although he could hardly be called a stage parent, Bruce's father did have a sense of his son's destiny—Lee's Chinese name, Lee Jun Fan, means "gaining fame overseas." But in the beginning, Bruce was just another kid actor, starring in a number of unspectacular films including *The Kid* in 1950, which was based on a popular comic book of the time. An interesting bit of trivia is that the cartoonist Yuan Buyun is the one who gave Bruce his nickname, Siu Lung—the Little Dragon.

Restless and feeling his career was going nowhere, Bruce returned to America when he was eighteen. A few years later he participated in a karate exhibition, which led to a screen test at Twentieth Century-Fox. He was the right man in the right place at the right time. Trying to capitalize on the Batman television phenomenon, Fox was preparing to debut a TV series based on the Green Hornet radio show, and thanks to his martial arts ability, Lee was cast as the kung fu fighting sidekick Kato.

The series was canceled after only one season, but it served as an attention-getting showcase for Lee. Many big-name actors like Steve McQueen hired him as a martial arts trainer, and although everyone knew he had star potential, nobody could figure out how to create the right vehicle for him, one that would showcase his remarkable physical skills as well as his acting.

While Hollywood scratched its head, Bruce worked as a journeyman actor, going from guest spot to guest spot on television episodes. Eventually Bruce returned to Hong Kong, where there was now intense interest in him among film-makers thanks to his years in Hollywood. Ng See Yuen, the same man who gave Jackie his big break in *Snake in the Eagle's Shadow*, believed Lee could be a major star, but at that time the producer lacked the financial means to develop a project for him.

The most insulting experience happened when Lee developed an idea for a television show but was denied the chance to star in it because he was considered too Chinese for American television audiences. The series Bruce created became known as *Kung Fu* and starred non-Chinese David Carradine.

No wonder Bruce went back to Hong Kong when opportunity came knocking. In the end it was Golden Harvest who won the Lee lottery, signing him to a three-picture deal. The good news for Bruce . . . he was finally going to get his shot at stardom. The bad news for Bruce . . . Lo Wei was going to be his director. Although Lee would become an international star after *The Big Boss* and *Fist of Fury*, in the beginning he had to fight the same constraints Jackie did.

Despite his obvious charisma on screen and superb kung fu abilities, Golden Harvest—and Lo Wei—were hesitant to give him too much control in choreographing, so they gave the job to a guy from the old school who wasn't too keen on Lee's newfangled ideas. After a lot of effort, Bruce was finally able to get some of his Jeet Kune Do choreography into *The Big Boss*, including the famous fight in the ice plant.

Unfortunately, the movie also features major trampoline

work that makes the fighters seem like they've got bionic-powered legs. *The Big Boss* is also the film with the often re-played scene where a villain is sent sailing through a wall and leaves a perfect outline of his body.

That kind of silliness seems out of place in a Lee film. What Bruce brought to his movies that set him apart was a disturb-ing realism that made the kung fu films of the past, filled with flying warriors and marauding ghosts, seem hokey, dated, and suddenly out of step with the times. To some, his films were too realistic.

It is ironic that a film industry that made a career out of on-screen bloodshed would get queasy over Bruce's films. The difference was that when the gore was caused by a warrior able to leap a tall building in a single bound, nobody took it to heart. Lee's films were so real the violence was disturbing. It couldn't be dismissed as unbelievable—it was all *too* believ-able.

As far as is known, not a single version of *The Big Boss* exists that includes the scene where Bruce splits a guy's head open with a cleaver—that scene was edited from every known print out of concern the image would be just too discomfiting.

Bruce modernized cinematic kung fu fighting in another way. Like Jackie, he used whatever was at hand for weapons instead of whipping out a couple of traditional swords or en-gaging in "gentleman's fighting."

Within a short time, Bruce was an international phenome-non, with the world his apparent oyster. But as everyone knows, it came to an abrupt end when Lee died on July 20, 1973. Bruce's death was as traumatic for his fans as Elvis's untimely death had been for the King's fans. And it's had just as many questions posed about what really happened. The most recent consensus is that Bruce died of an allergic reaction to marijuana.

According to *Hong Kong Action Cinema* author Bey Logan, the truth had been hushed up to protect his image, so instead the story about him dying after ingesting the painkiller Equagesic was circulated. Jason Lee, the actor who portrayed

Bruce in the biographical film *Dragon*, also claims Lee's widow admitted to him what had happened.

Even if the whole truth about his death is never known, it remains a solid fact that Bruce has passed from the realm of actor and legend to myth. His name will forever be synonymous with the modern kung fu film, with *Fist of Fury* and *Enter the Dragon* his epitaph.

Selected Bruce Lee Filmography

The Big Boss (1971)
Fist of Fury (1972)
Way of the Dragon (1972)
Enter the Dragon (1973)
Game of Death (1973)

Lau Kar-leung
(Liu Chia-liang)
(b. 1934, Canton)

Although his name is often overlooked when talking about groundbreaking forces in Hong Kong cinema, Lau is considered by many as one of the all-time great directors—anywhere.

Lau comes from a distinguished kung fu and movie family. His actor father, Liu Charn, studied with one of Wong Fei Hung's more famous students, Lam Sai Wing. Lau himself began learning martial arts skills when he was nine, often enduring grueling training under the stern instruction of his father.

Lau began working as a stuntman and bit actor in the 1950s, joining his father and brothers in show business. He joined Shaw Brothers as a fight choreographer, and after a long internship under director Chang Cheh, Lau began making movies and quickly became recognized as an innovative filmmaker.

A year before *Drunken Master* made Jackie Chan a star, Lau directed a film called *The Spiritual Boxer* which also happened to feature a drunken kung fu master. Many believe this was the "inspiration" for Jackie's *Drunken Master.*

Like most Hong Kong action directors, Lau starred in most of the films he directed, a practice at odds with the Hollywood way, where there are very few true actor-directors other than Woody Allen. Allen is actually an apt comparison because both men have a very less-than-macho screen visage. The difference is that Lau, of course, is hardly Mr. Milquetoast once the fighting starts.

Lau continued making films under the Shaw Brothers' banner for almost twenty years, until changing audience tastes made their type of traditional kung fu movies obsolete. The studio went out of the motion picture business, switching to television production instead, and Lau formed his own production company.

Since then, Lau has continued to make movies that show a flair of innovation, including Chan's *Drunken Master II.* Unfortunately, Lau locked horns with Jackie on that film over style, and he was eventually fired, although he retained the directing credit.

Shaw Brothers had a curious policy of not rereleasing their films, and because of this, a lot of Lau's early work isn't generally well known. Some feel that he doesn't always get the full credit he deserves as an innovator. And others point out that some of the fighting techniques and other novel ideas he used in his films were subsequently "borrowed" by others, who then took credit for them. For example, Lau was the first filmmaker ever to portray Wong Fei-hung as a young man—every other cinematic depiction prior to that had Wong middle-aged and older. But it is Jackie Chan, not Lau, who is most closely associated with that story innovation.

In recent years, however, with the increased interest in Hong Kong cinema, Lau's work is being dusted off and released on video, giving the world a chance to see just how great Lau's contribution to the genre has been.

Selected Lau Kar-leung Filmography

The Spiritual Boxer (1975)
Challenge of the Masters (1976)
Executioners from Shaolin (1976)
36th Chamber of Shaolin (1978)
Shaolin Challenges Ninja (1978)
Dirty Ho (1979)
Return to the 36th Chamber (1980)
Martial Club (1981)
Legendary Weapons of Kung Fu (1982)
Tiger on the Beat (1988)
New Kids in Town (1990)
Scorpion King (1992)
Drunken Master II (1994)
Drunken Master III (1994)

Ti Lung

(a/k/a Delon Ti Lung)
(b. 1946, Hong Kong)

This handsome actor began his career in 1968 and is still going strong, nearly a hundred movies later. A Shaw Brothers contract player, Ti learned the ropes under noted director Chang Cheh and made his film debut in the director's 1968 film, *Return of the One-Armed Swordsman.*

During the height of his career, Ti became the most beloved of Hong Kong actors. But like many other Shaw Brothers actors, Ti was left in the lurch when the studio abruptly switched over to television production in the early 1980s. At that time, there was a glass wall between film and television actors—once you were identified with a particular medium, crossover was virtually impossible.

So Ti suddenly found himself a star searching for a movie to act in. With no work, he turned to alcohol, and for several years he fought a drinking problem. It wasn't until the mid-

1980s when John Woo came calling that Ti Lung was able to turn his life around and enjoy a career comeback.

Since appearing in Woo's classic, *A Better Tomorrow*, Ti has once again been in constant demand. He still has a legion of loyal fans today and continues to appear in important action films, including *Drunken Master II* where he plays Jackie's father—even though he's only seven years older than Chan.

Selected Ti Lung Filmography

Duel of Iron Fists (1968)
Wandering Swordsman (1970)
Duel of Fists (1971)
New One-Armed Swordsman (1971)
Dynasty of Blood (1973)
Heroic Ones (1974)
Savage Five (1974)
Young Rebel (1975)
Five Shaolin Masters (1975)
Death Chambers (1976)
Legend of the Bat (1978)
Ten Tigers of Kwangtung (1978)
Tiger Killer (1981)
A Better Tomorrow (1986)
Tiger on the Beat (1988)
City War (1989)
Drunken Master II (1993)
Blade of Fury (1994)

Jimmy Wang Yu

Wang Yu is one of Hong Kong's more colorful film personalities and has forged a lengthy career out of average looks, mediocre talent, passing martial arts skills—not to mention close movie ties to the Triads. One of the first Shaw Brothers stars, Wang Yu made a name for himself in *The One-Armed Swordsman* and its many sequels.

Wang, a former swimming champion, is one of the few actors who has worked for both Shaw Brothers and Golden Harvest, but despite his many years in the business, it's hard to gauge the success of his career. While he has appeared in some important action films over the years, he wasn't really an innovator the way many of his contemporaries were. Nor was he ever beloved by audiences. He was just always around the action until his career finally fizzled and he concentrated instead on his Triad work in Taiwan, where he still resides, while still occasionally dabbling in moviemaking.

Selected Jimmy Wang Yu Filmography

Temple of the Red Lotus (1965)
The One-Armed Swordsman (1967)
Sword and Lute (1967)
The Chinese Boxer (1969)
One-Armed Boxer (1970)
Invincible Sword (1971)
One-Armed Boxer II (1975)
Fantasy Mission Force (1982)
Island of Fire (1990)

Lo Wei

Of all the words that come to mind about Lo Wei, *auteur* is not one of them, although he directed over sixty-five movies. Nor is visionary. He's been linked with two of Hong Kong's biggest stars of all time—Bruce Lee and Jackie Chan—but Lo's contribution to their careers was minimal, and in the case of Jackie, detrimental for a while. Many in fact might argue Chan and Lee succeeded *in spite* of Lo Wei, whose legacy will largely be one of mediocrity and missing the brass ring—twice.

Lo actually began his career in front of the camera and was once considered a matinee idol. He joined the Shaw Brothers family in 1965, and during his five years there put out a string of undistinguished films, like *Wang Yu's Seven Magnificent Fights.*

Lo's career took an upswing when he followed Raymond Chow to the latter's newly formed Golden Harvest. A short time later, someone—after the fact, everybody took credit for it—saw Bruce Lee on a local television show, and he was eventually signed to a contract by the fledgling studio.

Even though Lo was at the helm of Bruce's first two films, he's given little credit in history for their success. And rightfully so, although he did his best to try and convince people otherwise, going so far as to claim he had to instruct Lee on how to stage an on-camera fight. Bruce was not pleased. Not surprisingly, Lo and Lee's collaboration ended after two films.

Instead of seeing his own career blossom through his association with Lee, Lo Wei's reputation suffered. But he was given a chance to redeem himself and his creative standing through a new protégé—Jackie Chan. But Lo failed even more miserably the second time around, helping neither himself nor Jackie over the many years Lo had Chan under contract.

Lo left Golden Harvest in 1975 to form the Lo Wei Company. But the autonomy didn't change his creative vision, and he continued to generate mostly forgettable products— driving Jackie crazy in the process.

In the end, it took another director, Yuen Woo-ping, to give Jackie his breakout role. Lo Wei tried, once again, to hitch his wagon to a rising star, but he only succeeded in alienating Jackie. Like Lee before him, Chan severed his professional relationship with Lo Wei as soon as he was in the position to, never looking back.

Lo Wei died in 1996. He was seventy-seven.

Selected Lo Wei Filmography

Mong Lisi, Daughter of the Apes (1961)
Dragon Swamp (1969)

Comet Strikes (1970)
The Hurricane (1970)
The Big Boss (1971)
Fist of Fury (1972)
Back Alley Princess (1972)
Shaolin Wooden Men (1976)
Kung Fu Kid (1977)
Snake and Crane Arts of Shaolin (1978)
Magnificent Bodyguards (1978)
Fearless Hyena II (1980)

Maggie Cheung

(b. 1964, Hong Kong)

Like a lot of other Hong Kong actresses, Maggie Cheung started her career as a beauty queen, appearing in the Miss Asia contest in 1983, then going on to represent Hong Kong in the Miss World competition later that year.

Cheung was born in Hong Kong, but her family emigrated to England when she was only eight, where she was educated in various boarding schools. Along with Michelle Yeoh, Maggie speaks perfect English—in fact, she sounds positively British. After the Miss World competition she was cast in a film called *Prince Charming* (a/k/a *The Frog Prince*).

Cheung kept on working steadily, then two years later she was cast in the role that would serve as her biggest springboard, playing Jackie Chan's girlfriend, May, in *Police Story*, a role she reprised in two subsequent sequels.

It's been rumored that Maggie and Jackie were an off-screen item as well, but then again, Maggie has been linked with a number of her costars. Cheung's also been dogged by catty remarks from other actresses about her having had an eye-opening procedure and breast augmentation surgery.

Maggie's attitude about these various allegations has largely been one of the sticks-and-stones variety—let them yip, she's too busy working to respond. And more than almost any other actress, Maggie works. She's been averaging almost ten films a year—somebody ought to call the Guinness people and get her in their record book.

Although Cheung is probably best known in the West because of her Chan action film collaborations, she has no martial arts ability to speak of and often requires the use of doubles. On the other hand, Maggie has become well known and respected in Asia as a dramatic actress, having won the Hong Kong Film Award in 1993 for her work in the film *Center Stage* after having won in 1992 for the acclaimed film *Actress*. She's also won two Taiwan Golden Horse awards for Best Supporting Actress and Best Actress.

Speaking of Chan, he and Cheung had a minor falling out when she demanded her regular salary for what Jackie says was two days' work on *First Strike*. But since then they've kissed and made up, as it were, and now Jackie says his *Police Story* character will marry May in the next installment.

Until then, Cheung remains sought after by a multitude of other Hong Kong productions. In addition, following the recent trend, Maggie now has her eyes turning westward. Considering she speaks better English than most American studio executives, it seems only right that she be given the chance to test the Hollywood waters.

Selected Maggie Cheung Filmography

The Girl with the Diamond Slipper (1985)
Police Story (1986)
Story of Rose (1986)
Heavenly Fate (1987)
Project A (1987)
Police Story II (1988)
As Tears Go By (1988)
Golden Years (1988)
My Dear Son (1989)
A Young Woman's Heart (1989)
Heart to Hearts (1990)

Red Dust (1990)
Farewell China (1990)
Days of Being Wild (1991)
Actress (1992)
Dragon Inn (1992)
Heroic Trio (1992)
Supercop (1993)
The Barefoot Kid (1993)
In Between Love (1994)
Sung Dynasty Family (1995)

Chow Yun-fat
(b. 1955, Lamma Island)

Everything about Chow Yun-fat screams movie star, so it's easy to see why he's often referred to as the Chinese Cary Grant. But in addition to his matinee idol looks, Chow has the dramatic chops that elevate his talent to the same level as a De Niro or Pacino. He is equally adept at comedy or drama, and unlike many other Hong Kong actors, he strives to avoid being stereotyped and in the process has become Asia's best overall actor.

Chow grew up on Lamma, a quiet island populated by fishermen and farmers.

His family left the island when Chow was twelve, moving to nearby Hong Kong. There the young boy was introduced to "the movies," and he fell instantly in love. In 1973 he answered a newspaper ad seeking young actors willing to intern at a local television station. Chow enrolled in the actors training program and began his career paying dues in television, appearing by his own estimation in over a thousand series, mostly soap operas and dramas.

Chow finally hit small-screen pay dirt in the popular series *Shanghai Town*. It made Chow a household name and brought him to the attention of filmmaker Ann Hui, who gave him his first movie role in *The Story of Wu-Viet*. In so doing, Chow made the rare jump from television to feature films—not that anybody noticed.

For years Chow worked steadily but unspectacularly—until an up-and-coming director and his producer cast him in their film over the objection of the production company. The movie, *A Better Tomorrow*, won the 1986 Hong Kong Film Award for Best Picture and was the fourth-highest grossing movie of the decade. It also made stars out of director John Woo and Chow Yun-fat. It's interesting to note that one of Hong Kong's most famous action stars is the first to admit he's not exactly a martial arts wizard. In fact, he's got two left fists.

But what he lacks in fighting skills, he more than makes up for in charisma. That, and his ability to speak English clearly, is what Chow is hoping will open doors for him in Hollywood. Like so many others acutely uncertain of Hong Kong's artistic future under China, Chow decided to move his base of operation to the United States, and he relocated to California in 1996 with his wife, Jasmine, who has produced several of his films.

Chow says that at least for now, *Peace Hotel* will be his last Hong Kong film. He feels the filmmakers there weren't concerned with quality anymore, they simply wanted to churn out as much product as possible before 1997.

"For a better career in the future, I had to move to the West. I waited until now because I was under contract with Golden Princess. But that's over and now—I'm unemployed."

Probably not for long. In his corner are John Woo and Quentin Tarantino, who are working on a project they hope will be Yun-fat's Hollywood debut. He is the leading contender to star in a remake of *Anna and the King of Siam*. Along with Michelle Yeoh, Chow has the best chance of any Hong Kong performer to make the transition to mainstream non-action Hollywood films.

Selected Chow Yun-fat Filmography

A Better Tomorrow (1986)
Autumn's Tale (1987)

A Better Tomorrow II (1987)
All about Ah-long (1989)
A Better Tomorrow III (1989)
Wild Search (1989)
Tiger on the Beat (1989)
Diary of a Big Man (1989)
The Killer (1989)
God of Gamblers (1990)
Once a Thief (1991)
Hard Boiled (1992)
Full Contact (1992)
Treasure Hunt (1994)

Tsui Hark
(b. Vietnam)

Called a genius by many, Tsui Hark is considered one of the top New Wave directors. Born in Vietnam and raised in Hong Kong, Hark studied filmmaking in America—one of the few Chinese filmmakers who had an opportunity to have an academic background.

After graduating from college in Texas, Hark filmed a documentary about Chinese garment workers in New York, then headed back home to Hong Kong, where he worked in television before moving on to features. But after learning the business in America, the transition to the Hong Kong way of doing things was difficult.

Tsui has his own unique style, which can butt heads with Western sensibilities. Many of his films are a throwback to the old kung fu films, with people flying all over the place, which takes a serious suspension of disbelief. But that's a minor hurdle compared to some of his other trademarks—in the first minutes of his film The Blade, a dog's head gets crushed in a steel trap and the animal howls in agony. This is no special effect; a real dog was maimed to shoot the scene. For many, it doesn't matter how important a filmmaker he is; the needless cruelty casts an indelible pall over his talent.

But to Hark, concern over an individual animal is missing the point when an entire nation may be at peril—he's one of the artists who have been most vocal in their concern that life will change for the worse under Chinese rule.

Social awareness of another kind is on display in *Once upon a Time in China* and its numerous sequels. Although the film is yet another take on Wong Fei Hung, as seen through Tsui's unique perspective, the film becomes a commentary on the creeping Western influence on Chinese culture. In the film, Jet Li portrays the legendary martial artist who watches as American soldiers facilitate opium addiction and coerce peasants to set sail for the United States to work for the railroad barons. They dream of a better life but what they'll find is misery and virtual slavery as laborers.

But Hark didn't let the message overpower the entertainment. The martial arts in *Once upon a Time in China* are dazzling, as are the costumes and overall visual style. The film began a new boom in kung fu movies and further established Hark as one of Hong Kong's more imaginative creative forces. It was a reputation that began with his first film, *Butterfly Murders*, a fantasy film that borrowed from old-time kung fu flicks and *Star Wars*.

Having gone to film school in America gave Tsui a leg up over most Hong Kong filmmakers when it came to special effects. In fact, he was the first to use techniques like superimposition to create cinematic illusion. Many consider *A Chinese Ghost Story*, which cleverly combines horror and romance, as his fantasy tour de force. In it, Hark creates a mystical world filled with strange creatures and beautiful spirits. The film was a huge hit internationally and spawned two sequels.

Naturally, as Tsui's reputation grew, so did Jackie's desire to work with him. The result was *Twin Dragons*, an experience that doesn't rank in Jackie's top ten. The production was beset with tension and conflict between the two men, who have very different visions and ways of working.

For now, Tsui is keeping his Hong Kong ties while setting himself up in Hollywood. He feels confident that he'll be able to reach American audiences—so somebody had better tell him to ixnay cruelty to animals. Unfortunately, though his first American-made film—Jean-Claude Van Damme's *Double Team* (1997)—received good reviews, it was a commercial disappointment.

Selected Tsui Hark Filmography

Butterfly Murders (1979)
Dangerous Encounters of the First Kind (1980)
Zu: Warriors from the Magic Mountain (1981)
Aces Go Places III (1984)
Peking Opera Blues (1986)
Twin Dragons (1992)
The Lovers (1994)
Love in the Time of Twilight (1995)
The Blade (1996)
Double Team (1997)

Michelle Yeoh
(a/k/a Michelle Khan)
(b. 1964, Malaysia)

Although she readily admits she never properly studied martial arts, Michelle Yeoh's moves have helped her become Hong Kong's most successful action movie actress. She credits her early ballet training for her ability to learn the kicks and fighting required of most actresses who appear in action flicks. But of course the grit necessary to endure the battering actors take is something one is born with.

Michelle won the Miss Malaysia crown in 1983 and soon after moved to Hong Kong to pursue films. It didn't take her long to land her first film, *Owl vs. Dumbo*, directed by none other than Sammo Hung.

From there, Michelle found that if she wanted steady work, she'd better be willing to suffer for her art and agree to participate in the full-contact fights of action films. In her next film, *Yes! Madam*, Yeoh earned her stunt stripes by jumping over a balcony and through a plate glass window to tackle two villains.

However, the head injury she received also made her decide to be more careful about the stunts she agreed to do. In fact it was the combination of an injury and love that brought about her early "retirement." For reasons particular to their culture, most actresses retire once they marry. In Yeoh's case, her beloved was wealthy producer Dickson Poon, whom she wed in 1988.

If the marriage fails, as Yeoh's did, the actress has a much anticipated comeback. For Michelle, that vehicle was *Supercop*. So much for trying to refrain from dangerous stunts. In *Supercop*, Michelle proved marriage and divorce hadn't dulled her edges—at thirty-two she's still got mega-guts, matching Jackie stunt for stunt, bruise for bruise, kick for kick.

One of the most uncomfortable scenes to watch is when Michelle is hanging for dear life onto the side of a van as it tears through the streets of Kuala Lumpur.

Like so many others, Yeoh is looking to settle more or less permanently in America after the Chinese takeover in 1997. She's already got one part of American life down—she's a fanatical basketball fan. Michelle accidentally chanced upon the sport after she was undergoing treatment for a bad knee with a team doctor for the New York Knicks. During her physical therapy, she met several of the Knicks players who were fascinated with the story of how she was injured.

Yeoh's performance in *Supercop* turned a lot of other heads, too, including those attached to studio executives. The timing couldn't have been better for Michelle, who is hoping to get her foot in the Hollywood movie door, and she has one distinct advantage over many other Hong Kong actors fleeing to America prior to the Chinese takeover in 1997—she speaks perfect English.

Michelle acknowledges that curiosity over her physical prowess may be what gets her in the door initially, but she's confident she can convince the powers that be in Hollywood she's a total package.

If not, she can always kick their butts.

Selected Michelle Yeoh Filmography

Owl vs. Dumbo (1984)
Yes! Madam (1985)
In the Line of Duty (1986)
Royal Warriors (1986)
Twinkle, Twinkle Lucky Stars (1986)
In the Line of Duty II (1987)
Easy Money (1987)
Supercop (1992)
Project S (1993)
Heroic Trio (1993)
Tai Chi Master (1993)
Wing Chun (1994)
Sung Dynasty Family (1995)

Jet Li
(Li Lin-jei)
(b. 1963, Beijing)

Jet Li was born to fight. Considered a martial arts child prodigy, Jet began training when he was eight years old. For six consecutive years, 1974 to 1979, young Li won the Chinese National Martial Arts Contest championship and was a member of the first Wu Shu team to tour the West, including a performance at the Nixon White House.

With his physical abilities and handsome looks, it seemed inevitable Jet would make his way into show biz, which he did. In a big way. Li's first movie made him an instant star. Released in 1981, *Shaolin Temple* caused a sensation in China and was one of the first Mainland films to come to America. The film, which was partially shot on location at the site of the temple, created a surge of newfound interest in Shaolin history and helped make the burnt-out remains a tourist spot for youngsters anxious to emulate Li.

After a brief time in America, Li hooked up with director Tsui Hark for the *Once upon a Time in China* films, the second and third of which are considered by many to be masterpieces. While filming the first in the series, Jet was injured and had to be doubled, but in the later films, his skill is showcased to near perfection.

Ironically, though, Jet Li is occasionally criticized because of his historically inaccurate cinematic fighting. The magazine *Hong Kong Film Connection* says:

> Jet Li had now played three of the most prominent characters in kung fu history—Wong Fei Hong, Hung Hey-kwun and Fong Sai-yuk. All three were hung gar stylists. Not once has Jet Li used hung gar in any of his performances. Hung Hey-kwun was famous for his skill with the staff. In *New Legend of Shaolin*, Jet Li's take on Hung Hey-kwun, he fights with a spear. Hung gar is famous for low stances, iron forearms and the Tiger and Crane Fist. Jet Li used high kicks, no animals forms and the ''no shadow kick'' which was a true movement but was instead performed as a stunt using wires to carry him. Completely inappropriate and totally inaccurate.

Regardless, Jet's skill and brutal intensity have made him a unique star among the action film crowd. His biggest strength, though, has proven to be his greatest weakness as a movie star—Jet's classic martial arts skills don't always translate to modern times. His biggest successes have been in period pieces, which is obviously limiting.

Selected Jet Li Filmography

Dragon Fight (1990)
Born to Defence (1991)
Kids from Shaolin (1991)
Once upon a Time in China (1991)
Once upon a Time in China II (1992)

The Master (1992)
Swordsman 2 (1992)
Fong Sai Yuk 1 (1992)
Fong Sai Yuk 2 (1993)
Once upon a Time in China III (1993)
Shaolin Kung Fu (1993) (Documentary)
Tai Chi Master (1993)
The Kung Fu Cult Master (1993)
Last Hero in China (1993)
Bodyguard from Beijing (1994)
Dragons of the Orient (1994) (Documentary)
The New Legend of Shaolin (1994)
My Father Is a Hero (1995)
Fist of Legend (1995)
High Risk (1995)
Dr. Wai in "The Scripture with No Words" (1996)
Black Mask (1997)
Once upon a Time in China and America (1997)

Anita Mui

(b. 1963, Guangshi Province)

The precocious youngest of four kids, Anita began performing at the tender age of six. It wasn't all youthful fun and
games, though—she needed to dance as fast as she could to
help support her family after the unexpected death of her father. Economic pressures also forced her to leave school before
she finished junior high to pursue her career.

But the hard work paid off, and in 1982 she won the Hong
Kong Amateur Singers Competition, singing "Season of
Love." At nineteen, she already had a platinum-selling album
under her belt. Since then, she's gone on to become regarded
as Hong Kong's most successful singer, inviting the title Madonna of the New Territories.

In Hong Kong, the singing and acting worlds overlap heavily, so it was expected that Mui would make the transition to

movies as soon as she could. Her first film appearances were in a series of unremarkable films but eventually she was handed meatier roles that culminated in 1988's *Rouge*. Playing a ghost who's come back to find her true love, Mui won the Hong Kong Best Actress award for her performance.

Mui has proven herself equally adept at drama, comedy, and action films, including her delightful turn as Jackie Chan's "mother" in *Drunken Master II*. But as often happens, she's more famous for her off-screen life, including her romance with Chan and a high-profile encounter with the Hong Kong Triads.

Through it all, Mui has persevered and continues to be one of Hong Kong's brightest stars.

Selected Anita Mui Filmography

A Week of Passion (1983)
Fate (1984)
Musical Singer (1984)
Song and Dance (1985)
Inspector Chocolate (1986)
Happy Stories (1987)
Rouge (1988)
Miracles: Mr. Canton and Lady Rose (1989)
Shanghai, Shanghai (1990)
Stage Door Johnny (1991)
Au Revoir, Mon Amour (1991)
The Heroic Trio (1993)
Drunken Master II (1994)
He's a Man, She's a Woman (1994)
Rumble in the Bronx (1995)

Cynthia Rothrock
(b. 1960, Delaware)

This blond-haired, blue-eyed American is a rarity in the Hong Kong action genre—a Westerner who is predominantly a good guy instead of the "evil *gwailo*" Caucasians are so often cast as. There probably couldn't be a more unlikely action star than this Delaware native who grew up in the blue-collar world of Scranton, Pennsylvania.

By Asian standards, Rothrock was old when she started taking martial arts training at thirteen. But she showed a natural ability, and within three years earned her first black belt. Given the choice between trying to make a career out of martial arts or going to work in a mill, Cynthia joined the martial arts demonstration circuit. She also wrote books on the subject that enjoyed moderate sales success.

A five-time U.S. Forms and Weapons Champion, Rothrock headed to California in 1983 to audition for a Chinese production company searching for new talent. They passed. But after getting some free publicity via a network news feature on her, Cynthia was wooed by several Hong Kong companies anxious to use her.

Cynthia's first film was *Yes! Madam*, costarring Michelle Yeoh—the only other person who could speak English on the set. And since Cynthia spoke no Cantonese, she became friends with Michelle by necessity.

The shoot was a difficult learning experience, especially physically. But Rothrock proved tough and earned the respect of her Hong Kong peers. As a result, she went on to star in two dozen films including American-made projects.

Like most action stars, Rothrock has had her share of injuries and close calls, including a particularly nasty situation that developed during the filming of *Blonde Fury*. One scene called for Cynthia to jump from a building holding a baby—happily, at least the kid was faked. Rothrock's resulting injury was not. When she landed, she slammed her face against her knee, knocking herself half-silly. Twenty-five takes later, she was on the verge of passing out. Doctors discovered she had "rearranged" her internal organs.

But after some rest, she was right back at it. In recent years, Cynthia's taken it a bit easier and cut back on the more risky stunts, although she continues to make films both here and abroad.

Selected Cynthia Rothrock Filmography

Yes! Madam (1985)
Righting Wrongs (1986)
Magic Crystal (1987)
The Inspector Wears Skirts (1988)
Blonde Fury (1988)
No Retreat, No Surrender (1989)
China O'Brien (1988)
Martial Law (1990)
Tiger Claws (1991)
Angel of Fury (1992)
Fast Getaway 2 (1993)
Undefeatable (1994)

Sammo Hung
(b. 1950, Hong Kong)

It's hard not to think of Sammo Hung and Jackie Chan in the same synapse, so intertwined are their personal and professional lives. Sammo and Jackie met when they were both youngsters indentured at the Peking Opera School in Hong Kong—except Sammo was there by choice.

"Both of my parents worked, so I was taken care of by my grandparents," Hung has stated. "When I was about ten years old I saw some kids training in the Peking Opera. It looked like fun so I begged my parents to let me go so I could become an actor.

"I was a handful as a kid, so I think they thought sending me to the school was a good idea."

Although stout in stature, Sammo's fighting skills are top-notch and he's gracefully agile on his feet. He also has a wonderful sense for choreographing action sequences on film, and it's often said Sammo brings out the best in those he directs. You need to look no further than Jackie to know it's true.

Sammo made his film debut when he was eleven but was already an experienced entertainer. Using the stage name Yuen Chu, Sammo was the lead number of the Seven Little Fortunes, a performance troupe of Opera children that included brothers Jackie and Yuen Baio. In 1989 Sammo starred in *Painted Faces*, a biographical film based on his and the other brothers' lives at the Peking Opera School.

Despite an impressive résumé both in front of and behind the camera, Sammo suffered a fall from grace that began after a rift with Golden Harvest in 1991. The point of contention was a Sammo-produced film called *Into the Fire* that was abruptly pulled out of its run. The confrontation with studio owner Raymond Chow left Sammo hurt—and bitter.

Sammo severed his relationship with Golden Harvest. Out on his own, several of his next films failed to generate much box office interest. It didn't help that he and Jackie had also had a falling out after they finished *Twinkle*, *Twinkle Lucky Stars*—a case of two big-time directors disagreeing on the direction a film should take. The spat didn't faze Chan's career, but it helped put another layer of chill over Sammo's.

But Sammo hung in there, and his banishment appears to be over, with both Golden Harvest and with Jackie. He was at the helm of Jackie's first English-speaking venture, *A Nice Guy*, and has several other projects lined up. As far as his acting career goes, Sammo admits the years have caught up with him—his body simply can't take the punishment it could in years past, which is why he's making noises about hanging up his thespian shoes and concentrating on directing.

Selected Sammo Hung Filmography

Hapkido (1972, chor/actor)
Game of Death (1973, chor/actor)
The Skyhawk (1974, chor/actor)
Enter the Fat Dragon (1978, dir/chor/actor)

The Iron-Fisted Monk (1978, dir/chor/actor)
Magnificent Butcher (1979, chor/actor)
Spooky Encounters (1981, dir/chor/actor)
Winners and Sinners (1983, dir/chor/actor)
Eastern Condors (1987, dir/chor/actor)
Shanghai Express (1987, dir/chor/actor)
Painted Faces (1989, actor)
Gambling Ghost (1991, chor/actor)
Blade of Fury (1993, dir/chor/actor)

John Woo
(b. 1948, Canton)

One of the brightest of China's New Wave filmmakers, Woo has created his own film subgenre. A "John Woo" film is any overtly bloody, violent, and nihilistic movie outing. His style of slo-mo gun battles and blood splatter has been especially embraced in Hollywood, where Woo has many supporters, among them Quentin Tarantino.

Woo grew up in extreme poverty, the son of an anti-Communist philosopher who moved his family to Hong Kong rather than live in what he considered intolerable conditions in China. John's interests ran toward religion and the movies—over time, filmmaking took precedence. Unable to afford school, John taught himself film technique and theory from stolen books.

To put food on the table, Woo did grunt work on any movie shoot he could find and in his spare time filmed a number of shorts. Eventually, he got a steady job as a script supervisor at Cathay Studios. After two years, he moved over to Shaw Brothers, working directly under Chang Cheh.

Woo finally made a breakthrough when he was twenty-six with *The Young Dragons*. Unlike some others who equated quantity with success, Woo made movies at a more moderate pace, filming twelve over the next ten years. Among his movies during that period was *Hand of Death*, in which Woo cast a very young Jackie Chan.

But it wasn't until 1986 that Woo made a film that propelled him to a new echelon—*A Better Tomorrow*. It was also the beginning of his many collaborations with Chow Yun-fat, whom Woo calls his alter ego. They would become a team akin to America's Scorsese and De Niro. Ironically, Woo says his violent *noir* effort *The Killer* is an homage to Scorsese.

What makes Woo unique is that although his films are considered Hong Kong action films, there's a very little kung fu or Jackie-style stunts. What "choreography" there is can be found in the gun battle sequences, the violent, bullet-ridden confrontations presented as a macabre ballet.

Like his father, Woo found the thought of working under Communist China rule intolerable, so he moved to Hollywood, where his reputation preceded him. His first film, the Jean-Claude Van Damme vehicle *Hard Target*, proved he could make a commercially viable, big-budget American movie.

Now firmly ensconced in Hollywood as an action film director, Woo is looking for a project that will reunite him with Chow Yun-fat, who also now lives in Los Angeles.

Selected John Woo Filmography

The Young Dragon (1973)
The Dragon Tamers (1974)
Princess Chang Ping (1975)
Follow the Star (1977)
A Better Tomorrow (1986)
A Better Tomorrow II (1987)
The Killer (1989)
Bullet in the Head (1990)
Once a Thief (1991)
Hard Boiled (1992)
Hard Target (1993)
Broken Arrow (1996)
Face/Off (1997)

THE
Quizzical

13

成
龍

JACKIE CHAN

*I*f you've made it this far, you must think you know just about all there is to know about Chan. Well, there are still plenty of obscure factoids or movie trivia that haven't been covered—and uncovered.

For those who just love minutiae, we'll end on a trivial note. Below are seven question meant to test your Jackie IQ. The answers and scoring follow.

Good luck, and remember—Jackie doesn't like cheaters.

成
龍
QUESTIONS
成
龍

---

1. In *Twin Dragons*, who played the "back" of John Ma/ Boomer when the scene showed one twin talking to the other?

2. Name the five films in which Jackie's character dies. Extra credit if you know how.

3. What are Jackie's favorite films of the ones he's made, performance-wise? Directing-wise? Which three films does he believe are the best introduction to his work?

4. How is *Fearless Hyena* historically inaccurate?

5. What famous action scene designed by Jackie did Sylvester Stallone obviously appropriate in *Tango & Cash?*

6. Name four members of the Seven Little Fortunes performance troupe besides Jackie. What was Chan's stage name?

7. What film does Jackie call his "luckiest" in terms of his not being "seriously" injured?

成
龍   ANSWERS   成
龍

1. Jackie's old pal Mars played the backside of whichever twin was supposed to be facing away from the camera. Scoring—2 points.

2. *Eagle Shadow Fist*—stabbed preventing the rape of a woman
    Island of Fire—blasted away during a shootout against a drug lord
    Hand of Death—killed by marauding Chinese
    New Fists of Fury—ambushed and shot by Japanese snipers
    Enter the Dragon—broken neck
    Scoring—1 point for each correct film. Give yourself 5 points extra if you get all the films and modes of death.

3. Performing—*Police Story, Drunken Master II*
    As an introduction to his work—*Police Story, Project A,* and *Rumble in the Bronx*
    Favorite directorial effort—*Miracles*
    Scoring—1 point for each correct answer.

4. In *Snake and Crane Arts of Shaolin,* look closely and you'll see Jackie is wearing a small pigtail beneath his famous floppy mop of hair. Fast-forward to *Fearless Hyena,* and Jackie sports no pigtail. So what? Here's what—during the Manchurian era when *Fearless Hyena* is set, pigtails were a mandatory fashion statement. The penalty for failing to

comply was death. Apparently Lo Wei was no better a historian than he was a filmmaker.
Scoring—4 points.

5. When Jackie stops a bus full of bad guys roaring down on him with just a gun in *Police Story*.
Scoring—1 point.

6. The best known of the original Seven Fortunes performance troupe are:
Sammo Hung: He used stage name Yuen Chu.
Yuen Baio: Unlike Sammo he retained his Seven Fortunes name professionally.
Yuen Wah: Started out in the movie business working as stand-in for Bruce Lee but has become a well-known actor in his own right the last several years.
Yuen Kuei: Now a well-known Hong Kong action director, he is best known for Jean-Claude Van Damme's *No Retreat, No Surrender*.
Yuen Mo: He has also carved out a living in movies as a stuntman and action director.
Ng Ming Choi: He used the stage name Yuen Choi. Former bit actor turned producer.
Yuen Tak: Decided to leave acting behind to become award-winning action director.
Jackie Chan: He used stage name Yuen Lau.
Scoring—2 points for each correct name, 14 points maximum. 5 points for Jackie's stage name.

7. Jackie says *Police Story II* was his luckiest. In that film he "only" gashed his head after diving through plate glass. Everything in life is relative.
Scoring—1 point.

Rate Your Jackie IQ:
1–5 points: What have you been watching—Jean-Claude Van Damme movies?

5–15 points: Even Lo Wei would have done better.
16–34 points: A solid Jackie fan—Dragons Forever!!!
35 + points: You are truly a Drunken Master.

14

Name Game

成
龍

As if trying to match the Cantonese translations with those in Mandarin isn't difficult enough for most
English-as-a-first-and-only-language people, many Asian
actors add an extra twist that further complicates figuring
out who's who. To make their names more familiar-sounding
to Westerners, Hong Kong thesps Anglicize their names—
which in fact becomes the name by which we often best know
them.

But there's more. Once you've mastered the Cantonese and
Mandarin translations and the Anglicized names, then you
have to add in the many aliases periodically used over the
course of their careers.

So what does all this mean in practical lay terms? That
people can get very confused—not to mention annoyed—
particularly when trying to decipher some video covers. But
fear not, help is on the way. The following list gives the multitude of appellations used by the top action film performers
and will hopefully clarify who's who.

So next time some Hong Kong action film know-it-all
starts prattling on about Sing Lung, you'll be able to say,
"Yeah, well, don't you think it's about time old Sing marries
poor Zhang Manyu in the next *Police Story* movie, hmm?"

That'll show 'em.

JACKIE CHAN:

CANTONESE—Sing Lung

MANDARIN—Cheng Long (Cheng2 Long2)

OTHER—Yuen Lau (his Seven Fortunes moniker), Ch'eng Lung, Chen Yuen-lung, Chung Long, Chen Lo, Cheng Lung, Chen Yuen Lung, Chu Yuan Long, Chen Yuen Long, Chen Yuan-lung, Chan Yuan Lung, and Paul (his chosen Anglo name until Lo Wei changed it to Jackie)

YUEN BIAO:

CANTONESE—Yuen Biu

MANDARIN—Yuan Biao (Yuan1 Biao1)

FRANKIE CHAN:

CANTONESE—Chan Fan Kei

MANDARIN—Chen Xunji (Chen2 Xun1 Ji1)

OTHER—Chen Xunqi

LESLIE CHEUNG:

CANTONESE—Jeung Gwok Wink

MANDARIN—Zhang Guorong (Zhang1 Guo2 Rong2)

OTHER—Leslie Cheung Kwok-Wing

MAGGIE CHEUNG:

CANTONESE—Jeung Maan Yuk

MANDARIN—Zhang Manyu (Zhang1 Man4 Yu4)

OTHER—Chang Man Yu, Cheung Man-yuk

CHOW YUN-FAT:

CANTONESE—Jau Yun Faat

MANDARIN—Zhou Runfa (Zhou1 Run4 Fa1)

OTHER—Aman Chou

TIEN FENG:

CANTONESE—Tin Fung
MANDARIN—Tian Jun (Tian2 Jun4)
OTHER—Paul Tien Feng

TSUI HARK:

CANTONESE—Chui Hak
MANDARIN—Xu Ke (Xu2 Ke4)

SIBELLE HU:

CANTONESE—Woo Wai Jung
MANDARIN—Hu Hui Zhong (Hu2 Hui4 Zhong1)
OTHER—Hu Hui Chung, Hu Hui Ching

KARA HUI:

CANTONESE—Wai Ying Hung
MANDARIN—Hui Yinghong (Hui4 Ying1 Hong2)
OTHER—Kara Hui Ying-hung

SAMMO HUNG:

CANTONESE—Hung Gam Bo
MANDARIN—Hong JinBao (Hong2 Jin1 Bao3)
OTHER—Hung Chin Pao, Hong Chinbao

WONG JING:

CANTONESE—Wong Jing
MANDARIN—Wang Jing (Wang2 Jing1)

KAM KAN:

King Kong

AARON KWOK:

CANTONESE—Gwok Foo Sing
MANDARIN—Guo Fucheng (Guo1 Fu4 Cheng2)
OTHER—Aaron Kwok Fu-Sing

ANDY LAU:

CANTONESE—Lau Dak Wa
MANDARIN—Liu Dehau (Liu2 De2 Hua4)
OTHER—Andy Lau Tak-Wah

BILLY LAU:

CANTONESE—Lau Naan Gwong
MANDARIN—Lou Nanquang
OTHER—Billy Lau Wam-Kwong

LAU KAR-LEUNG:

CANTONESE—Lau Ga Yung
MANDARIN—Liu Jiayong (Liu2 Jia1 Yong3)
OTHER—Liu Chia-Yung, Lau Ka Wing, Bruce Lau

BRUCE LEE:

CANTONESE—Lei Siu Lung
MANDARIN—Li Xiaolong (Li3 Xiao3 Long2)
OTHER—Lee Jun-fan, Lee Shao Lung

WAISE LEE:

CANTONESE—Lee Ji Hung
MANDARIN—Li Zixiong (Li3 Zi3 Xiong2)

ANGILE LEUNG:

CANTONESE—Leung Wan Yui
MANDARIN—Liang Yunrui (Liang2 Yun4 Rui3)

JET LI:

CANTONESE—Lei Lin Git
MANDARIN—Li Lianjie (Li3 Lian2 Jie2)
OTHER—Li Lin-jei

BRIGITTE LIN:

CANTONESE—Lam Ching Hsia
MANDARIN—Lin Qingxia (Lin2 Qing1 Xia2)
OTHER—Brigite Lam, Venus Lin, Lin Ching-hsia, Bridget Lin

LO WEI:

CANTONESE—Loh Wai
MANDARIN—Luo Wei (Luo2 Wei2)

RAYMOND LUI:

CANTONESE—Lui Leung Wai
MANDARIN—Lu3 Liang2 Wei3
OTHER—Lui Wai-min

ANITA MUI:

CANTONESE—Mooi Yim Fong
MANDARIN—Mei Yanfang (Mei2 Yan4 Fang1)
OTHER—Mui Yim-fong

RICHARD NG:

CANTONESE—Ng Yiu Hon
MANDARIN—Wu Yaohan (Wu2 Yao4 Han4)

JAMES TIEN:

CANTONESE—Tin Jun
MANDARIN—Tian Jun (Tian2 Jun4)
OTHER—Tien Chun

STANLEY TONG:

CANTONESE—Tong Gwai Lai
MANDARIN—Tang Jili (Tang2 Ji4 Li3)
OTHER—Stanley Tong Kwai-Lai

ERIC TSANG:

CANTONESE—Chang Ji Wai
MANDARIN—Zeng Zhiwei (Zeng2 Zhi4 Wei3)
OTHER—Eric Tsang Chi-Wai

BILL TUNG:

CANTONESE—Dung Piu
MANDARIN—Dong Piao (Dong3 Piao4)

JIMMY WANG YU:

CANTONESE—Wong Yue
MANDARIN—Wang Yu (Wang2 Yu3)

DICK WEI:

CANTONESE—Dik Wai
MANDARIN—Di Wei (Di2 Wei)
OTHER—Ti Wei, C.L. Tu

KIRK WONG:

CANTONESE—Wong Ji Keung
MANDARIN—Huang Zhiqiang (Huang2 Zhi4 Qiang2)
OTHER—Kirk Wong Chi-Kung

JOHN WOO:

CANTONESE—Ng Yue Sam
MANDARIN—Wu Yusen (Wu2 Yu3 Sen1)

YUEN WOO-PING:

CANTONESE—Yuen Woh Ping
MANDARIN—Yuan Huopin (Yuan2 Huo4 Pin2)
OTHER—Yuen Ho-ping, Yuan Heping, Yuan Dayan, Yuan Ho-
  ping

MICHELLE YEOH:

CANTONESE—Yeung Ji King
MANDARIN—Yang Ziqiong (Yang2 Zi3 Qiong2)
OTHER—Yeung Chi King, Michelle Yeoh (married name), Michelle Kheng, Michelle King, Yeoh Chu Kheng

FRANÇOISE YIP:

CANTONESE—Yip Fong Wa
MANDARIN—Ye Fanghua (Ye4 Fang1 Hua2)
OTHER—Francoise Yip Fong-Wa

ANITA YUEN:

CANTONESE—Yuen Wing Yee

15
成龍

THE
Fanatical
JACKIE CHAN

*I*f you want even more information on Jackie, write to one of the fan clubs listed below:

(HEADQUARTERS)
Jackie Chan International Fan Club
The J.C. Centre
145 Waterloo Road
Kowloon
Hong Kong

(USA)
Jackie Chan Fan Club, USA
P.O. Box 2281
Portland, OR 97208
(503) 299-4766
chanfansus@aol.com

(CANADA)
3007 Kingston Road
Box 109
Scarborough, Ontario
M1M 1P1

(JAPAN)
#1001 Nagatani Mansion
26 Banchi
Sakamachi, Shinjuku-ku
Tokyo 160

(AUSTRALIA)
P.O. Box 1668
Bondi Junction
New South Wales 2022

(UNITED KINGDOM)
92 Ambleside Road
Kingsway, Bath
BA2 2LP